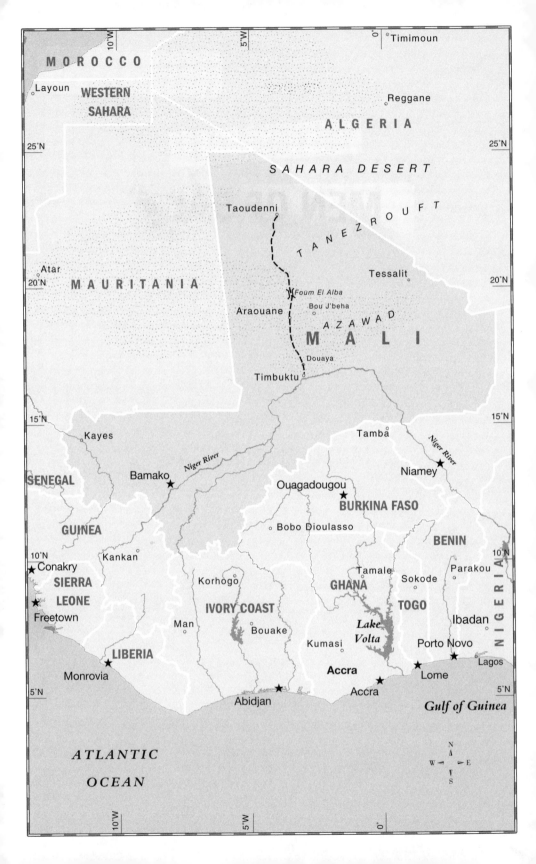

MEN OF SALT

CROSSING THE SAHARA
ON THE CARAVAN OF WHITE GOLD

MICHAEL BENANAV

THE LYONS PRESS
Guilford, Connecticut
An imprint of the The Globe Pequot Press

The Lyons Press is an imprint of The Globe Pequot Press.

10 9 8 7 6 5 4 3 2

ISBN 978-1-59921-164-0

Printed in The United States of America

Designed by Maggie Peterson

Photographs by Michael Benanav

The Library of Congress has previously catalogued an earlier (hardcover) edition as follows:

Benanav, Michael.

Men of salt : across the Sahara with the caravan of white gold / Michael Benanav.

p. cm.

Includes bibliographical references.

ISBN 1-59228-772-7 (trade cloth)

1. Sahara—Description and travel. 2. Caravans—Sahara. 3. Salt industry and trade—
Sahara. 4. Salt mines and mining—Sahara. I. Title.

DT333.B46 2006

916.604'329—dc22

2005023205

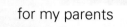

for my parents

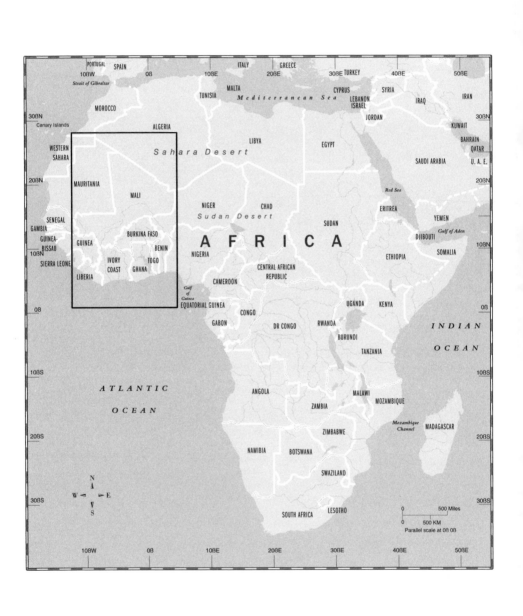

CONTENTS

PREFACE

For the past thousand years, the Caravan of White Gold has plied the desolate sands of the Sahara. Its mission: to penetrate deep into the heart of the world's largest desert and return to civilization bearing gleaming slabs of solid salt. Men clad in turbans, threadbare robes, and the occasional sports jacket lead strings of camels over some of the most severe terrain on earth, from the fabled city of Timbuktu (in the West African nation of Mali) to the remote salt-mining outpost of Taoudenni, nearly five hundred miles to the north, in the middle of nowhere. There they load their animals with tons of edible ore, then travel back across the desert to bring it to market. Their ancient, arduous way of life has hardly changed in the millennium since the salt caravans began.

Today these men and camels work one of the last of the caravan routes still active in the Sahara. The rest of the complex caravan network that once crisscrossed northern Africa has virtually vanished, victim to modern means of transportation; most goods, which in centuries past would have been carried across the great desert on camelback, are now flown over it, driven through it, or shipped around it by sea. Yet the Caravan of White Gold marches on, spared by its isolation.

The caravan route passes through one of the most notorious stretches in the Sahara, known as the Tanezrouft—the oldest and driest part of a desert bigger than the continental United States. Along the northern two-thirds of the trail, there are no human habitations or even nomad camps; the earth is simply too parched to support life. There are no oases, just a few solitary wells spaced days apart. Temperatures regularly surpass 120 degrees. Sandstorms sweep unchecked for hundreds of miles across the flat expanse. Entire caravans have left their bones there, including one time, in 1805, when some two thousand men and their camels arrived at a dry well and didn't make it to the next.

Taoudenni itself is in arguably the harshest spot in this harshest of regions. On an utterly barren plain hundreds of miles from the nearest village, miners hack tombstone-sized blocks of rock salt from hand-dug pits using semi-primitive tools. Living in Stone Age–style huts, they survive on a meager diet of rice, millet, and briny water; they have no medical facilities, no electricity, and no way of contacting the outside world but through those who travel back to it with salt.

Though I'm a great lover of deserts, I had never heard of the Caravan of White Gold or the salt mines of Taoudenni until one night while I was surfing the Internet, researching the evolutionary advantages of one-humped versus two-humped camels in their respective environments. Having recently returned from a trip to Mongolia, home to the Bactrian camel, I wondered how its two humps could possibly serve it better than the single hump of its cousin, the Arabian, or dromedary. I eventually discovered that the Arabian evolved from the Bactrian, and had fused two humps into one for the same reason it had developed shorter hair, longer legs, and a leaner physique—to keep its body temperature a few critical degrees cooler in the extreme deserts of the Middle East and Africa where it lives.

It was while following a divergent trail of camel-related Web links that I stumbled across an article about the Caravan of White Gold. The caravan, the article asserted, was in its dying days, as trucks had recently begun competing for the salt trade. With their superior speed and carrying capacity, they would soon drive camels into obsolescence. It sounded like a Saharan John Henry story with a predictable ending—the death of the caravans and the iconic, age-old caravan culture. The noble ships of the desert, it seemed, were bound for dry dock.

As I read, my mind filled with exotic scenes of desert-hardened nomads leading camel trains over a vast, undulating landscape. Enthralled, I read the piece again, my thoughts racing headlong into the Sahara. I hurriedly searched for more information on other Web sites, but was too excited to really focus—not because the caravans were doomed, but by the thought of joining one before they disappeared from the planet once and for all. Suddenly, my mental image of the caravans included me, galloping on camelback alongside the nomads, my head and face wrapped in coils of cloth like some archetypal Desert Man. I sensed that before long this vision would come true, even if I wouldn't ride as well as I had in my imagination. It was that feeling known by those of us who don't so much take journeys as are taken *by* journeys: hearing the call of a particular place for a particular purpose that will not be denied. And I was hooked. Too hyped up to sit at my computer any longer, I told myself it was the kind of trip I was born to take.

When I was nine, my father gave me an old hardbound biography called, simply, *Lawrence of Arabia*. I read it over and over, entranced by the deeds of a man who seemed to transcend the limitations of the possible, both culturally, by integrating with a fierce foreign people, and physically, by leading a band of underdogs to victory over the Turks and beating the British to Damascus. My desert traveling fantasies had been ignited.

In my twenties, I picked up *Seven Pillars of Wisdom*, Lawrence's autobiography. After reading it, I made a pilgrimage of sorts to Wadi Rumm, in Jordan, partly to walk in Lawrence's footsteps, mostly to see with my own eyes the stunning desert corridor that he described as a "processional way greater than imagination."

Once there, I wandered alone for a week across salmon-colored dunes and among sandstone massifs intricately hewn and varnished by the elements. I spent time under the woolen tents of Bedouin families, drinking tea, talking Arabic, and eating fresh goat meat. Charmed by their hospitality, intrigued by their culture, I became hopelessly infected by a fascination with nomadic peoples.

Though Lawrence never traversed the Sahara, joining a salt caravan would in many ways realize my lifelong dream of traveling the way he had traveled, minus, of course, the Turks, which was one element of his story I was just as happy to do without. The geography was less important to me than was traveling with desert people for a long period of time, and with an actual purpose. Taking a scenic camel tour wouldn't have satisfied me, since it would have been all too apparent that I was engaged in an act of pretend. By walking and riding step for step with working camel drivers, eating what they ate, sleeping as little as they slept, and helping with their labors, I believed I could get a taste of what their lives were like. I wanted to immerse in their customs, listen to their stories, and learn about the ways of the Sahara from the bearers of generations' worth of collective wisdom before they took their final ride.

Aside from my qualifications as a dreamer, I had been a wilderness guide in the western United States for about ten years and had spent weeks at a time roaming its deserts by foot. Without a pack animal, I had carried all my supplies, even gallons of water, on my back, and had become expert at ignoring pain while hiking for many miles with shredded feet. The thought of not showering or changing my clothes for the estimated forty-day camel journey struck me as, at worst, a minor inconvenience and, at best, a chance to set some new personal benchmarks for sustained filth.

Moreover, I reminded myself, I had first ridden camels not long after I learned to walk—though on further reflection, I doubted that being led around a pen at the Bronx Zoo counted for much. In my late twenties, I'd settled for a couple of months in a village at the base of the Giza Plateau, and my friend Omar and I occasionally rode his camels through the desert around the Pyramids for a couple of hours at a time. While I did learn how to get a camel to go faster with a rapid series of slurping sounds, the most important thing I took away from those experiences was a deep respect, even a fondness, for those strange-looking animals so often characterized as ornery or oafish. To me, camels were regal, remarkable, and, when their lips were closed in a Mona Lisa smile, seemed to be laughing inside at some private joke that we humans would never get. Nonetheless, I had to admit that I knew next to nothing about traveling on them.

As my ideas about joining a caravan evolved from an inspired notion to the practicalities of getting plane tickets and vaccinations, my initial enthusiasm was tempered by the daunting realities I was going to face. Despite—indeed *because* of—my knowledge of deserts, I took the risks of the journey very seriously. I knew there'd be no chance of rescue if anything went wrong, and wanted to be as prepared as possible.

I embarked on a makeshift physical training program that consisted mostly of walking barefoot on the dirt roads near my home in rural New Mexico to toughen my feet, and chopping cords of wood, which my girlfriend would need to heat the house while I was away. I brushed up on my French—Mali's colonial tongue—which I mistakenly hoped the camel drivers would speak (fortunately, I took my Arabic phrase book plus a sheaf of handwritten vocabulary notes along with me). Seeking background information on Saharan nomads, I contacted an anthropology professor who had spent many years among Tuareg tribespeople and who kindly sent me copies of her published papers.

I also looked into the history of salt in West Africa, wondering why people would go to what sounded like absurdly extreme measures to obtain this most common of commodities. But centuries ago, I learned, in the heyday of the Saharan salt trade, rock salt from the desert was exchanged "measure for measure" with gold—hence the name of the caravan. Though some scholars dispute whether the salt was literally worth its weight in gold, as is advocated by others, there is no question that it was extremely valuable. In fact, until French colonizers introduced paper money to West Africa around the turn of the twentieth century, salt was the dominant form of currency throughout the region, thanks in part to its hardness and durability. It served the same purposes as money and "could be bought, sold, stored, loaned or 'rented,' inherited and consumed, sharing the same monetary functions and more than as silver coins." "Everything one finds in the Sudan," a local historian wrote (referring to Mali by its colonial name, not to the East African country), "is bought with salt: horses, cloth, millet, and slaves." At various times, the price of a slave was a piece of salt the size of the slave's foot; later, a slave's value increased to an entire bar of salt.

Hence, until paper money took hold in West Africa, the Saharan salt mines were literal money pits. What's more, as I was soon to learn firsthand, there are places in the desert where salt remains the dominant form of currency to this day.

Aside from its fiduciary uses, salt was so valued because, as Cassiodores, the Roman senator, once said, "Man can live without gold, but not without salt." The people of West Africa needed salt for spicing and preserving food, and to feed to their animals. Despite the labor involved in its extraction and transport, the desert was the best place to get it.

While there were other sources of salt, including evaporated sea salt from coastal areas and vegetable salts, which were ashes from burned millet stalks, these were less highly prized than solid Saharan rock salt. Vegetable salts were inherently inferior and couldn't be fed to livestock. Sea salt was difficult to transport; it changed color and taste when subject to excessive heat and humidity; it didn't store well over time; and it wasn't as good as rock salt for livestock.

The salt from Taoudenni, on the other hand, met all the nutritional and culinary needs of both people and animals. It traveled well, and could be stored for so long without deteriorating that slabs of it were commonly handed down from one generation to the next. It cost no more than sea salt, due to the problems with transporting sea salt into the West African interior. One French salt company, looking to strike it big in the West African market and aware of the regional preference for rock salt, went so far as to compress sea salt into bars resembling those mined in the Sahara. The introduction of *sel agglomeré* was a commercial fiasco—of the first shipment of three thousand bars, in 1897, 20 percent were lost or ruined in transit. Much of the rest arrived damaged, and the cases in which they were stored proved less than weather-tight, allowing rain and dust to further degrade the salt while in storage. What's more, West Africans could no more be fooled into buying fake rock salt than a rancher could be fooled into grilling up a Spam steak.

Today salt from Taoudenni is still the people's favorite and is found everywhere in Mali and other parts of West Africa, though its value has diminished so greatly that it's now more on a par with that of the table salt commonly sold in American grocery stores. But because each caravan returns from each trip with many tons of it, the journey remains a profitable one in contemporary Mali, where the average person earns less in a year than a minimum-wage worker in the United States earns in a few weeks.

While digging around for facts about the salt caravans, I came across the name of an archaeology professor who had journeyed with the Caravan of White Gold one-way, from Taoudenni to Timbuktu (he had taken a Land Cruiser to the mines). I phoned him, believing that some firsthand information would be both valuable and reassuring. I was right about the first, wrong about the second.

John began by telling me he'd had trouble finding a caravan that would accept him. Most camel drivers were afraid he wouldn't be able to keep pace, and they weren't going to slow down on his account.

When a crew finally agreed to take him along, they did so on one condition: that if anything "major" befell him, the camel drivers could leave his body in the desert and continue on their merchant mission with all possible speed.

"There are lots of ways you can get hurt out there. Sure, you might die of thirst or hunger," he said casually, as though this were a given, "but you're more likely to fall off a camel and break a leg." Whether or not such an injury would lead directly to death by infection or blood loss, he gave me the impression that it would qualify as something "major" enough to warrant abandonment.

He cautioned me about the unbelievable heat, the eternally long days and nights on the march, and mentioned that he had become sick from the water. That led me to inquire more or less tactfully about what he used for toilet paper.

"Sand," he replied.

I knew that many desert peoples did use sand to clean themselves, but I never quite understood how it worked; I always envisioned it as an unpleasantly messy operation. Without prying too deeply into the potentially gross experience of a man I had never met, I tried to get some details on the mechanics of it, but came away from the conversation no clearer—John simply said something about how quickly everything dries in the Sahara. I made a mental note to bring a roll of toilet paper with me.

The camel drivers, John continued, were friendly and helpful. Most important, they understood that he was different—"different," in this case, being a synonym for "less desert-worthy"—and accepted the fact that he had to eat more than they did. "Bring extra food, like peanuts and dates," he cautioned. "There's not a lot on the caravan, and there's hardly any protein. I lost twenty pounds on the trip."

"Twenty pounds!" I marveled, realizing I'd be traveling twice the distance he did.

Overall I got the impression that he was glad to have done it once, glad to have only gone one-way, and glad that he wasn't going back again anytime soon.

When I hung up the phone, I had a clearer picture of what I was getting myself into and was considerably more anxious. Perhaps I should have been encouraged that someone twenty years older than me had survived the voyage without permanent injury. But my mind kept circling around the deal I believed I'd have to make—the one about being left for dead in the desert.

MEN OF SALT

Lachmar, my camel.

CHAPTER ONE

The boat coasted slowly into the port at Kourioume, on the Niger River, maneuvering its way into an open space among the other wooden crafts already moored there. It was ten o'clock on a late-October night. Only a few scattered lights glowing in the houses on shore broke the total darkness. The air was hot and still except for the faint wakes stirred up by circling swarms of mosquitoes.

Hand-hewn canoes were poled alongside the boat—which itself looked like a canopied canoe the size of a subway car—to carry people, luggage, and cargo to land. Passengers mobbed to the lip of the ship, queuing as if in an experiment in natural selection. They thrust nylon duffel bags, cardboard boxes tied with string, and bundles wrapped in rice sacks into the outstretched hands of the shuttle boat drivers, then climbed quickly down into the shallow hulls of the leaky dugouts. The man I'd been sitting next to for the previous two days waved for me to follow him, so I passed my backpack over and stepped aboard the wobbly little canoe. Once on land, I waited with other passengers for a shared taxi to arrive to take me the last eleven miles of my nine-day journey to Timbuktu—the southern terminus of the Caravan of White Gold, which I hoped to join on its trek through the Sahara along the ancient but still active salt-trading route.

I'd flown first to Dakar, Senegal, where I spent one night in a cheap hotel that doubled as a local brothel, then hopped a plane to Bamako, Mali's capital. I spent a week making my way across the country to Timbuktu, traveling by bus, minivan, pickup truck, and, lastly, cargo boat down the Niger River. In all, it was a slow, cramped, dirty, sweaty journey—a fairly typical third-world public transportation experience. I looked upon the discomforts as a good opportunity to stretch my tolerance in advance of traveling with the caravan, which I knew would be leagues more demanding.

Along the way, I quickly saw that Mali is a very poor country. Close to 70 percent of the land within its borders is covered by the Sahara, and is known as *Mali inutile* (useless Mali). Most of the rest of it lies within a swath of semi-desert savannah-land called the Sahel, a transitional zone between true desert to the north and forest to the south that is particularly vulnerable to the whims of climate fluctuation. Eighty percent of Malians rely on the marginal lands and erratic river flows to sustain simple agricultural lives of small-scale farming, fishing, or herding. Most work is performed by hand, whether planting and harvesting, casting fishing nets, doing laundry, or crushing the millet that is the staple of the Malian diet. Food, even in many restaurants, is cooked over charcoal or wood. The hands and feet of nearly everyone I'd seen were cracked and callused, tough as hide. It was readily apparent why Mali is placed fourth from last on the United Nations Human Development Index, which ranks the standard of living of 177 countries based on a combination of factors, including per capita gross domestic product (Mali's is about $250 per year), literacy rate (about 45 percent), and infant mortality rate (a quarter of Malian children die before age five).

But I also quickly realized that it's the type of country in which I like best to travel: one in which much of daily life takes place outside; where things function with no concern for liability lawsuits; where the local version of order closely resembles the Western notion of chaos; and where poverty does not equal shame, partly because so many people are poor, partly because riches don't increase one's status in the eyes of Allah.

The cacophonous, colorful markets; the sense of solidarity that forms among passengers crammed together in the back of a battered pickup truck that sputters like a wounded turtle along rutted roads; the groups of men arranging prayer mats on the sidewalks at sunset, kneeling and casting long shadows before them as the calls of the muezzins roll from minarets; even the littered streets and putrid gutters that are a regular feature of towns in the developing world—all these reminded me of other places I'd been, other places I'd loved. I felt an instant fondness for the country, a sense of homecoming, though I'd never been there before.

I approached Timbuktu filled with anticipation. It was a destination of mythic proportion, whose name had been part of the popular lexicon since at least 1863 as a synonym for "the most distant place imaginable." Arriving at Kourioume, with Timbuktu a short taxi ride away, I was tired but excited. I was a little anxious, too. The thing was, I had no idea how easy or difficult it was going to be to join a salt caravan; if it would take me a day, or a week, or if it was even feasible at all. If it wasn't, my trip to the proverbial end of the earth was going to be a bust.

I tried to address this critical uncertainty before I'd left home by contacting a Timbuktu-based tour company whose e-mail address was listed in my guidebook. I told them I wanted to ride with a caravan round-trip to the salt mines at Taoudenni, and asked if they knew how I could arrange such a thing. The agency director wrote back, telling me it would be no problem; he could easily find me a place on a caravan for a mere five thousand dollars.

Even if I had that kind of money to spend on a trip, it was an insane amount to pay for what promised to be six weeks of Hell. I wrote back, telling him there was no way I could afford it. He responded, asking what I could pay. I felt like I had stepped into a cyber-bazaar. Rather than haggling via e-mail, which would have robbed me of seeing the all-important body language cues that are so much a part of the bargaining ritual, I told him I'd wait until I got to Timbuktu to talk to him, though I didn't know when exactly that would be. I imagined he was giving me the "tourist over the Internet" price, and believed it would drop significantly when I arrived in person and had the option of shopping around. If it didn't, I'd be out of luck. Five thousand dollars was about twice my entire savings.

The taxi that arrived at the port was a decrepit white Toyota Land Cruiser. The seats had been pulled from the back, replaced by wooden benches fitted against the sides. The only way in was through the back door. Among the others inside was a young man who introduced himself and asked me if I knew where I was staying that night. When I named a cheap hotel from my guidebook, he told me I could stay at his family's house for half the price, claiming that many tourists, especially Peace Corps workers, did so. Since it was late, and I'm never one to turn down a bargain, I took him up on his offer.

I'm not sure what I expected to experience upon first arriving in Timbuktu, but because it was dark and quiet when we got out of the Land Cruiser, I felt like I could have been just about anywhere. Any mystique would have to wait until morning. My companion and I walked along dirt streets, zigging right then zagging left, the lanes becoming narrower and the buildings more densely packed. Just as I began to wonder if I'd been lured into some sort of a scam, we were at his house.

He opened the heavy wooden door. We stepped into a large unlit foyer with a round, defunct fountain in its center, then went up a stone staircase that could have been in a medieval castle. While we ascended, he told me that he was a tourist guide. If I wanted to arrange any kind of sightseeing trips, or spend a night or two in the desert, he could set it up for me.

What I really wanted, I said, was to ride with a camel caravan to Taoudenni and back.

"I can arrange that, too," he said.

I set my backpack down on the terrace where I was going to sleep.

"Tell me your name again," I asked.

"Alkoye. Alkoye Touré."

I pulled out my guidebook and found the page I was looking for, the one with the contact information for the guide I had e-mailed from home. And there, circled in red pen, was the name *Alkoye Touré* .

Alkoye was about five foot five, with a head that was shaped like a peach pit and topped with black fuzz. His skin was dark brown, and his droopy-lidded eyes always seemed half closed. In the morning, he recommended that we go over to the tourist agency office first thing, find out when the next caravan was leaving, and get me on it. It sounded simple. I could hardly believe how smoothly things were falling into place, though I steeled myself for what was sure to be a rigorous bout of haggling.

We walked down lanes lined by houses like Alkoye's, two stories tall and as solid as fortresses, whose carved, heavy wooden doors lent them a deceiving air of affluence. We cut through twisting adobe-walled alleyways that resembled severely eroded sandstone slot canyons. Some of the mud-brick buildings, thanks to unusually heavy rains in the previous months, had recently collapsed into ruin; others had lain that way for many years. The dirt streets, even the nice ones, were rutted by wastewater runoff from the houses, which collected every so often in murky, smelly pools.

The office he led me to was like a windowless walk-in closet whose door opened onto the main paved thoroughfare into town. It had high ceilings, but was just big enough for a desk and a few chairs. Rudimentary xeroxed maps of routes in the Sahara were taped around the room at eye level. I shook hands with the chief, a well-weathered yet well-groomed Tuareg who looked to be about sixty and wore a long, loose robe called a *boubou*, and a turban, both white. When we were all seated, the games began.

The chief said there was a caravan leaving the day after next, and I could get on it for $1,750. This would include a guide, one camel for each of us, and all the food for the trip. I asked how much it would cost without a guide, saying that if I was traveling with a caravan, I wouldn't need one. No, I was told, I absolutely needed one. No caravan would accept me without a designated minder—someone, essentially, whose job it was to make sure I stayed alive and out of trouble, so the rest of the *azalai*—the local word, both singular and plural, for "camel driver"—could focus on their jobs rather than on the foreigner who got in over his head. Besides, Alkoye pitched in, the azalai only speak Hasinaya, their Arabic dialect, but the guide would speak French and could translate for me. And $1,750 was the best price I could get.

Though it was more than I wanted to pay, it was much less than the five thousand dollars I'd been quoted over the Internet—which I refrained from mentioning—and was low enough that I knew we'd be able to come to terms. I was excited but tried to hide it, not wanting to weaken my bargaining position by appearing over eager. Instead, I feigned shock at the price and lowballed the chief with a counteroffer of less than half the amount he'd named. He reacted as though I'd just blasphemed against Allah Himself. Back and forth we went. Despite my efforts to keep a poker face, I couldn't quite corral my feelings. Riding with a caravan was the reason for this entire trip, and I was being offered a chance to leave with a string of camels in two days. My long-held dream was nearly within my grasp; I badly wanted it to be in my pocket. So I lost my cool. Somehow I forgot the part of the ritual where you stand up and say, "Thanks, but it's too expensive and I'm going to go see if I can get it cheaper somewhere else." I made the deal then and there for twelve hundred bucks (which I later learned was a fair price).

Once we settled on the specifics, we drew up a contract. Alkoye, the chief, and I all signed it. Though I couldn't help thinking this was little more than a procedural farce, written contracts have been a part of Saharan trading culture for centuries and have always been legally binding. Merchants used them to record the terms of the deals they made with each other and their employees—the traders who actually shuttled the cargo across the desert. As the nomad saying goes, "What leaves the head does not leave the paper." The importance that Saharans attached to their contracts is evident by the fact that they bothered to write them at all, since paper was rare, very expensive, and never used frivolously.

Paper had such power that something like traveler's checks had been an integral part of the Saharan trading system. Rather than crossing the desert with the wealth required to purchase goods in a far-off place and potentially losing it to bandits en route, a trader often gave money to a merchant in his hometown who had connections with another merchant in the destination city. In return, the hometown merchant gave the trader a handwritten note—called a *suftaja*—redeemable for that amount once he reached his destination. A suftaja could also be exchanged with other traders like money, and could pass through countless hands before finally being cashed in. Thus, traders could successfully cross vast distances, including entire continents, carrying little more than an IOU. Unlike traveler's checks from American Express, however, if a trader lost his suftaja, he was out of luck.

I spent the rest of that day and the next getting ready to leave. Timbuktu felt like a true frontier town, a place ever conscious of its smallness and vulnerability beneath searing heat and desert gales. Accessible from the rest of Mali only from the Niger River, by air, or over hours' worth of dirt tracks, it exudes an island-like sense of isolation, giving the impression that one has come to both the metaphorical and actual end of the road. With its dusty streets, general stores filled with provisions for life in town and on the range, and swarms of dubious—though generally harmless—characters, each trying to hustle a few bucks, I felt like I had stepped into an African version of the Wild West, with cowboy hats replaced by turbans, boots by flip-flops, whiskey by green tea, and horses by camels and beat-up Land Cruisers.

Timbuktu was founded around 1000 AD. Situated on the southern border of the Sahara and along the northern bend of the Niger River, which flows in a twenty-six-hundred-mile arc through West Africa, Timbuktu could have been the prototype for the aphorism about location, location, location. It became the trading nexus for goods traveling between black Africa and the Magreb, Europe, and Egypt, beginning in the eleventh century. Among the slaves, ostrich feathers, ebony, and salt exchanged in its markets were boggling quantities of gold.

Its legend began in 1324, when Mansu Musa, the emperor of Mali, traversed the Sahara en route to Mecca, making the hajj required of all faithful Muslims. When he arrived in Cairo, accompanied by perhaps the richest caravan the city had ever seen, tales of the staggering amount of gold he carried from Timbuktu quickly spread across the civilized world. Accounts by the great Arab explorers Ibn Battuta, who visited Timbuktu in the 1350s, and Leo Africanus, who visited in 1526, further stoked the European imagination. In his book *A History and Description of Africa*, Africanus wrote that the king of Timbuktu "owns great wealth in gold piastre and bullion, some of which weigh 1300 pounds" and that the residents "are exceedingly rich . . . in place of money, [they] use pieces of pure unadulterated gold. . . ."

In Europe, Timbuktu became mythologized as an African Eldorado. Its houses, rumor had it, were sided and shingled with gold. But for centuries, only one white man had ever been there: a Florentine merchant named Benedetto Dei, who made it to the city in 1470 when it was near the peak of its prosperity. Dei, however, left little record of his experience, and Timbuktu remained shrouded in such mystery that European geographers didn't even know where to draw the fabulous city on their maps.

Lured by its wealth, hundreds of explorers died trying to find it between the sixteenth and nineteenth centuries. Those who approached from the west, attempting to follow the Niger River, succumbed to disease or were killed by hostile natives. Those who came from the north were thwarted by the vast desert and the tribal warriors who dwelt there.

Then, in July 1825, Major Alexander Gordon Laing, a thirty-two-year-old British army officer of Scottish birth, set out from Tripoli, intending to caravan-hop his way some twenty-six hundred miles southwest across the Sahara. He began his expedition with an Arab guide, a Jewish interpreter, a servant from Sierra Leone, and a couple of West African boatbuilders who, if all went well, would help convey him down the Niger River after reaching Timbuktu. But all did not go well. In the middle of the desert, Laing was double-crossed by his guide, who sold him out to a group of Tuareg bandits. Armed with guns and sabers, the Tuareg pounced upon Laing and his small entourage while they slept. Laing was jarred awake by a bullet in his side moments before a sword sliced into his thigh. Defenselessly absorbing a flurry of blows, he was slashed repeatedly across the face and neck, which left him with a broken jaw, a severed ear, and a fractured skull. One strike to the back of his neck penetrated so deep that it scratched his windpipe. He either lost the use of—or completely lost—his right hand, with which he had shielded his head. His left arm, wounded in three places, was broken.

A mangled, bloody mess, he incomprehensibly survived, owing no small debt to the sterility of the Sahara. So feeble he had to be strapped into his saddle, Laing trailed the caravan for four hundred merciless miles to the village of Sidi Mukhtar, where he was struck with a yellow-fever-like illness. After nine days hovering near death, he recovered, then set out to cross the remaining two hundred miles to Timbuktu. By this time, all of his original companions were dead.

When I picture Laing limping through the gates of Timbuktu on August 13, 1826, I like to think that he had enough of a sense of humor to laugh through his tears at the cruel joke he must've felt had been played upon him. For, after completing his Herculean quest, he became the first European to discover that Timbuktu was a greatly overrated destination. Between the time of Benedetto Dei's visit and Laing's arrival, Timbuktu had been sacked by Moroccan forces. Then, European nations longing for direct access to sub-Saharan markets began establishing ports along the West African coast. As a result, the sea replaced the Sahara as the primary trade route between Europe and black Africa, diverting the lucrative intercontinental trade away from Timbuktu. Though it remained an important center of intra-Saharan trade, especially in salt, it had long since fallen from riches to ruin, and was a city of crumbling mud. The Timbuktu I arrived in wasn't all that different from the one discovered by Laing, though it did have intermittent Internet service.

Laing headed home after spending nearly six weeks in Timbuktu, traveling north with a guide and a small caravan. He didn't get far before his new guide betrayed him; three days into the journey, Laing was beheaded and buried beneath a thorn tree. He was not alone in his fate; numerous other explorers en route to Timbuktu, both before and after Laing, were turned on by their guides, stabbed or strangled to death by the very men they had trusted to see them safely across the sands.

I was a bit uneasy about the historical precedent of guides killing their clients in the middle of the desert. I reckoned I would be in the same position as the explorers—a lone white man, rich by nomad standards, wholly dependent on my native companions in a place beyond the reach of law. Moreover, this was the fall of 2003. Six months earlier, the United States had invaded Iraq and was actively waging war on terrorism—which many Muslims (and some evangelical Christians) perceived as a sequel to the Crusades. It was a new low point in Arab–American relations. Images of Arabs burning the Stars and Stripes and threatening death to America saturated the media. My father, who had a friend in the U.S. State Department, relayed warnings to me about anti-Americanism in Mali, particularly among the Arabs and Tuareg in the north—precisely the people to whom I'd be trusting my life. Though I knew that most people in most places easily distinguish between individuals and their government, I was wary of how I'd be received as an American at that time; it'd be best, I concluded, not to let anyone know that I was Jewish, too.

I used my time in Timbuktu to buy some essentials for the trip through the Sahara, including a set of nomad-style clothing that would help me fit in with the azalai and make me more comfortable as I faced the sun, wind, and sand of the desert (a pair of baggy pants; a boubou; a shirt; and three meters of cloth for a turban—all made from the same lightweight sky-blue cotton fabric). I bought a kilo of tobacco to pass out as a gift to men I'd meet along the trail. Perhaps most important, I picked up a few supplementary kilos of dates and peanuts, as well as a box of black tea. I took seriously the warning that John, the archaeology professor, had given me about the Spartan caravan diet. I was startled by the dramatic amount of weight John had lost; I didn't have twenty pounds to spare.

While at home, pondering how best to prepare for weeks of undernourishment, I developed two completely contradictory theories of physical training. The first was that I should promptly halve my normal food intake, so that by the time I was on the caravan my body would be accustomed to functioning on less and wouldn't torture me with hunger pains. The second was that I should begin eating all the time, in order to enter the desert with more weight to lose.

I polled all of the doctors I knew, asking which approach was most medically sound. They unanimously advised me to eat, a lot, since bulking up would give my body more time before it went into "starvation mode." Since the last biology class I had taken was seventeen years earlier, and I had been encouraged to drop out rather than fail, I had no idea what "starvation mode" was, but it sounded bad. I imagined it as a form of cellular cannibalism, as though my body would be throwing a molecular Donner-themed party at which my cells would draw lots and the losers would sacrifice themselves to the winners, becoming microscopic martyrs for the cause of my survival. I hoped the peanuts and dates I bought would help stave this off as long as possible.

The day before I was scheduled to begin the journey across the desert, I met briefly with my guide on the shaded patio of a coffee shop next to the tourist agency office. Walid, an azalai by trade, had the typically slight frame and leathery skin of Saharan nomads. His face was lean, his cheeks angular and clean-shaven. His black mustache curved down around his lips and joined with a close-cropped goatee. A black turban was wound atop his head and under his chin, so it could easily be pulled up over his mouth and nose. Contrary to Alkoye's promise, Walid couldn't speak French. Though I was confident we'd be able to communicate in Arabic, which I'd once studied in Cairo, it was a disappointing revelation nonetheless, since I spoke French much better.

Walid was accompanied by his uncle, Lamana, who was fluent in French, which he'd learned over the course of many years of guiding tourists into the desert around Timbuktu. He was Walid's mentor, and was helping him build a guiding career for himself—one that was easier and paid better than shuttling salt across the desert. Walid was relatively new at leading foreigners and had only taken a handful out on short excursions before he got the call to accompany me on the most grueling trek that either tourist or nomad could make.

Sitting around the wooden table on the café's patio, Lamana warned me about the hardships I was going to face. The heat would be insufferable. The caravan would march fifteen, maybe twenty hours at a stretch with no rest. Walid and I, Lamana said, would have some flexibility in our daily schedule before we met the caravan at the good grazing grounds where it was mustering six days to the north, but once we joined up with it, I'd have to keep up or be left behind. If I fell ill or got injured, there was no way out. I shouldn't underestimate the dangers of the crossing, he continued; most local people would think I was nuts for voluntarily embarking on this trip. He said he was nervous for me, and felt responsible for my safety.

I was nervous for me, too, and wondered to myself if I was nuts for signing on to a caravan. Before heading to Mali, I'd scrutinized the risks of the journey—from starvation to injury to murder—through a mental magnifying glass, blowing them up to terrifying proportions. For a week, I forgot everything that drew me to the caravans; I lost my curiosity about the exotic culture in which I was going to immerse; I just wanted to come back alive. I finally broke out of this neurotic eddy, putting the dangers back into a more rational, manageable perspective. They were still substantial, but I was nonetheless swept forth again by visions of camels and nomads and desert.

Trying to ease Lamana's concerns, I told him I knew what I was getting into and that I'd traveled many a mile through other deserts. I'm not sure I convinced him that I could in fact hack it, but he certainly got the picture that my mind was made up.

"One last thing," Lamana said. "Do you eat meat?"

When I said yes, of course, he laughed and said he never knew what to expect from foreigners' dietary habits; many, he continued, inexplicably engaged in a bizarre practice called vegetarianism.

As we rose to leave, I shook hands with Lamana and Walid and said, "See you tomorrow."

"*Ensha'allah,*" Lamana replied—meaning "God willing"—the standard Muslim reply to every statement about the future, even the most mundane.

Moments after leaving the café, I was approached by a black man in a Polo-type shirt, jeans, and sneakers, who asked if I was the American who was going to Taoudenni.

"Yes," I said, surprised that my plans were known by people I had never met. The old adage about news traveling fast in a small town seems to be a universal truth.

"Why didn't you come see me?" he asked.

"What are you talking about?" I wanted to know.

"You e-mailed me from your home, asking about joining a caravan, and you said we'd discuss it when you got to Timbuktu. My name is Alkoye Touré. And now I learn that you've already decided to go with someone else."

"You are Alkoye Touré? Then who did I arrange my trip with?"

"That was the other Alkoye Touré. There are two of us here in town. Everyone calls him 'Le Petit' because he is smaller than me. Did he tell you he was me?"

"No, no," I said. "I thought he was you because your names are the same, but he never pretended to be you."

Alkoye "Le Grand" didn't believe me and chided me for breaking my promise to him. How was I supposed to know, I asked him, that there could possibly be two guides with the same name in the same town? But ignorance of Timbuktu's unwritten laws was no excuse; guides there lay claim to tourists as though they are property—whoever makes first contact owns them. While I was in the desert, Alkoye "Le Grand" actually complained to the local authorities about this simple matter of mistaken identity, basically accusing Alkoye "Le Petit" of tourist theft. And he won his case—"Le Petit" had to pay "Le Grand" about thirty dollars in compensation for what amounted to trademark infringement.

With everything set for my departure into the great desert, all my nervousness and excitement disappeared. I felt, essentially, blank. Despite all that I had heard and read about crossing the Sahara, I recognized on the deepest of levels that I had no idea what to expect; that the experience of doing it would be so altogether different from reading about it that I wouldn't really know what it'd be like until after I had done it. I accepted that my course had been set and found myself naturally adopting a calm, open-minded attitude, in which I felt prepared to receive whatever lay ahead, as ready as I could be without knowing exactly for what.

Then, that evening, I felt myself getting sick. Suddenly, starvation was the least of my concerns.

I awoke in the morning with sinuses swollen and tender. My nose was so clogged, I had to gulp for air like a beached catfish. Mucus trickled steadily from my nostrils; I was chain-sneezing; my neck and shoulders ached. And I was hot, really hot, and not just because of the ambient air temperature. I felt like the NyQuil poster boy.

Had I been at home, I would have lain around nursing myself. I was hardly fit to strike out into the Sahara. I briefly and seriously considered delaying my departure for at least a day. I'm no reckless adventurer; I like to come back from my trips alive. But I knew that the caravan wasn't going to wait for me. If Walid and I arrived late at the grazing grounds where we were supposed to meet it, it would likely be gone. It was a risk I didn't want to take. After getting final approval from my internal actuary, whose job it is to coolly weigh the probabilities of all possible disasters, I decided to go for it. By the time I reached Lamana's house on the northern edge of town, sweat was seeping from my every pore and through my clothes.

Lamana, Walid, and I followed the cratered dirt lanes past the last of the mud-brick houses and into a dusty clearing strewn with torn plastic bags, scraps of fraying, fading fabric, and the heaped remains of slaughtered goats. Thorn trees quivered in the hot breeze under morning skies milky with haze. Children pumped water from a well into bright green-and-yellow buckets, pausing to shout, smile, and wave their dark, skinny arms as we passed. This was the shore of civilization, where the sands of the Sahara washed up on the outskirts of Timbuktu. The children, I thought, were like the throngs that bid farewell to cruise ships, tossing confetti from the docks, only this ocean was made of sand and our ships had four legs and humps.

Our two camels were loaded with enough rice, millet flour, biscuits, green tea, and sugar, plus a few kilos each of peanuts and dates, to last two people for forty days—a biblical-sounding length of time. All of our food fit into two watermelon-sized rice sacks, except for the meat—half of a raw, freshly skinned goat carcass that was lashed to the outside of our cargo. Four rubber inner tubes, cut in half and with their ends tied off, would hold just enough water to sustain us between wells.

Our supplies were divided between our camels; each had a load slung over its back, resting atop pads made of desert grasses that equalized the baggage over the camels' ribs. We carried neither a tent nor a tarp. We had no saddles, just the blankets we would later sleep on tied over our camels' humps. I had my backpack, while Walid brought a knockoff nylon duffel printed with the word ABIDAS.

For a journey of nearly a thousand miles across some of the toughest terrain on earth, it looked like we had underpacked.

The tail of the lead camel was tied to the lower jaw of the second with a rope of handwoven grasses. Another rope was cinched around the lead camel's jaw, which Walid carried over his shoulder. We marched north, into the open desert. Thinking superstitiously of Orpheus and Lot's wife, I didn't look back.

Lamana accompanied us over the first series of dunes. Before he sent us off and returned to town, we paused. Lamana called Walid aside and gave him a few minutes' worth of hushed, last-minute counsel, like a concerned coach about to watch a young athlete take the field for a big game. Then he turned to me.

Shaking my hand warmly, an expression of true caring on his face, he cautioned me one last time about the dangers ahead. If I wanted to back out, he said suggestively, this was the time. Seeing I had no intention of doing so even though I was obviously physically unwell, he advised me to meet the desert with courage and offered a final, perplexing warning: "Allah is compassionate, but He doesn't speak French." I didn't bother to ask if He spoke English.

Lamana, his blue robe flapping in the wind, turned back toward Timbuktu. Walid and I continued north, side by side. I was wearing my new blue pants, a light, long-sleeved buttondown shirt, my turban, and a pair of sandals. Walid wore his black turban, lime-green plastic flip-flops, and a blue, green, and white striped caftan that hung to the middle of his calves. We made small talk in Arabic to break the silence. Since I hadn't spoken it in five years, I had to keep things simple.

Walid, I learned, was thirty years old. He had grown up in the desert among the Berabish tribe, living in cloth tents, moving with herds of goats, sheep, and camels from one sparse pasture to the next, and had ridden with the salt caravans since he was fifteen, making two or three trips to Taoudenni each year. Like most nomads, Walid was completely unschooled. I found he did know a tiny bit of French—the phrases *C'est bien, Ce n'est pas bien,* and the words *grand, petit,* and *chameau.*

Walid's camel was aptly, if not creatively, named L'beyya, which means "white" in Walid's dialect. Mine was called Lachmar, which means "red," though he was more of a rusty brown with a tuft of white on his hump and a little under his chin from age. At fifteen, Lachmar was five years older than L'beyya. Neither was old for a camel—they can live to thirty—but L'beyya was at his physical peak. Lachmar, on the other hand, had slid into middle age. He had at most a few more trips to Taoudenni left in him, and this, Walid said, might be his last.

Our simple dialogue required more effort than I like to admit. I was forced to improvise with the random remnants of my Arabic vocabulary that remained accessible; the bulk of it lay buried beneath the sands of forgetfulness like ancient Egyptian relics, which I hoped I'd be able to dredge up before too long.

Thankfully, I could already tell that Walid and I had a natural linguistic connection. When speaking a foreign language, I find that some people are much easier to talk to than others, for no reason I can explain. I've been in situations where I've sat with two people, one of whom I can communicate easily with, the other hardly at all. At such times, the person to whom I can relate serves as a translator of sorts: I'll say something in Arabic (or whatever language I'm trying to speak), he'll repeat the same Arabic words I've just spoken, and the third person will then understand. That person will reply in Arabic and the translator will repeat those words to me, again in Arabic, which I then understand. It makes no sense at all. But the fact of the matter is that the connection is either there, or it isn't. That Walid and I could already communicate as well as we did was a good sign, considering that I was speaking a crippled Egyptian Arabic and his native dialect was Hasinaya. We also shared silence comfortably. When our first conversation ran its natural course, I retreated into my own mental world, which revolved entirely around my health, or lack thereof.

Walking briskly alongside Walid, my nose demanded perpetual wiping and blowing. The inside of my mouth, which I had to keep open in order to breathe, was parched from the arid air. Though the overcast sky buffered us from the glare of the sun, I felt dangerously hot from the inside out.

Thus my long-dreamed-of odyssey began. Rather than feeling the thrill of setting off on a great adventure, I just felt like crap. Instead of contemplating the immense desert I was entering, I was busy hyper-scrutinizing my physical state, trying to divine whether each minute change in my body foreshadowed an imminent recovery or a slide into full-blown illness. I tried to assuage myself with rationalizations: If Gordon Laing could traverse the desert after being hacked up by his Tuareg assailants, surely I could survive a sinus infection. But I couldn't talk myself out of the fear that I'd made a potentially fatal mistake by starting the trek in such a debilitated condition. I was already breaking that perfunctory promise I'd made to loved ones to "be safe."

My girlfriend, Karen, was less than thrilled with this undertaking to begin with, but since she'd stuck with me four years already, she understood that there was no holding me back and was as supportive as she could be. A year or so earlier, when I had set out to pioneer a solo trek through a remote mountain range in Mongolia, she was less so. Then, since I was completely alone for weeks on end and had no way of contacting home, she was afraid I would die in an accident and simply vanish in the wilderness.

This time, even when considering the objective dangers involved in crossing the Sahara, she was much more relaxed. "At least you'll be with other people," she said, explaining her attitude. "In the worst-case scenario, someone will know what happened to you, and I'll be able to find out." Thus I learned that my death wouldn't be such a tragedy to her as long as she could have some closure around it.

Some of my friends and family had urged me to carry a satellite phone, or at least a GPS, in case of emergency, but since the camel drivers never used them, I felt like that would be violating the spirit of the adventure. I remembered an interview I'd once read, given in 2001, by the then ninety-year-old Wilfred Thesiger, author of the classic *Arabian Sands* and arguably the most intrepid desert explorer of the twentieth century. At one point, he was asked what he thought of biologist J. Michael Fay's two-thousand-mile-long trek through the jungles of Africa with a bunch of pygmies. Fay, Thesiger was told, carried a satellite phone and could have supplies air-dropped if he needed them. "Well, you see, that wrecks it!" Thesiger pronounced. "Then you know he's in no danger." Referring to his own excursions through Arabia's Empty Quarter in the 1940s, during which starvation was more than once a looming possibility, he said, "A telephone would have ruined the whole thing."

I agreed with Thesiger wholeheartedly. Part of true adventure—and the way explorers traveled by necessity until recent times—is pushing beyond the reach of outside aid, managing situations with the resources one has, being smart while praying for a touch of divine grace. You perceive your environment and yourself differently if help is merely a phone call away. I didn't want the safety net. But feeling as miserable as I did heading into the desert, I wondered if I'd end up regretting that decision.

I also began to question whether the personal goal I'd set for myself was laughably unrealistic.

One of the essential tensions in my life is the conflict between the love I have for my home and the insatiable wanderlust that provokes me to leave it for the farthest corners of the earth. I find my kindred spirit in the character of Sindbad the Sailor, who revels in his life in Baghdad surrounded by family and friends, yet can't resist the lure of travel. Time and again he is drawn to the port city of Basra, whence he sets sail across the sea. Inevitably, he stumbles into the most fantastic and calamitous of adventures.

In his most famous exploit, Sindbad finds himself shipwrecked on a deserted island that happens to be the nesting ground for the Rukh, a bird so huge and terrible that it blocks the sun when it spreads its wings and "feeds its young on elephants." Its eggs are as big as a house. Sindbad concludes that his only way off the island is with the Rukh, so while the great bird sleeps, he lashes himself to its talons with his turban. The next morning, the Rukh takes off in search of food, soaring high above the earth while Sindbad prays for his life. At last it lands in a valley teeming with serpents the size of palm trees. When it touches down, the terrified Sindbad quickly unties himself before the Rukh soars away with a snake in its claws.

As it is told, the floor of the Valley of Serpents is littered with precious gems. Men from the surrounding area have learned to harvest the riches without having to face the snakes—they slaughter sheep on the mountain above and cast the skinned animals down into the valley, where diamonds stick to the meat. Eagles and vultures swoop down and carry the jewel-laden carrion up to the mountaintop, where the men chase them away and pick the diamonds from the flesh. Sindbad, desperate, binds himself to a carcass and is lifted along with it to safety by an eagle. With the help of the gem dealers, he finally makes it back to Baghdad.

In the midst of adventures like these, Sindbad's only thought is returning home alive. He is always grateful when he arrives there safely, but sooner or later is inevitably infected with the urge to set sail again.

In the novel *Arabian Nights and Days*, which is loosely based on *1001 Arabian Nights*, Nobel Prize–winning author Naguib Mahfouz points out Sindbad's greatest flaw: As Sindbad is about to leave on another journey, a wise doctor says to him, "Go in peace, then return laden with diamonds and wisdom, but do not repeat the same mistake." A puzzled expression crosses Sindbad's face, and the doctor continues: "The Rukh had not previously flown with a man, and what did you do? You left it at the first opportunity. . . ."

"I hardly believed I would make my escape," Sindbad replies in defense.

"The Rukh flies from an unknown world to an unknown world," the doctor says, "and it leaps from the peak of Waq to the peak of Qaf, so be not content with anything for it is the wish of the Sublime."

Sindbad's mistake was his failure to appreciate the rarity of his circumstance, so preoccupied was he with saving himself. It was a message that resonated deeply with me. Reflecting on my own adventures alone in the Mongolian wilderness, I saw I'd made the same one. While the experience was deeply rewarding in many ways, I had failed to squeeze everything possible out of it. I struggled with a gnawing anxiety over being so far from civilization for weeks on end, with no possible aid but that which nomadic herders—who didn't even have aspirin—could provide. I felt rushed, as though the sooner I could complete the trek, the greater chance I'd have of emerging safely from the mountains. I could have explored its canyons, meadows, and ridges for weeks more, but was compelled by this low-grade fear to get out sooner rather than later. Once I returned home and slowly evaluated my experiences, I regretted the opportunities I'd forsaken due to my own preoccupation with escaping alive.

I took to heart the advice given to Sindbad by the doctor; I was determined not to repeat my mistake in the Sahara. I likened traveling with a caravan to flying with the Rukh; I set myself not only to survive, but to enjoy and derive value from the journey, to appreciate being exactly where I was, no matter how difficult it became.

Struck with fever, feeling like my head was packed with lead as I walked my first miles in the Sahara, I couldn't help scaling back my lofty goals. Not even an hour into the forty-day voyage, I already felt like I was in trouble. I just wasn't sure how much.

Walid.

CHAPTER TWO

After an hour or so on foot, Walid decided it was time for us to mount our camels. We stopped, and Walid grasped Lachmar's lead while softly uttering, "Shhh. Shhhh. Shhhh." The camel complied by kneeling to the ground. I clambered onto my blanket, but before I was settled, Lachmar took to his feet, steeply lurching forward and back, nearly pitching me off. Half panicked, I instinctively grabbed for the rope that crisscrossed the cargo pads in front of me. Once Lachmar was standing and I'd regained my composure, Walid told me to take off my sandals—for true cameleers ride barefoot—which he then tied onto a dangling piece of cord.

After making sure that Lachmar was still tied securely to L'beyya's tail, Walid took L'beyya's lead and walked a few steps to get his camel moving. Then he grabbed the animal's left ear with his left hand. In a sequence so smooth and rapid that all the motions blended into one, L'beyya lowered his head to the height of Walid's, and Walid sprang gracefully up onto the camel's neck, landing on it with his shin. L'beyya raised his head, and Walid along with it, while Walid turned to the right so he faced backward, the front of his body pressing against the camel's. He rode like that for a minute, making a few adjustments to his improvised saddle, then slid effortlessly up on top of the hump. It was a feat worthy of any trick rodeo.

Thanks to Lachmar's long legs and arced back, my head was twice as high as it had been when I was on the ground. From my new perch, I had commanding views of the landscape around me. The desert spread out in all directions like a giant rumpled carpet, its patterns woven with green and beige. Long, low rolling ridges broke up the flat desert plains, running parallel to each other and giving the level areas between them the feel of shallow basins. Clumps of tall, slender grasses sprouted from the sand, speckling the sandy earth like leopard spots. Here and there, thorn trees grew; their bony branches spread from twisted trunks, forming crowns that resembled cumulus clouds with flat bottoms and bulging, rounded tops. In each of the valleys between the hills, nomad tents were pitched. With broad roofs flaring out like wings from a peaked center and one side open like a gaping mouth, they looked like giant white manta rays. Herds of goats wandered untended. Lone camels lifted their heads to watch us pass. Though I knew that the southernmost part of the desert—called the Azawad—was the most livable, I was surprised to see the earth dusted with a fine layer of grass—a blessed result of the recent rains. But even it was far more arid than the Sahara of ages past.

In prehistoric eras, parts of the Sahara were covered by rain forests, mangroves, and swamps. Rivers flowed, emptying into large inland seas that expanded in wet years and retreated in dry ones, leaving behind layer upon layer of mineralized sediment with each major cycle—the process responsible for creating the salt beds of Taoudenni. All of this water was a key contributor to an ecosystem that, until the first millennium BC, teemed with life.

Dinosaurs thrived in their day, including the plant-eating *Paralititan*, the second largest dinosaur ever discovered, whose skeleton was pulled from the sands outside Bahariyya Oasis, Egypt, in 2001. Prehistoric fish eaters have been unearthed in regions that now are among the driest in the world. In the barren wastes of Niger, a Tuareg chief once told a paleontologist that he knew "where a lot of big camel bones were lying around." For generations, the Tuareg had told their kids that the bones were the remains of a fabled monster called Jobar; in tribute, the newly discovered dinosaur species was named *Jobaria tiguidensis*.

In times closer to our own, elephants, giraffes, lions, ostriches, leopards, and gazelles—among many other animals—roamed the lush Sahara. Crocodiles, hippopotami, and fish filled its waters. Many of the early Saharan peoples were hunters, as depicted in Algeria's primitive rock art. Others were fishermen; bone fishhooks and harpoon tips have been discovered deep in the desert. When in Dakhla Oasis, in Egypt, I came across fossilized shark teeth scattered among the surrounding plateaus, and found fossilized snails atop the mesas near Siwa.

Today the bulk of the Sahara is so dry that annual rainfall is measured in millimeters, and some places wait many years between showers. Of course, the Sahara's aquatic life has all but disappeared; now even few large mammals can survive there. Jackals stick close to water sources; gazelles have a much greater range, but the only large wild mammal truly fit for life in the heart of the desert is the addax antelope. Like the camel, the body temperature of the addax can surpass 110 degrees before it breaks into a sweat, helping it conserve water. Also like the camel, the addax's respiratory system is designed so that the air it inhales through its nose cools off the blood flowing to its brain to prevent it from overheating. Blessed with an ability to glean all the moisture it requires from the vegetation it eats, an addax has no need to drink water, ever. The one element of Saharan life to which the addax cannot adapt is its hunters, who prize the animal for its long, black, spiraled horns, its hide, and its meat.

The people who once dwelt across the length and breadth of the Sahara are now confined to its fringes, where just enough grass grows to support their livestock; along the route to Taoudenni, herding families range no farther than Araouane, an isolated village 150 miles north of Timbuktu. The salt caravans, however, penetrate the desert far past the limits of normal human—and even animal—habitation.

Figuring out how to get comfortable on Lachmar's back temporarily distracted me from my obsession with my health. Timidly, so as not to lose my balance while the motion of the camel rocked me forward and backward and up and down, I experimented with different positions. I laid my legs to the right of the hump, then to the left, then tried straddling it. Each shift earned me only short-lived relief from the pounding friction between my camel and my ass. As Lachmar—a promiscuous eater, like all camels—lunged his head toward every small plant we passed, I had to fight to maintain my equilibrium against his sudden thrusts to the side. I looked with envy at the ease with which Walid was nonchalantly perched atop L'beyya, his posture perfect.

Meanwhile, I was constantly blowing my nose. Concerned that I'd burn through my small supply of tissue, I was as conservative with it as possible. After each blow, I'd hold the soggy paper up in the air, which was so arid that the tissue dried completely and was able to be reused in less than a minute.

After a few hours, we stopped for lunch in a sandy hollow. We unloaded the camels and loosely tied their front ankles together so they could graze unburdened but couldn't stray far. By this time I was spent. We spread our blankets under the thin shade of a thorn tree, upon the spikes of which Walid had impaled our goat carcass. He quickly set to making a batch of *dorno*—the nomad version of an energy shake—scooping handfuls of millet flour into a stainless-steel mixing bowl, then adding water from one of the inner tubes, plus a little bit of sugar. When it had attained the consistency of watery gruel, he stirred it with a cassette-sized chunk of solid salt. He raised the bowl to his lips, sipped it, and, satisfied, passed the bowl to me and urged me to drink. What on this day struck me as a good substitute for papier mâché paste soon became something I loved, even craved. Hundreds of sand-colored grasshoppers flecked with tiny brown triangles, as though they were wearing desert-issue army fatigues, swarmed in from nowhere, drawn to the few drops of water that had dribbled on the ground.

Until this moment, I'd had the fantasy that I would purify all the water I drank with iodine. Realizing it would be impossible to do so and that it'd be pointless to treat just some of it, I handled the threat of waterborne bacteria the most intelligent way I could think of—by ignoring it. I hoped my gut was strong enough to take care of itself.

Once the dorno was finished, Walid began gathering dead branches over which to make tea and cook a pot of noodles. I made a feeble effort to help him, but was so exhausted I was dizzy. He urged me just to sit and rest, so I went back to the blanket, more than a little ashamed. I felt like the kind of tourist I never wanted to be—useless—relaxing while the native guide did all the work—the quintessential white man. But I also knew that the best thing I could do for both of us was to recover as quickly as possible. I swallowed four ibuprofen and promptly passed out.

Walid woke me about fifteen minutes later, holding out a small glass and repeating *"Kess, kess,"* which I quickly learned was the nomad call to tea. Had I been in his position, I would have just let me sleep, but to these desert people, tea drinking is one of life's non-negotiables, taking precedence over virtually all else. It is such an ingrained ritual, it seems as though it's been part of their culture since prehistoric times.

In fact, tea was first imported into this part of Africa in the early 1800s. For nearly a hundred years, it remained a luxury item, consumed mostly by the wealthy. Only in the early twentieth century was it adopted by the culture at large. It was so popular, and addictive, that Muslim scholars wrote long opinions on whether drinking it was permitted by the Koran.

Historically and today, the everyman's brew in this region is green tea from China—though not because the nomads were aware of its myriad health benefits. The British deemed green tea to be undrinkable, so their merchants used crates of it as ballast for their ships. When they docked at the Moroccan port of al-Swaira, the tea was unloaded and sold off cheaply, then the holds of the vessels were filled with African goods.

After drinking three shot-sized glasses—the number required by the ritual—I fell back to sleep.

When lunch was ready, Walid woke me again and passed me a metal plate heaped with noodles and slivers of goat meat, drizzled with goat butter and palm oil, sprinkled unintentionally with sand. I was hardly hungry but the food wasn't bad, so I stomached what I could, prodded by Walid's Jewish mothering. "Eat, eat," he urged, "for your strength." With only one spoon between us, which was used for serving, I began my longest-ever streak of eating only with my fingers. Walid dined directly from the charred metal cauldron; though the Muslim holy month of Ramadan had begun a few days earlier, the azalai and the Taoudenni salt miners are exempt from observing the monthlong sunrise-to-sunset fast, with no divine repercussions, due to the rigors of their jobs. In the end, my leftovers were dumped back into the pot, covered with a lid, and saved for later.

Thanks to my nap, I felt energetic enough to attempt a conversation. I pulled out the few photos I'd brought from home, figuring that if they were even close to being worth the proverbial thousand words, we'd be communicating pretty successfully. Since most of the images were of things that were once part of my vocabulary—family members, girlfriend, house, pets, landscapes near my home—talking about them gave me a chance to use the words I remembered and refresh some that had slipped my mind, with the help of my Arabic phrase book. When I showed him a shot of one of my dogs, taken at White Sands National Monument, Walid took it from my hands, his eyes wide with surprise. It looked like parts of the Sahara, he said, hardly believing it was a picture of America. I explained, in the broadest of strokes, that the States were filled with a mixture of deserts, forests, mountains, cities, rivers, and seacoasts. He nodded thoughtfully, as though absorbing something of great importance. At everything I said that he understood, he made a clucking sound from the back of his throat, which I quickly learned was the nomad's way of signifying comprehension or agreement—like the American *uh-huh*.

Near four o'clock, when the worst of the day's heat had passed, Walid said he was going to round up the camels. Trying to make up for my earlier uselessness, I went with him. They had wandered about a quarter mile away and were munching on a bush. Their split, prehensile upper lips worked like hands, grasping and tearing away prickly leafed twigs, then passing the fodder back between their teeth. I took Lachmar's lead and guided him back to our gear. For the first time all day I was overcome with elation, looking at myself as though from the outside, towing my camel across the Sahara. This was the dream coming true.

I helped load the camels, hoisting and holding a bag in place on one side of the hump while Walid held a bag on the opposite side and secured them to each other over the cargo pads. Tied just to each other, not to the pads, the bags relied only on the integrity of the knots and the laws of physics to remain in place. I'd expected the azalai to use specialized knots for rigging their loads, but Walid was content with the simplest twists that would likely do the job. Given that most of the ropes were split, frayed, mended, and generally unsound, I was glad that there was no rock-climbing component to this adventure.

We set off on foot, then mounted after a few miles, as would be our pattern. The air was cooler now, and though I was still perpetually wiping my nose, I felt hopeful. The sky had cleared above us. We marched through the glow of a lustrous copper sunset and into the ghostly light cast by the almost half-moon. The world was shades of indigo and steel. The hills before us rose like rollers in a dark sea. To the south, shadowy plumes obscured the stars and lightning flashed, but the storm was far from us.

While we rode through the night, Walid occasionally gave a shout, an abbreviated "Hoy!" I intuited that I was supposed to answer in kind, and did. I wasn't sure if this was his way of feeling less alone, or if the call and return was simply his way of making sure that I was okay and still with him. It inspired in me a sense of true companionship, cementing the knowledge that we were in this together.

By the time we made camp atop a sandy dune, the moon had long since set. We unloaded the camels and laid out our blankets. Walid built a tea fire, and I collapsed, my resources drained and my head still draining. I didn't bother pulling out my sleeping bag; wearing my boubou, which was like being wrapped in a sheet, provided enough warmth.

Though I was sure to be wakened for tea, I couldn't help myself from drifting off. But before I fell asleep, I was jolted by a blaring noise that abruptly broke the absolute silence of the desert; Walid was searching for stations on a shortwave radio. Each one was awash in static, but he was not easily deterred. Because I never carry a radio when I'm in the desert, that Walid had one out here took me by complete surprise. I think of going to into the wilderness as a time to leave the civilized world behind and immerse solely in the natural. Walid, however, had no purist ideals about what it was supposed to mean to be in the desert; to him, this *was* the civilized world.

Walid paused for a moment on the Voice of America. I almost asked him to leave it there, but quickly realized I didn't care about knowing what was going on elsewhere. I'd long since reckoned with the phenomenon of being completely out of touch for weeks at a time, and the understanding that familial or global tragedies could occur while I was so sequestered. I was glad when he turned the dial to an Arabic music station.

When we finished the tea session, Walid jammed his camel stick into the ground at a sharp angle and hung the pot of lunch leftovers from it over the low, lapping flames. Before it was warmed, I fell asleep.

I woke up a couple of hours later to blow my nose and hawk up phlegm. The fire had burned down to small pile of embers. Walid was asleep. Hungry, I ate from the pot of noodles, now cold, and guzzled some water. Before going back to sleep, I wandered some thirty yards off to go to the bathroom. Relieved with the results, I praised Allah (something that comes instinctively after some time in Muslim countries, even for a non-religious Jew) that at least my gastrointestinal works were in good shape. More miraculously, even before I finished my business, four dung beetles converged upon me like black, bite-sized tanks surrounding a target.

I was astonished that the beetles could have so quickly homed in on a fresh deposit of food, drawn by their keen sense of smell. With no true nose, the beetles detect and distinguish a wide variety of odors through their antennae, the palps on their jaws, and even the hairs on their legs. They shape excrement into balls about as big as a beetle is tall, then roll them across the sand and cache them underground. The buried balls are saved for future eating and used as incubators inside which female beetles lay their eggs. When the larvae hatch, they feed on the dung they sprang from. A single beetle can clean up 250 times its own weight in one night; it was once recorded that a three-and-a-half-pound pile of elephant poop was consumed and buried by beetles in less than two hours. The claim has been made repeatedly that, but for dung beetles, of which there are nearly eight thousand species dispersed across all continents except Antarctica, the planet would have long ago been covered in shit.

The beetle's hard exoskeleton makes it well adapted to the parched conditions of the Sahara. Aside from preventing water loss to the air, some beetles use their shells to collect water; by pointing its head to the ground and abdomen toward the sky, the beetle allows water vapor to condense on its shell, which then rolls down in a precious droplet into its mouth.

We rose before the sun. In the crepuscular predawn light, we appeared to be part of the world's dream as it hovered in that fluid middle space between slumber and wake. Adding to that effect, an unexpected call to prayer wafted eerily from the north, as though rising from the desert itself. As it turned out, the village of Agouni was just over the next hill, out of sight. It was the last permanent settlement we'd pass until we reached the solitary village of Araouane five days later.

As Walid prayed, I stoked the fire. Though a steady stream still flowed from my nose, I felt much better than I had the day before. When he finished with his devotions, Walid came over to make tea.

He took a fistful of tea from a cardboard box a little bigger than a Rubik's cube and dumped it into a green pot so small that its base fit easily in the palm of his hand. He added water and set it atop the coals. Once it boiled and simmered for a few minutes, Walid scooped a shot glass of sugar from a small leather pouch and added it to the brew. He poured the tea into the glass and dumped it back into the pot, raising the glass high and thrusting it downward to increase its stirring force. He repeated this until it was well mixed, then he filled the bottom of the glass with about a centimeter of the yellowish liquid, swirled it around, and tasted it. Satisfied, he served us each a glass, refilled the pot with water without removing the leaves, and put it back on the coals. There is nothing arbitrary or whimsical about the tea-making process—it is the same every time, practiced with the orthodoxy of a religious rite. While we waited for rounds two and three, we ate a handful of peanuts and dates and a few biscuits—the so-called Tuareg breakfast.

The Tuareg are the famed "Blue Men" of the desert, so dubbed because the dye from their indigo clothing bleeds into and stains their tanned but otherwise fair skin. Of Berber origin—North Africa's indigenous race—their language, Tamashek, is a Berber tongue quite distinct from Arabic. They dwelt in the Sahara long before the arrival of the Arabs, who migrated to North Africa in two major waves, in the seventh and eleventh centuries, bringing with them their language, the word of Islam, and the gumption to launch the era of the great camel caravans.

Though they came first as conquerors, the Arabs who moved into the Sahara were eventually absorbed into the existing Saharan culture by way of intermarriage. Tribes of the western Sahara who today are commonly identified as "Arab" are considered as such because they speak Arabic dialects, which they adopted as the lingua franca for both religion and trade. Genealogically, however, these "Arabs" have largely Berber roots, like the Tamashek-speaking Tuareg. Their identification as Arab is both an oversimplified label given to them by Western scholars and a myth perpetuated by a number of the tribes themselves, since this allows them to more legitimately claim direct descent from the Prophet.

Saharans themselves historically classified tribes, regardless of their roots, into two types: the *hasani*, or "people of the sword," and the *zwaya*, "people of the book." The hasani, among whom most Tuareg were counted, were warriors and raiders who lived from pillage and by exacting tribute from caravans in exchange for Mafia-like protection. The zwaya were followers of religious clerics who engaged in study, trade, herding, and some farming. Yet even these categories were far from airtight. There were hasani groups who traded and studied, and many who herded, as there were fierce zwaya militias. While these two types of groups sometimes lived in enmity, they also formed alliances for mutual benefit.

Rather than thinking of the people of the Sahara as Arab or Tuareg, the notion of a broad Saharan culture with individual variations among tribes who share fundamental similarities is more persuasive. Recognizing this, the French, in the 1950s, even considered scrapping the political boundaries that they had imposed upon North and West Africa in favor of creating an independent Saharan state from parts of the colonies that became Mali, Niger, and Algeria. Though it never came to fruition, dreams of such a homeland festered among the Saharans, providing part of the fuel for future rebellions against the governments of Mali and Niger.

One of the unique features of Saharan culture that separates it from the rest of the Muslim world—and an example of how Tuareg practices were carried over with varying degrees of orthodoxy by so-called Arab tribes—is that the *men* traditionally veil their faces while women do not. Though there is a practical aspect to wearing a turban that wraps around the head and covers the face like a shield against sand and sun, the Tuareg veil, called a *tagelmoust*, has deep cultural connotations—as does the fact that women boldly show their faces to the world.

The tagelmoust symbolizes the Tuareg emphasis on personal reserve and respect for self and others. It serves as the ultimate poker face, through which emotional expression becomes completely opaque. According to Dr. Susan J. Rasmussen, an anthropologist who has lived with Tuareg tribes on and off for more than twenty years, veils "are props in a masquerade to protect one's status and interests. They remind the wearer of the need for caution and self-control, [and] underline status. . . ." Men adjust the level of their tagelmoust to reflect the social hierarchy within a particular gathering, with the highest-ranking man wearing his veil the lowest. Exceptions to this general rule include *marabouts* (holy men), who often cover as much of their face as possible, and smiths or artisans, who are said to lack the quality of reserve, and thus may do away with the veil (and a number of other social pre-scriptions) altogether. Another reason for the veil is that the mouth, like other bodily orifices, is considered by the Tuareg to be dirty, a so-called "zone of pollution" meant to be covered. As such, they say "the veil and the pants are brothers." Shrouding the mouth also safeguards against the evil spirits who seek to enter the head and cause madness. According to some Arab wits, however, the real reason Tuareg men cover their faces is to "hide their ugliness."

A man usually adopts the tagelmoust sometime around his twenti-eth year, at a time determined by his father. It is a major rite of passage; after a man takes on the veil, he is deemed ready for marriage and war.

The head scarves worn by women also represent their reserve. That they are not expected to cover their faces entirely is due to the belief that it's appropriate for them to be more emotionally expressive than men. Though of course Tuareg dress codes were not established for this reason, when I think about the veils and burkas that other Muslim peo-ples require women to wear, I can't help but see the headdress practices of Tuareg women as a symbol of the relative independence and auton-omy that they enjoy.

In stark contrast with the customs of Middle Eastern countries, many of which forbid women from holding passports independently of their husbands, Tuareg women can travel freely. They interact socially with men, and, though discouraged, can even have premarital affairs without fear of being ostracized (let alone stoned to death). Since the Tu-areg understand that both men and women may be infertile, childless-ness is not a black mark against a married woman. What's more, wives have the power to divorce their husbands, and divorced women are not looked down upon.

Social status in this traditionally matriarchal culture is determined by the lineage of one's mother, and a significant portion of any family's property is explicitly owned by its women, including herds of goats and sheep. The tent in which a couple lives is part of the bridal dowry and belongs to the wife, who keeps it even in the event of divorce. While Tuareg women generally inherit half of what their brothers inherit (based on the principle of Islamic law that states that, for legal purposes, a woman is equal to half of a man), one Tuareg chief told me that in his clan, family property is divided such that half goes to the daughters and half to the sons, meaning that if a family has one daughter and two sons, the daughter, who inherits the entire female share, gets twice as much as either son, who split the male share between them.

Though this relatively liberal attitude toward women is shared by both Tuareg and non-Tuareg tribes, it has its roots in the Tuareg's pre-Islamic, animist traditions—the practice of which first inspired the Arabs arriving in North Africa to dub them *Tuareg*, which means "abandoned by God." The Tuareg refer to themselves as the *Kel Tamashek* (Tamashek people) or *Imashagen*—"the free." Living up to that name, they've managed to blend animist and Islamic customs in an unorthodox manner that is often complementary and sometimes contradictory, but functional within its own context. The so-called Arab tribes retain some animist superstitions, but have generally forsaken the array of prescribed animist rituals in favor of a more traditional Muslim perspective, as well as a lineage system based on patriarchal descent.

The reading I'd done before leaving for Mali, which was a somewhat hasty survey of all things Saharan, more popular than scholarly, had inaccurately overemphasized the involvement of the Tuareg in the salt trade; I had been led by it to believe that a trip to Taoudenni would likely be made with Tuareg tribesmen. But the Tuareg, I found, virtually never drive salt caravans.

Since they historically ruled the region through their military prowess, the Tuareg left the running of caravans to others, from whom they collected tribute in exchange for safe passage through the desert, raiding those who didn't pay. The three main groups involved in the Taoudenni salt trade were "Arab": the Tajakant, the Kunta, and the

Berabish—Walid's tribe. Though ascendancy among these groups shifted through the years, the Berabish were the dominant force by the end of the nineteenth century. They held exclusive control over the southern end of the route, between Araouane and Timbuktu, in part because of an arrangement they'd made with the Tuareg. Rather than paying tribute, the Berabish became the tribute collectors for the Tuareg, gathering payment from other clans for a free pass through the desert and a small percentage of the take. Though the Berabish were a mighty hasani clan in their own right and had fought sporadically with Tuareg tribes over the ages, this alliance allowed them to devote their resources to trade rather than battle.

Due to their specialized role in Saharan society, the Tuareg bred and owned different kinds of camels than the trading tribes did. Tuareg herds were composed largely of riding camels, which are lean and fast—the Corvettes of the desert—giving raiders a significant tactical edge over heavier, slower-moving cargo animals, which are more like pickup trucks. Of course, if you're hauling heavy loads you'd rather have a pickup than a sports car, and the Berabish and Kunta raised huge herds of baggage camels, which were bred specifically for endurance under severe stress. They could carry more and travel longer on less food and water than the riding camels. Since preeminence in desert trade hinged on who had the baggage camels, the Berabish and the Kunta kept a lock on their propagation and possession in this part of the Sahara; when long-distance caravans from other regions entered Berabish territory, they were forced to abandon their own animals and buy or rent new ones from the Berabish.

Today the Tuareg wouldn't have the camel-power to run caravans even if they wanted to. Their herds were decimated during the Great Drought of 1973–74, when the sparse pasturelands on the fringes of the Sahara disappeared as the true desert advanced some sixty miles southward. Before the drought, it wasn't unusual for Tuareg families to own a few hundred camels and cows, along with a thousand sheep or goats. Afterward, a family was fortunate to have any animals left at all. Another drought hit in 1984; then, after the Tuareg Rebellion broke out in 1990, the Malian army severely curtailed nomadic movement, making it difficult, if not impossible, for desert dwellers to approach Timbuktu and other towns that they relied on for supplies. As a result, many families were reduced to eating the few animals they had. Though the war ended in 1995, Tuareg herds have not recovered much. And the Tuareg people, who suffered greatly through it all, are just beginning to.

Though the Berabish were subject to the same circumstances, their hardier camels made it through the drought a little bit better. More important, with their extensive trading networks, the Berabish were able to sell many of their animals to merchants in Morocco and Algeria, then use the money they received to buy new ones later on, once the droughts and the war abated. Though they suffered right beside the Tuareg and have far fewer camels than they did fifty years ago, they still have enough with which to trek to Taoudenni.

We finished our breakfast and were loaded and on the trail by seven o'clock. Walid led the camels as I kept pace beside him. His steps were quick and light, his lithe legs hardly thicker than my arms (and "burly" isn't on the list of adjectives that describes me). Though my strides were longer, my feet sank and slid backward in the sand while Walid's padded nimbly over the surface. Walking through the desert with a nomad was like swimming with a seal.

That I was where I was, marching next to a turbaned nomad puffing smoke from a stubby, antelope-horn pipe, leading a couple of camels through the Sahara into which we were heading ever deeper, felt like exactly what I was meant to be doing. With my health definitively on the mend, I was swept with a heady surge of hubris. *One day down, only thirty-nine to go*, I thought. *I've got this caravan thing licked.*

Before long, our path merged with that of a lone camel driver and his string of five camels. His name was Nashuf, and his camels were burdened with coils of rope, wooden tent poles varying in length from about three to ten feet, bolts of cloth, metal cooking pots, rice sacks, and goatskin water bags. The camels looked like desert versions of the loaded jalopy driven by the Beverly Hillbillies.

Nashuf was heading to his family's desert camp, then on to Araouane. As is the custom with the azalai, we would travel together while our routes overlapped—for greater safety and company. When he asked where we were going, Walid said, "Taoudenni."

"*Wallahi?*" Nashuf asked—Arabic for "really?" or "You swear to God?"

"Wallahi," Walid confirmed.

Nashuf didn't reply immediately, but looked at me with an expression that conveyed a mild skepticism. He shook his head and chuckled.

"It's very far," he said.

"I know," I said, the confidence I was feeling at that moment coloring my tone, which probably made me look like an idiot.

"Where are you from?" he asked.

"America," I answered, with some hesitation.

"Welcome!" Nashuf said brightly, without the slightest trace of animosity.

Some two hours after leaving camp, Walid indicated it was time to ride. We stopped to couch Lachmar so I could get on; Walid and Nashuf, of course, could leap on and off their camels at will without causing them to break their strides.

They rode side by side, absorbed in conversation, until Nashuf looked back and saw that he was missing a camel. The last one in line had become untied from the one in front of it; with no inborn compulsion to stick with the other camels, when one gets loose it usually stops where it is to graze—if there's anything to eat. By now, the lost camel was out of sight.

Nashuf dismounted, untied the three camels behind the one he was riding, and tied them to Lachmar's tail. Then he remounted and rode off in the direction whence we came while Walid and I continued on. Within half an hour, Nashuf was back with his maverick.

With none of the cloud cover of the previous day, the morning heated up early. The landscape was similar to the one we'd passed through the day before, though the flats between the hills grew wider and wider and the terrain appeared much less hospitable under the fierce glare of the sun. As the hours passed, the air grew so hot, so heavy, it sat on me like a rhinoceros. It seemed like we'd already hit the predicted high for the day, which I'd seen on a weather report back in Timbuktu—about 115 degrees. Meanwhile, my ass felt like it was being pummeled with a splintery club. My earlier confidence began to ebb.

Walid asked what time it was at around eleven o'clock. When I told him, he said we'd take a break at noon. At eleven thirty, with my body revolting against the impact between it and the camel, I decided to get down and walk the last half hour. I told Walid, who guided Lachmar to his haunches, and I dismounted.

The camels walked about half a pace faster than Walid and I normally did, but every ounce of extra effort was worth it for the relief of not riding on one. And despite the soaring temperature, the uneven terrain, and my runny nose, if there was one thing at which I knew I could push myself, it was walking long distances.

By the time it was noon, however, I was thirsty and overheated. Here, the trees were few and far between, so when I saw one ahead that offered good shade, I told Walid the time, hoping he'd take the hint. He said we'd continue for another fifteen minutes. Fifteen minutes came and went. Half an hour passed. We didn't even slow down. The sun pounded through my turban, sapping my energy, bringing to mind those old anti-drug ads with the frying egg—*this is your brain in the Sahara*. Thinking we'd break at any time, I didn't want to ask Walid to stop the camels so I could get on. I began imagining the unlikely possibility of running into a convoy of tourists in Land

Cruisers with coolers of cold drinks. So much for having this caravan thing licked.

We didn't stop until after one. Exhausted, I managed to help unload the camels and gather an armload of firewood before collapsing in the pool of shade cast by a tree. Small birds that looked like miniature falcons had taken shelter in its branches. Legions of grasshoppers alit on my arms and face, sucking invisible amounts of moisture from my skin.

I greedily downed the dorno Walid mixed up, its salty-sweetness slaking my thirst, its sheer quantity sating my hunger. While the tea was brewing, I lay down with my eyes closed, thinking. One of the reasons why the last hour had been so tough was that I had only prepared myself to walk until noon. Trusting Walid's word, I hadn't saved any mental reserves, which are far more crucial to endurance than physical strength. Had Walid told me we weren't going to stop until one, I could have paced my expectations and walked it willingly, rather than as though every step taken past noon was an effort beyond the call of duty.

It dawned on me that one of the most challenging aspects of this journey was going to be my total lack of control. Not only was I conclusively not in control of my circumstances, I hardly even knew what was going on. I had only the vaguest sense of where we were; I had no idea what the lay of the land looked like up ahead or how far we needed to travel in a day. It would have helped if Walid could've explained it to me, but obviously even when he tried to in terms of time, his estimates were unreliable. I wondered if this was what it felt like for the groups of teenagers I led in the wilderness before they got used to the routine and learned to read maps; I was filled with empathy for them.

Accepting the reality that I was not in control, I saw that I had to mentally steel myself to travel onward forever. I couldn't afford to hope that we would stop to rest or eat at any given time, since when that hope is dashed, desperation sets in and endurance wanes. I decided then and there that the only way to survive this trek without going insane was to be prepared to continue on into eternity, with no known goal, never allowing false expectation to drain my will again.

We set out again at around four. Nashuf struck off to the west, leaving Walid and I to head north alone. My spirits were rejuvenated by the rest and the water I'd consumed, like a parched plant sprung back to life after a rain shower. Walid and I talked while we walked. He told me he had a wife, who was twenty-one, and two sons, ages one and three. Usually they lived in the desert, he said, but sometimes they stayed in Timbuktu, when he was selling the salt he returned with from the mines. Right now, his wife was at her family's camp a few days north of where we were, where she and the kids were spending the month of Ramadan.

"Which do you like better," I asked, "the desert or Timbuktu?"

"Ah, Timbuktu," Walid said without a shade of doubt.

"Why?"

"It is easier there. There are houses and stores. I hope one day to live there, mostly so my sons will be able to go to school."

"You don't want them to be azalai?"

"No," Walid said, shaking his head. "That life is hard and dangerous. I want them to have good jobs and live long."

After a pause, Walid said, "Maybe in a few years you can take one of them to America with you so he can learn to speak English? Then he could surely have a good life."

"Okay," I agreed, knowing it would never happen.

As the sun began to set, slipping behind a gauzy curtain of haze that hung over the horizon, Walid and I took to our camels once more. In a final show of strength, the sun amped up its assault, blazing intensely before finally giving up and dropping below the rim of the earth. The searing breeze turned deliciously cool. The desert breathed a sigh of relief. At last I could let down my guard and revel in my environs, watching happily as the sky turned into a swirl of pink and violet and bronze as darkness slowly seeped from the east. I realized that the safest place in the Sahara was not a place at all, but a time: night. Making it to sunset, I thought, was the one goal I could pin my hopes on every day, since it would never disappoint. I unbuttoned my shirt to let the refreshing evening air wash over as much of my skin as possible.

We rode late into the night. Again, with each passing hour, it became increasingly painful to stay on Lachmar's back. But my new attitude of riding on forever was already serving me. I accepted my suffering as yet one more thing to ignore, refusing to let it break my spirit. I sang songs to pass the time and tried to identify the constellations that appeared in the clear, haze-free circle of sky directly overhead. So far, we had been following relatively distinct tire tracks much of the time. When they disappeared in sandier ground, as they surely would, which stars would be our markers? And how would we be able to stay on course if the whole sky was obscured? I was eager to learn.

At last, some seven hours later, we stopped to camp. We performed the typical tasks of unloading the camels and foraging firewood.

Joining Walid by the fire, my butt was so tender I had trouble sitting down. I put a hand down my pants to inspect myself and discovered two sticky, bloody wounds the size of half dollars, where the friction had been most constant. Never having been much of a horseman, I always thought the term "saddle sores" referred to muscle pain, not actual sores. Though they were distressing enough as they were, my main concern was preventing them from getting worse.

While waiting for the rice to cook, it occurred to me that this scene—two men sitting around a small fire in the Sahara after traveling all day with nothing but their clothes between them and the elements, moving at a pace no faster than a camel's—could have been lifted, virtually unchanged, from any time over the past thousand-plus years. It was as though I'd crossed a bridge spanning a millennium into a land hardly touched by the passage of time. The minor modernizations that had been adopted, like the stainless-steel bowls that had replaced hollowed gourds, or the rubber inner tubes that sometimes replaced goatskin water sacks, were small refinements to the existing culture, changing nothing essential about it. And many of the technologies—handmade ropes, fire, the camels themselves—were the same as they'd always been. Though I had hardly begun to immerse myself in it, there was an obvious air of permanence about this way of life; change was gradual and served to fine-tune a system of survival that had worked for so long in the world's harshest inhabited lands. The roots of this age-old lifestyle were hardy and deep.

Only a radical intrusion from the modern world, I thought, could shake its foundations—like trucks taking over the salt trade.

*Taking a break in the heat of the day,
with a blanket for shelter.*

CHAPTER THREE

Pain. Melancholy. Resignation.

These were the stages I passed through in the minutes after Walid woke me, as I lay wrapped in my blanket staring blankly at the cool slate sky. The pain was purely physical, twisting the muscles of my lower back and stabbing through the sores on my ass. Knowing I would have to get up, melancholy set in; I longed to return to sleep like a lover parted from his beloved. Finally, I resigned myself to the reality that this was my reality. Accepting it grudgingly, I steeled myself for the day and rose. The teapot was already on the fire. I packed my bag while it brewed, then sat with Walid and ate our humble Tuareg breakfast.

Walid told me we were about twenty kilometers south of the well at Douaya, where we would refill our inner tubes and let the camels drink. Then he stood and said he was going to round up the camels. They had disappeared out of sight, yet Walid walked off confidently, as though he had long-distance X-ray vision that enabled him to see beyond the horizon line formed by a low ridge of sand. Of course he must have followed their tracks, but there were so many camel tracks from others that had passed this place that discerning those of Lachmar and L'beyya was a feat nearly equal to that of seeing through the earth.

While he was gone, I chugged a liter of water, then refilled my two bottles. I fumbled with the mouth of the inner tube, trying to tie it securely. No matter what kind of knot I tied, water still leaked from between the tube's pursed lips. When Walid returned with Lachmar and L'beyya, I asked him for help. He quickly assessed my work, untied my knot, then folded the open end of the tube over so it capped itself. He rolled it tightly across the fold, then tied a knot like a clove hitch, but not quite. He made no effort to show me how to do it; he was only concerned with doing it fast.

Speed is an ingrained value in Saharan travel, since the faster you move, the better your chance of making it to your destination alive. Everything Walid did, apart from making tea, he did quickly, and the same held true with the other camel drivers I would soon meet. It was as though they had two settings—High and Off. Thus Walid, adhering to the desert ethos of "the quicker the better," didn't take the time to teach me anything. This was no Outward Bound course; he clearly thought of himself as a guide, not an instructor, and had little interest in developing my self-sufficiency (and even less in facilitating my personal growth). If I wanted to learn how to travel like an azalai, I realized, I was going to have to watch Walid closely, then try things myself and learn from my mistakes.

When we loaded Lachmar, Walid arranged the bags and positioned my blanket farther back on the camel's hump. This, he assured me, would be much more comfortable. Once our gear was slung, we headed north.

Here, rather than flat plains broken by hills, the ground was pitched at a low incline, forming gradual mile-long ramps that fell sharply on their lee sides, then slowly rose again. Thorn trees were scattered more sparsely than before, but enough grass still grew to tinge the earth a faint green. As the vegetation thinned, nomad tents became fewer and farther between.

My head, though still dripping slightly, was much improved. And once we established a rhythm, the pain in my back disappeared and my sores itched but didn't hurt. Even so, when Walid suggested we mount up after a couple of hours, I told him I was going to stay on my feet. I felt I had to play to my strength—my ability to walk—and compensate for my weakness—my tender butt. Walid shrugged and leapt atop L'beyya.

Immediately I had to double my pace in order to stay even with the camels. I walked as fast I could without breaking into a run, my legs whirling in a blue blur of motion, my heart arace, my feet sinking into the soft earth before striking ground solid enough to propel me forward. I realized that the previous day, when I had walked while Walid and Nashuf rode, Walid had slowed our camels' natural gait to match the pace of Nashuf's string of loaded animals. On their own, L'beyya and Lachmar moved at the limits of my ability to keep up.

Soon I had to measure my breathing, inhaling as I took four steps, then exhaling for the next four. My upper body felt disconnected from my legs; I began to imagine myself with the torso of a man, the legs of a machine; a sci-fi centaur. Meanwhile, though I wasn't yet overheating, I became unbelievably, unquenchably thirsty. My mouth felt like it was coated with glue. I considered giving up and getting on, but knew that every hour I could stay off Lachmar gave my sores another hour to heal.

Each successive ramp of earth was virtually identical to the one before it; there were no prominent landmarks. I had no way of judging how much progress we were making, and there were certainly no signs indicating how many kilometers remained to Douaya. To stave off the feeling of hopeless desperation to which I'd succumbed the day before, I began controlling my experience the only way I could—with my watch. Though I couldn't set geographic goals for myself, I *could* set temporal ones. If the well was about twenty kilometers from where we had camped and we were covering about five kilometers per hour, that worked out to four hours of travel, which would put us there a little after 11 AM. Figuring in the distinct possibility that Walid had been less than exact in his estimate, I imagined we'd more likely arrive between noon and 1 PM. Without investing much in reaching the well at any particular time, I decided I would walk until eleven, then ride the rest of the way, however much longer that was. This allowed me to set a mental destination for the speed-walking portion of the morning and, after going for about four hours nonstop, would give me a needed break just as the day moved into the hottest hours.

As I struggled to keep up, I told myself that this was the last trip I would need to take that was even close to this physically demanding. From here on out, I'd be content to travel to places that were fascinating and foreign, but not so tough. As I mused about where those places might be, I laughed silently. I was sure Sindbad had said the same thing to himself many times.

Precisely at eleven, I told Walid I was ready to ride. He stopped, couched Lachmar, and I got on. Sitting farther behind the peak of the hump made all the difference in the world. The friction between my body and Lachmar's was drastically reduced and my legs fell naturally into positions of relative comfort. Perhaps, I rationalized, it was good that I had suffered so for the first two days, since now, in comparison, the ride was nearly tolerable.

As the sun neared its zenith, some divine hand cranked the cosmic thermostat all the way up. The heat battered me around the head, and though my turban softened the blows, I was soon reeling like a boxer after a rough round. Gradually overcome with lethargy, I swayed back and forth limply, as though my bones had begun to melt. Once noon passed, I stopped looking at my watch. Time didn't matter anymore; we would get there when we got there.

At last, as we gained the crest of a ridge, a deep valley of sand stretched before us from the eastern to the western horizon. This was Douaya. It was completely barren, grazed to the last blade of grass by animals that came to drink—hundreds of which were clustered together in groups, camels with camels, goats with goats, sheep with sheep, donkeys with donkeys. They kept a respectful distance from the mound that rose in the middle of the basin, waiting to ascend and take their turn at the troughs.

The wells between Timbuktu and Taoudenni were originally dug by nomads hundreds of years ago. They were known to run dry, to collapse, or be buried by sand according to the whims of the weather. Among the other uncontrollables of traveling this route, the wells were perhaps the wildest cards of all. In earlier days, caravans rationed water strictly in case they had to travel farther than expected before arriving at a good well. This strategy was far from foolproof, as many a desert traveler perished when wells they relied upon proved unreliable. In an effort to increase safety in the region while winning a few Saharan hearts and minds, the French dug the wells deeper and lined them with cement.

Walid and I stopped about fifty yards from the well. A few gangly men in black turbans and threadbare boubous scampered over to help us unload. They knew Walid, shook his hand vigorously, and launched into the ritual Saharan greeting. Composed of a series of prescribed queries and responses, the greeting can literally last for minutes as the same questions and answers are repeated over and over:

"No problems?"

"No problems."

"Are you well?"

"I'm well."

"Praise be to God."

"Praise be to God."

"What's the news?"

"Praise be to God."

"No problems?"

"No problems."

"Are you well?"

"Praise be to God."

"What's the news?"

"I am well."

"No problems?"

"No problems."

And on and on and on it goes until, at some subtle cue, both parties agree that God is to be praised and they can move on to talking about other things. When there are more than two people saying hello, the questions and answers overlap—which hardly seems to matter, because it often seems like the greeting is being read from a script without any true interest in how the other person is actually doing. When I asked Walid why they repeated themselves over and over, he said you couldn't trust a man who only asked each question once.

I carried our depleted inner tubes while Walid led the camels to the top of the mound, in which the well was set. One group of thirty-odd camels, including a few babies, was queued behind troughs made from sawed-off fifty-gallon drums half buried in the sand. Around the well's foot-high cement rim, four pairs of stripped tree limbs stood at angles over the hole. The tops of the limbs were forked. Resting in the forks between each pair was a grooved wooden dowel that spun around a smooth stick and served as a pulley. A long rope of braided goat hide ran over the groove. One end was tied to a collapsible, round, goatskin bucket that flattened when it was empty, expanded when it was full, and seemed a lot like a leather jellyfish. The other end of the rope was attached to a camel that stood near the well.

The empty bucket was tossed down the well. When it hit the water, one of the men gave a few tugs on the rope to make sure the bucket had opened and filled. Then another man gave a loud grunt and led the camel out into the desert. As the camel trotted away, it pulled the rope over the dowel, raising the bucket from the depths. When it emerged, Walid and one of the well men grabbed it and shouted. The camel stopped, and Walid and the well man hefted the heavy, sloshing leather sack over to a trough. They dumped the water in, and three camels plunged their heads into the metal drum. They sucked up the water so quickly that within moments only a shallow puddle remained in the barrel's bottom. The bodies of the camels swelled before my eyes.

Camels can go for many weeks without drinking anything at all. The notion that they cache water in their humps is pure myth—their humps are made of fat, and water is stored in their body tissues. While other mammals draw water from their bloodstreams when faced with dehydration, leading to death by volume shock, camels tap the water in their tissues, keeping their blood volume stable. Though this reduces the camel's bulk, they can lose up to a third of their body weight with no ill effects, which they can replace astonishingly quickly, as they are able to drink up to forty gallons in a single watering. Such a feat, even in relative terms, would be impossible for any other mammal, since all but the camel have round red blood cells, which would explode if suddenly forced to absorb so much water; the camel, however, has oval red cells, which can expand as needed without bursting. Regardless of how much water is available, the camel will only drink what it needs to replenish itself.

Walid beckoned me to the side of the well and invited me to peer down into what looked like a pipeline to Hades. Far, far below, I could just discern a pool of rippling, reflected light. The voices of the men around me were drawn into the well, ricocheted around its walls, and bounced back out, amplified. Water from so deep in the earth, I thought with relief, was probably safe to drink.

The men at the well were gruff and unfriendly. They clearly had no use for me and made no pretense of welcome. I was taken aback by their brusqueness, since I'd never before met a nomad who shunned a stranger. I tried my best to stay out of their way.

Walid helped the others with a few rounds of watering, then it was our turn. Lachmar and L'beyya slurped heartily from the barrel, downing an entire bucketload and half of the next. Then Walid, using one of our metal bowls, scooped the leftover water directly from the trough into our inner tubes, which I held open as they were filled with camel backwash and floating cud particles. So much for bacteria-free drinking.

At the bottom of the mound on the side opposite where Walid and I had left our things, three men were lying down in the shade of a ten-wheeled cargo truck. The truck was an old mechanical beast that bore the scars of scuffling with the desert year after year. The light blue paint on the cab had been sandblasted down to bare metal in places. The low walls that enclosed the flatbed were dented and bent. The bed was empty, save for a few large drums of fuel. It was the first vehicle I'd seen since leaving Timbuktu. Though perhaps faster than a camel, this truck was neither graceful nor exotic. While camels feel like an integral part of the desert, their presence amplifying its innate character, the truck seemed alien, like a malignant mutation in discord with its surroundings. While I faulted no one for preferring a truck to camel, it struck me that the day the camel caravans finally die will be the day the Sahara loses a piece of its soul.

It would also be a triumphant comeback for wheeled transportation in a centuries-old contest with the camel that camels had once seemed certain to win. In fact, though chariots and carts were commonplace in North Africa and the Middle East in ancient times, they were universally abandoned in favor of the camel, which proved so much more practical than anything with wheels that the wheel completely disappeared from those regions for more than a thousand years.

Between 3000 and 2500 BC, while the Egyptians were busy creating their most enduring legacy to future generations—the Great Pyramid—the semi-civilized people across the Red Sea, in southern Arabia, were also producing theirs: the domesticated camel. Initially prized only for its milk, centuries passed before the camel was used as a beast of burden. Though the exact year that they were first loaded with goods is a subject for scholarly debate, it's clear that sometime around 2000 BC (give or take a couple of hundred years) the incense traders of southern Arabia rigged their dromedaries with bundles of frankincense and myrrh and headed north toward Syria in the world's first caravan.

As Semitic tribes spread from the Levant into southern Arabia during the second millennium BC, they took over the incense trade and shared camel technology with their kin in the north. By the eighth century BC, camels were toting supplies for Sargon II's Assyrian army and had become popular pack and herd animals across the Middle East.

Camels were introduced into North Africa at a much later date. Beginning in the first or second century BC, their range gradually expanded westward from Egypt and Sudan. The people of the Sahara and its border regions recognized the animal as the ultimate form of desert transport, appreciating its stamina, speed, and strength; a camel could travel farther in a day while hauling twice as much as a mule- or ox-drawn cart. Since they were more efficient than anything with wheels, the enthusiasm for building and maintaining roads—upon which wheeled transport was dependent—fell with the Roman Empire.

Thus, before the seventh century, and possibly as early as the third, the wheel vanished entirely from North Africa and the Middle East (except for isolated pockets in Tunisia). Great cities, such as Fes, were built with no consideration for the needs of wheeled vehicles; its streets are so narrow and twisted that, today, goods are off-loaded from trucks at the old medina's gates and transferred to the backs of mules, which successfully negotiate the maze of alleys.

Far from being a backward culture, the wheel-less Arab civilization made countless contributions in mathematics, astronomy, medicine, and many other fields from architecture to literature to optics. While wheels were still used as pulleys and for other mechanical purposes, as a means of transportation they were simply outdated.

European colonists reintroduced the wheel perhaps twelve hundred years after their disappearance, but their adoption by local peoples was far from instantaneous. According to historian Richard Bulliet, streets in nineteenth-century Cairo were still being built based on the width of two loaded camels standing side by side, a dimension too narrow for the easy maneuvering of carts or carriages. Bulliet also points out that, to this day, wheelbarrows are conspicuously absent from Middle Eastern construction sites, even in urban areas; loads are instead carried on litters or in buckets, which he identifies as a throwback to the "pervasive non-wheel mentality."

The French brought the wheel back to the Sahara. This time, however, it wasn't pulled by horses or oxen; it was pushed by the internal combustion engine. On January 7, 1923, a team driving ten-horsepower Citroën half tracks made the first successful crossing of the Sahara by automobile, completing the journey from Algiers to Timbuktu in three weeks. They averaged nearly a hundred miles a day, about three times what a camel would cover. Today cars, trucks, and motorcycles racing across the desert in the annual Paris–Dakar Rally drive daily stages more than four times that distance. Perhaps more surprising than the fact that trucks now operate along the ancient salt route between Timbuktu and Taoudenni is that it took them until the end of the twentieth century to do so.

With our tubes filled and properly tied, we balanced them over L'beyya's back for the short walk back to our bags. We thanked the well men, loaded up, and said good-bye. It was a little after two when we left. I was hot, hungry, and tired. Fortunately, we stopped to rest after only half an hour, at the first tree we came across.

As usual, by the time we hit the trail again I was rejuvenated. Walid and I walked side by side at an easy pace, talking. Wondering how far American pop culture had crept into the Sahara, I asked Walid if he had ever heard of McDonald's. To my great satisfaction, he hadn't.

"But you know Coca-Cola, yes?" I continued.

"Sure, there is Coca everywhere in Timbuktu."

Though I rarely drink the stuff at home, thinking of it in these circumstances made me crave it.

"Can I buy it in Araouane?"

"No," he said. "There's no Coca there."

"Really?"

"Really."

I could hardly believe it. I'd been in isolated mountain hamlets in places that never see foreigners—where children burst into tears when they saw me, where even adults hid behind trees and peered out curiously at me—and Coke, like a corporate Kilroy, had been there first. Of all the remote villages I'd been to in the world, the only ones where Coke was absent were in the farthest reaches of Mongolia—and getting there before Coke felt like a major triumph. It seemed reasonable to think that someone could easily throw a couple of cases in the back of a truck that was going from Timbuktu to Araouane.

"What about at the shops?" I asked.

"There are no shops in Araouane," Walid replied.

I paused to digest this information, then, continuing with my inquiry and recalling a report I'd once read that named Harrison Ford as the most seen movie star in the world, I asked Walid if he'd ever seen *Star Wars*—the seminal film of my youth (okay, and my adulthood, too).

"What's that?" he said.

"It's a movie," I answered, then, wondering if I'd made a huge assumption, I asked Walid if he knew what movies were.

"Yes, I've heard of movies." Hesitantly, he said he thought he'd seen one once on somebody's television in Timbuktu.

Thinking of quintessential American icons, I took one last stab at naming one he might be familiar with.

"Do you know Superman?" I asked.

"No. What's that?"

"He's like a man," I explained, "but he's very strong and he flies around."

"Ah," Walid said, "he is a djinn."

"Well, sort of," I said. "But Superman is good. He helps people and he fights against evil."

"Yes," Walid said, "he is a djinn. Many djinn are bad and try to hurt people, but other djinn are good and serve the will of Allah. Your Superman must be one of the good djinn."

"Yes," I said, "he must be," figuring this was as about as common a term for "superhero" as we were going to arrive at.

The *djinn*—whence the word "genie" is derived—are the spirits that inhabit the Muslim world, and dwell in the Sahara alongside the local, animist spirits, called the *Kel Essuf* (*kel* meaning "people," *essuf* meaning "wild," "solitude," or "nostalgia"). Though some are beneficent, most are evil and are deeply feared, since they seek to possess people, driving them insane. "When possessed by the *essuf*," writes Dr. Rasmussen, "people are said to be 'in the wild.'" Thinking about this as I traveled through the desert, the notion of being infected by wildness or solitude struck me as profound; Saharans live in the wild, in the most solitary places on earth, all the time—what they fear is that the wild, the solitude, will live in them.

When someone goes mad, marabouts are called in and given money, livestock, or other goods in exchange for reciting Koranic blessings over the victim. I was told that often, when the spirit is finally exorcized, the sick person will dream of a cat walking away from him or her. If the marabouts prove ineffective, the Tuareg turn to healers known as friends of the Kel Essuf—non-Koranic healers who serve as mediums with the spirit world, and are often women. They might use music or herbs to chase off the Kel Essuf, or perhaps sacrifice a goat while intentionally refraining from uttering any Islamic blessings.

I smiled at the irony of imagining Superman, the protector of Truth, Justice, and the American Way—which at that moment was in an epic cultural clash with Islam—as a mystical servant of Allah.

As the sun slid over the horizon like a weary eye unable to stay open, the sky faded from bleached blue to smoky violet. We mounted our camels. Once again, the night came as my redeemer, lifting my spirits higher than they'd been all day. As darkness shrouded the heavens, the waxing moon cast a pale, diffuse glow that lit the sand the color of snow. I sang an inspired (though not necessarily pretty) rendition of that old blues hymn "When That Evenin' Sun Goes Down." I took off my turban and let the breeze tousle my hair with what felt like affection. I was, maybe for the first time all day, happy.

Except for my singing and Walid's occasional shout, which I answered in kind, the night was silent. It felt like we could have been the only people on earth. We continued on for hours, until Walid's shout of "Hoy!" was answered by another voice in the darkness up ahead. We veered slightly from our course to check it out and came across two people, one sitting, the other sleeping. Walid dismounted and approached while he and the stranger launched into the ritual salutation.

Once I was down from my camel, I shook hands with the nomad and asked, "No problems?"

"No problems!" he answered glee, surprised at being so greeted by a foreigner.

"You are well?"

"I'm well!"

"Praise be to God!"

"Praise be to God!"

"What's your name?" I asked, unable to get into the spirit of asking the same questions ad infinitum.

"Sali. And yours?"

"Michael."

"You speak Arabic?"

"A little," I said.

"Eeeeee! Praise be to God!" he said, laughing.

"Praise be to God!" and I laughed, too.

Woken by our voices, Sali's sleeping companion stirred and raised his head. I recognized him instantly.

It was Anselm, a nineteen-year-old German traveler who had been the only other tourist on the cargo boat I'd taken down the Niger River. He had wavy, shoulder-length blond hair parted in the middle and tucked behind his ears. Pimples speckled his cheeks and forehead. We had run into each other a few times in Timbuktu, and he'd booked a camel trip to Araouane, also through Alkoye "Le Petit." Alkoye had asked us whether we wanted to travel that leg of the route together, and we'd decided against it, not out of any dislike for each other, but to immerse more completely in the nomad experience, perhaps to live in the illusion that we were each the only Westerners in the desert.

Anselm had spent the previous two months working at a German-run orphanage in Burkina Faso. Now he was getting in a bit of traveling before returning home, where he hoped to enter a university, get a degree in psychology, and use it to work with at-risk teenagers, which is exactly what I had done in my twenties. He was earnest and idealistic, and I saw in him more than a little of myself when I was nineteen. I think back on that period of my life as a time when I was my most pure self, with both a solid sense of my core nature and a yet-untrammeled spirit of idealism. I spent my nineteenth summer hitchhiking around the Pacific Northwest, going from place to place and picking up work for a few days in a cherry orchard and a fish cannery, and for a few weeks at a fruit stand, and then a restaurant. I hiked in the Cascade and Olympic Mountains, lived on a fishing boat in the San Juan Islands, and befriended artists and alcoholics. My summer on the road was as much an act of faith as it was an adventure; despite the well-advertised dangers of sticking your thumb out and getting into a stranger's car, my naive notions of the divine permitted me to trust that the Universe would take care of me if I could align my intentions with its intentions for me. In the fourteen years that had passed since then, I'd come to appreciate the whimsy, caprice, and cruelty that are as essential to the functioning of the cosmos as are order and grace; I no longer trust it as blindly or as easily, and regularly question whether such a thing even exists. It was refreshing to meet someone who hadn't yet lost his innocence in the world. But the cynic in me couldn't help wonder what form Anselm's fall would take and how he would sound after he'd been bruised up a little.

Walid and Sali talked for a minute, and decided that since we were on the same route, we should travel together. Walid wanted to make yet more progress to put us nearer the well we would pass the following morning, and Sali agreed that that was a good plan. He tried rousting the dazed Anselm, who wanted to know what was happening. I explained it to him, so he got up. Walid and Sali quickly packed up the camp and loaded the camels, and within ten minutes we were back on the trail, our four camels strung together in a single line led by Walid.

We walked together side by side, Walid and Sali talking in Arabic, Anselm and I in English. Neither of us was disappointed that we ended up crossing paths. We empathized with each other about the daytime heat and our posterior pain. In many ways, we'd had similar experiences, but since Anselm spoke no Arabic, his journey had been a silent one. Sali was nice, he said, knew what he was doing, and was able to communicate the essentials by pointing and miming, but they really hadn't been able to talk about anything. He was disappointed, since he, too, had been promised a French-speaking guide by Alkoye.

"How did we end up in the same place?" Anselm wondered. "I don't mind, but we were supposed to take different routes to Araouane."

"I don't know," I said. "Are there different routes?"

"Yeah. Sali and I were supposed to go the long way by taking a detour through a place called Bou J'beha, then come back the direct way, hopefully with a caravan on its way to Timbuktu."

"We can look at my map later," I said, referring to the map of Mali that I carried, on which the major wells and subregions of the Sahara were marked, "but I'm sure that this is the direct route to Araouane, and that it doesn't pass through Bou J'beha." Sometimes, when we sat around the fire, Walid would list the landmarks—mostly wells—that we would pass on the way to Araouane, making me repeat after him, drilling me as though for an exam. Douaya; Harseini; Touerat; Taganet; Sidi Mukhtar; Araouane. I knew them by heart.

"Hmmm. I didn't want to travel there and back over the same ground . . . ," Anselm said.

While we were immersed in these logistics and wondering whether Alkoye had lied to Anselm about this, too, Sali suddenly sprang forward, grunted, and smashed the ground with his camel stick. To me, it looked like he was making a particularly emphatic point to Walid, but when he lifted his stick it was draped with the limp form of a lifeless serpent. It was clearly a horned viper—the deadly nocturnal Saharan sidewinder. Though it couldn't harm us now, my body surged with adrenaline. How many more might we encounter? Sali casually flung his kill to the side and we kept walking, I, for one, glad to have this human Riki Tiki Tavi on my team.

When we stopped an hour or so later and laid out our blankets, I scouted the area for firewood, which was scarce. Gathering a few dead twigs here and there, I realized I still had some energy left in me. My back hardly hurt and my sores had scabbed over. My body seemed to be adjusting to the rigors of desert travel after all.

In the daylight, I got my first good look at Sali. He wore a gray djellaba over a blue boubou, cinched around the waist with a rope into which was tucked a long, sheathed knife. His chestnut-colored face was lean and angular, his ears pointy, his smile sharp. His hair was cropped nearly to the scalp; a goatee shot from his chin like an arrow, completing his devilish appearance.

We came upon the well at Harseini after less than an hour of walking. There were only three other people there—an old man, a teenage boy, and his younger sister—and their two camels, two donkeys, and handful of goats. While Douaya had felt like the Saharan equivalent of a truck stop along an interstate, Harseini was more like a mom-and-pop service station on a rural two-lane road. The well wasn't quite as deep, but still plummeted far into the terrestrial abyss. The troughs were shallow cement basins. The surrounding area was a broad sandy waste; dust whipped through the air, flung by a vigorous breeze.

Since we'd arrived at Douaya while others were watering, I hadn't realized that the ropes, dowels, and goatskin buckets weren't fixtures of the wells, but were carried by travelers. Walid and I didn't have any of those things, but Sali did. He rigged the system, tied a thick grass rope to one of his camels, and, once the bucket had hit bottom and filled with water, led the camel away. The taut rope rode smoothly over the dowel, creaking with a sound that reminded me of the scene in *The Little Prince* when the pilot and the prince find the well; the little prince pulls the rope over a squeaky pulley, raising a bucket, and says, "We have wakened the well, and it is singing."

Our dowel sang sweetly until it suddenly fell silent as the rope went slack. Walid called out to Sali, who ran back to the well. We peered over the edge and saw the broken end of the rope swaying in the void below. Anselm and I glanced at each other, saying, "Oh, shit," with our eyes, then looked at Walid and Sali. They looked at each other, saying, "Oh shit," with their eyes. Then they looked around for the boy.

He was sitting on a blanket about twenty yards away with his sister and the old man. Sali called him to us and explained the situation, pointing down into the well. The boy pulled his beige djellaba off over his head; underneath, he wore lapis-blue nylon shorts and a navy T-shirt. Being the smallest one present except for the girl, he was the logical choice to send down after the bucket.

The end of the rope that just broke was tied around one of the boy's skinny thighs. Another rope that looked just as unreliable was tied around his other thigh and set over a second dowel, provided by the old man. A strip of cloth was tied around his chest, over the ropes, to keep him from flipping upside down. The boy pushed off the edge of the well as the ropes tightened in Walid's and Sali's hands. He hovered over the gaping hole, then was slowly lowered into it as Walid and Sali let the ropes out.

The boy, rigged to frayed ropes.

CHAPTER FOUR

Kneeling, I pressed my palms down on the rough lip of the well and watched the boy disappear into the darkness. Gripped with dread, I waited for the scream, followed by the splash, that I knew was coming. For anyone to trust their life to these ropes of twisted grass that had been spliced and respliced up and down their length was totally insane. If the boy fell, how would they get him out? Send someone else down on the very same ropes to rescue him? It was like *The Three Stooges* meets *Touching the Void*.

After a couple of very long minutes, a shout echoed up from the depths. Sali tied his rope to his camel and led it out; Walid took up the slack in his rope with his hands. At last, the top of the boy's head emerged from the shadows into the light. I exhaled for what felt like the first time since he'd entered the well. A few seconds later, he was sitting on the edge of the well, his lips parted in a smile of relief. But he was empty-handed. The leather bucket, weighted with water, had sunk beyond his reach.

The old man, who had been watching nervously, offered to lend us his bucket. Sali tied it to the rope, then dropped it into the well. He led the camel away, and this time the bucket rose to the top, full. Walid and I grabbed it, then, with water sloshing over our legs, heaved it over to the trough, from which the three camels drank. Though they could have gone many more days without touching water, Walid was being conservative, looking out for their best interests and ours. By keeping them well watered now, Lachmar and L'beyya would stay stronger and have an easier time later on when they'd have to go without it. When the trough was empty, the camel on the rope was switched out so he could drink as Lachmar hoisted the bucket.

With the camels taken care of, we filled our tubes. Sali carried a traditional leather water sack, which looked like the skinned goat it was—its legs were tied closed at the feet; the places where the tail, penis, and anus would have been were sewn shut; water was poured through its headless neck, which was lashed closed when not in use. Goatskins keep the water inside cooler than do rubber tubes, since as the water slowly seeps into the leather, evaporative cooling takes effect. The disadvantage of the leather is that it needs to be oiled, which makes the water taste a little queer. These days, many nomads use goatskins in the summer and inner tubes in the winter. Both are known as *guerbas*.

As Sali, Anselm, and I began walking north again, Walid stopped to talk with the old man; it was clear they were having a disagreement, but we were too far ahead for me to tell what it was about. Walid caught up to us quickly and continued on as though nothing had happened; within a minute, we heard a shout from behind, and turned to see the boy running to catch us, dragging a goat on a rope behind him. We paused, and when he reached us he and Walid exchanged a few words, then he handed Walid the goat's lead and Walid gave him some money.

As though it knew what was in store, the goat struggled against the rope. As Walid tugged it forward, it bleated like a baby in distress. Finally, Walid asked me to smack the animal with my camel stick to keep it moving. Putting aside my notions of animal ethics, which seemed utterly bourgeois in this setting, I struck it firmly on its hindquarters. It scampered along so Walid no longer had to yank on it, then it resisted again. I struck it again, and it moved again. This routine went on for about half an hour, until we came to a thorn tree that cast a wide web of shade.

The goat was small, its head just higher than my knees. It was short-haired and white with light gray freckles, brown ears, black eyes. The tip of its tail was frayed like a worn-out paintbrush. It had no horns. Walid tied it to the tree while we unloaded and hobbled the camels. It bleated incessantly, as though pleading for its life.

Walid led the doomed goat a few yards away, took off the rope, and held the animal down in the sand, tilting its head backward. Sali unsheathed his steel knife and drew it across the goat's throat, hard and fast, with neither mercy nor malice. Blood shot in an arc from the severed jugular, splattering and pooling on the sand. Walid held the head back for a few moments, then left the goat lying on its side to bleed out. The four of us scavenged fallen branches from underneath the tree; Walid built a fire three times as big as any we'd had yet and, once a sufficient base of coals was established, put a pot of water on to boil.

Sali went back to the goat, cut its head clean off, then began skinning it. He tore the hide as little as possible, essentially peeling it downward, separating it from the flesh with short, precise strokes of his knife. The legs gave him the most trouble, so, while sitting on the ground, Walid held the goat's fleshy body while Sali grasped the skin, and both of them leaned back, pulling against each other until each leg was stripped bare. Though the raw meat would dehydrate and keep well for a long time, the organs wouldn't, and had to be cooked immediately.

The heart, lungs, kidneys, and liver were tossed into the pot of water. The intestines were cut into finger-length pieces, then the stomach was sliced open, revealing a huge blob of putrid, partially digested grass. The lining was rinsed off and sliced up, then it and the intestines were added to the stew. Half of a leg was hacked off and placed directly on the hot coals. The rest of the carcass was rinsed, halved lengthwise, and stuck on the tree's spikes to dry, along with the hide.

Walid, and Sali much more so, were so enthusiastic about everything involved in cooking this goat, it seemed like they'd caught meat fever. They didn't seem to notice the blood and other fluids that splashed on their clothing and covered their hands. They rebuffed Anselm's and my offers to help, so we hovered around, watching with interest and taking pictures.

While we sat in the shade waiting for the organs to cook, Sali took the goat's milk sac and kneaded it with his hands. After a few minutes, he opened it and offered the contents around; the milk inside had congealed to the consistency of yogurt. I tasted it tentatively, expecting something sour and foul, but it proved to be delicious, refreshing and clean, an appetizer better than the course that followed.

Walid stuck his knife into the pot, chopped up the larger organs, scooped a heaping pile of steaming offal onto a plate, and passed it to Anselm and I. We looked at each other with an expression similar to the one we shared when the bucket got lost at the bottom of the well. Neither of us really wanted to eat it, but we felt we couldn't refuse. In the past, when I'd been confronted by similar culinary situations, there was always other food served as well, so I could nibble a little at the organs, eat other things, then claim to be full without having to experiment with the parts that struck me as most disgusting. This, however, was the all-entrails special.

Using our fingers, Anselm and I picked at the plate like we were eating from a box of mixed chocolates, searching for the pieces we liked best—or disliked least—while Walid and Sali hungrily devoured what was left in the pot. In the end, we were left mostly with intestines and stomach lining. Fortunately, Anselm preferred the stomach—which was like a rubbery tongue with outsized taste buds—and I preferred the intestines—which required very little chewing before swallowing.

While Sali and Walid were cracking the roasted leg bones with their knives and greedily sucking out the marrow, I reminded myself that billions of people in the world regularly eat offal; that dead animal parts are dead animal parts and there's nothing objectively gross about eating any of them. But aside from their off-putting taste, texture, and appearance, I couldn't quite shake the prejudices of my first-world upbringing, which were decidedly anti-guts. I resorted to slurping down the intestines, pretending they were made of Jell-O, but it only helped a little. When the plate was clean, Anselm and I shared a moment of silent relief, then cleansed our palates with succulent roasted leg meat.

Before we knew it, noon was upon us. Rather than strike out into the heat on full (and in my case semi-nauseated) stomachs, we opted to rest and digest for a few hours. I read, dozed, and wrote, appreciating every moment of this day that, while gastronomically challenging, was turning into something of a holiday.

Once on the move again, we soon left the grassy, pastoral-feeling flats behind us and entered a land of sand. Orange dunes rose like whales breaking the surface of the sea, which we maneuvered around like sailors in tiny skiffs. Serpentine ridges of sand cut sharp profiles against the bleached-out sky. The landscape was far more barren, yet far more captivating, than any we had yet traversed. Before, the unchanging terrain numbed my eyes; here, the sensuality of the dunes entranced me, satisfying a hunger for beauty that I hadn't realized I was craving.

For the first time, we traveled with our camels unhitched, meaning that I was in full control of driving Lachmar. Holding his lead in one hand as I sat atop his hump, I could finally picture myself as a true desert traveler rather than a tourist on a tether. Lachmar proved to be a

willful beast, and riding him was akin to driving a car with poor align-
ment, no power steering, and minor transmission problems. Disin-
clined to follow along with the others, he forced me to actively goad
him with my camel stick while clucking and slurping until my mouth
went dry. I felt some initial pangs of guilt when slapping his hide, until
my frustrations at him for forcing me to do it absolved me of any re-
morse. He occasionally veered to the sides, aiming for anything that
looked edible instead of staying on course, requiring me to redirect him
by pulling his lead to one side or another. I had the distinct sense he
knew that I was a less-than-confident driver and was trying to take advantage of my uncertainties. Over the next few hours, my technique
improved as I learned to handle him more firmly, and we rode into the
night under a clear sky ashimmer with stars.

Inspired by attaining the next level of camel mastery, when we
stopped a few hours after dark, I dismounted from Lachmar while he
was still standing, sliding awkwardly off the front of his hump and
dropping to the ground. It was another threshold clumsily crossed, and
I never again couched Lachmar before getting down.

Walid said we would cook a small dinner, sleep for just a few hours,
then get up and leave. He asked me to set the alarm on my watch for 1 AM.

Sleeping was one thing I never had trouble doing. Between the effort of riding and walking for hours, and simply enduring the pummel-
ing heat, sleep was more precious to me than food or even water. Every
night, as soon as I laid down on my blanket, I passed out, wearing the
same clothes I had worn all day, day after day.

The alarm jarred me awake at one. I called Walid's name a few
times before he stirred. When he did, he mumbled to reset it for five,
then rolled over and went back to sleep. I was grateful for the reprieve.

In the morning, we soon left the dunes behind us and entered a world
as flat as a pane of glass. The landscape looked exactly the same in every
direction: a level floor of sand stretching to the horizon line, which was

perfectly horizontal. Clumps of tall yellowed grasses sprouted here and there, as did the rare thorn tree. Because all sense of depth was devoured by the extreme flatness, the trees up ahead, which were scattered quite far apart, appeared to form a thick forest; like the stars in the night sky, it was impossible to tell that they were situated at varying distances from us. As we traveled, passing trees one by one, the edge of the illusory forest never neared, because it didn't exist.

Anselm and I talked while we walked. He was mildly obsessing over the fact that he wasn't traveling through Bou J'beha, and needed to voice the frustrations that had been running amok in his mind during the many silent hours we spent on camelback. Alkoye had clearly offered Anselm what he'd wanted with little concern for whether or not it would be delivered. It made me wonder if I might be the rube in an even bigger con job; I began to fear that Walid and I would arrive at the good grazing grounds only to find ourselves without a caravan to join, meaning I'd have traveled to the middle of the Sahara for nothing. I kept these concerns to myself, however, and focused instead on Anselm's situation. We discussed his options at length, and he finally decided that if it turned out to be impossible to travel back from Araouane to Timbuktu with a caravan (another promise of Alkoye's that he'd all but lost faith in), he'd offer to pay Sali more money to return through Bou J'beha, and deduct that amount from the remainder that he owed Alkoye.

Once we had thoroughly pulverized the subject from every angle, I figured it'd be a good idea to get his mind off it—and mine off my own doubts—so I enlisted his help in developing an idea I'd had the day before: writing a cookbook of authentic Saharan recipes. It would be a slim volume, to match the paltry variety of dishes on the nomad menu, and would be titled *Cooking with Sand*, since that was the one common ingredient in everything we ate.

For a versatile snack or easy-to-prepare appetizer, we had Lightly Sanded Peanuts and Dates, and the less exotic Dry Sandy Biscuits. We naturally included the ubiquitous Saharan Rice (made with slivers of goat meat, sun-aged goat butter, and anywhere from a tablespoon to half a cup of sand), and featured a few other specialties: Offal (Awful) Stew with Sand, Gritty Millet Gruel, and Soft Noodles Al Dente. Not to leave out the drinks, our book would teach people how to brew Sweet Green Tea (Served in a Sandy Glass); to complete the genuine dining experience, we'd recommend Warm Water Mixed with Camel Spit.

When it was time to ride, I decided to try mounting Lachmar while he was still standing. While Walid and Sali looked on with amused expressions, I stood by Lachmar's head and paused to gather myself. I grasped his ear lightly with one hand, then reached up and took hold of one of the cargo ropes with the other. When Lachmar lowered his neck, I leapt up onto it and nearly toppled over the other side. Walid and Sali hooted with laughter, and I quickly flung myself to my right and grabbed the cargo pad with both hands to steady myself. While I balanced precariously on his neck, Lachmar let out a frightening, leonine roar and started to walk. Fighting the swaying of his body, I scrambled in a panic up the front of his hump and more or less dove onto my blanket, landing on my stomach. Gingerly, my heart pounding, I righted myself and faced forward. Walid still had a grin on his face, but he nodded with approval. Sali raised a fist and gave a celebratory shout. I felt like a kid being praised by his father for learning to ride a bike without training wheels.

We rode on through the parched wasteland for a couple of hours, then stopped. Walid hobbled the camels while I untied Lachmar from L'beyya's tail, but this time we left them loaded. We weren't staying here long, Walid said, and, by way of an explanation, said that this was the last of the trees. Sali set to making a pot of tea while Walid, Anselm, and I gathered branches to carry with us for fuel. Half an hour later, with the tea finished and the wood secure on the camels, we left.

Walid was right. After this point there were no more trees. But for a few that had been planted in the village of Araouane, I wouldn't see another until I passed this place again, some four weeks later.

The desert remained as flat as a tabletop. Without the trees, it became even starker. Riding in silence through pure desolation, mile after mile after mile, staring into the face of utter emptiness with nothing to fill the mind but its own raw contents, it seemed we were traversing the earthly manifestation of the existential void. Starved for stimulus, my eyes scanned the vastness and locked on watery mirages that pooled like ponds and flowed like rivers across the sand. They were so tempting, it was easy to imagine delusional travelers madly leaping toward them to quench their thirst. No wonder, I thought, that the Tuareg fear the Spirits of Solitude.

We had long ago left any remnants of tire tracks behind, yet Walid led us across the desert in an unwavering course. He had neither map nor compass, and the only possible landmark was the sun, which would have been a vague one at best even if he'd had a watch. Yet just a few degrees of error over the distance we were covering would take us fatally wide of our destination. Though I'm an accomplished wilderness navigator, I was utterly baffled by how he knew where he was going without a single topographic cue. It was as though he had the powers of a migratory animal—a salmon that innately knows how to find its spawning grounds; a bird that flies thousands of miles back to the same nest. Awed, I tingled with the sense that I was rubbing up against one of the mysteries of the desert, revealed but not explained. When I asked him later how he did it with no map, no nothing, he smiled, pointed to his head, and said, "The map's in here."

When we stopped at about 1 PM, with no shade anywhere and the sun ravaging us from above, Walid and Sali erected a makeshift shelter, propping a blanket up over a few sticks, and tying its corners out to our heavy bags. The roof was hardly big enough to cover us all, so I decided to enlarge it. There was more to my motivation than creating a shadier space: unfamiliar with the techniques of nomad life, I'd been struggling with feeling totally inept. Sure, I could make a fire, but when it came to most things, even as small as pouring water from the rascally inner tubes without spilling a drop, or tying bags together over the camels, I did them slowly, hesitantly. With speed ever of the essence, Walid (and now Sali, too) would intervene and take over, brushing off my efforts, making me feel useless and incompetent. Having set up tarps probably a thousand times, building an annex onto our shelter was something I knew I could do right; I wanted to do it for my own sake, and to show Walid and Sali that I wasn't a total idiot.

When I brought my reed mat over, Walid urged me to sit down and forget about it. I ignored him. Anselm, who had been feeling much the same as me and taking it far more personally, jumped up eager to help. We tied the mat over one edge of the blanket, angled it down to the ground, and weighted the corners. Within minutes we had doubled the size of the shelter and scored a small but satisfying victory. It was better than the way I usually recovered my esteem following a particularly humbling moment, when I would imagine leading a helpless Walid through the streets and subways of Manhattan.

No food was cooked, which was okay with me, since it was too hot out to eat, and the cool dorno was all I wanted anyway. Sali busied himself deftly twisting a bundle of grasses into an inch-thick rope that materialized before my eyes. I asked to try it myself, and though I could get the individual strands to bond together, when I tried to lengthen the rope by meshing the ends of the grasses together, they fell apart under the least bit of strain. Oh well, I thought of my latest failure, at least our annex was still standing.

Since we had overslept that morning, we headed out earlier than we had from previous afternoon breaks. The sun still seethed overhead, crippling in its force. I focused my energy on putting one foot in front of the other. Stepping ever farther into the nothingness, with no way to mark our progress, was like walking into infinity. At last Walid paused and asked if I wanted Lachmar to couch so I could get on. I said no, leapt upon his neck, and crawled up his back. Though still graceless, it was a better performance than earlier that morning. I soon found it much easier to mount a standing camel than a sitting one, and within two days was able to do so while Lachmar was walking slowly.

Once again, night came like a blessing from the Merciful One. Rejuvenated and clearheaded, I reflected on some of the things I had seen thus far. As the nomad tents were pitched ever farther apart, as the vegetation became ever more scarce, it occurred to me that the way Saharans live closely mimics the patterns of the natural desert ecosystem they dwell within. They camp away from one another so their herds won't have to compete for sparse pasture, just as thorn trees and clumps of grass are spaced far apart to avoid overconsumption of precious water. There is even a rootless plant, the rose of Jericho, that blows across the desert from place to place, bearing tiny fruit and spilling seeds where it stops, like a biological metaphor for nomadism. Only by working with the desert on its own terms, just like other plants and animals, have Saharan peoples been able to survive. The key to their success is an ethic of mutual sustainability: If the scant resources are overused, everyone dies.

This, of course, makes perfect sense, but as I tossed it around in my mind, a question began to nag: Why bother? The environment is so unrelentingly brutal, it's hardly the optimal place for anything to live. Why then are plants, animals, and people so driven to eek out an existence in such a place? What's the point? Certainly neither money nor glory. The answer, it seems, is survival simply for its own sake. The deepest urge of all. And by adopting strategies that adhere to the laws of the desert, they can.

This, I saw, was about as far as one could get from the American proclivity for outsized consumption. Unlike the Saharans, who know the need for balance with the natural world because they live in it, we live as though we're separate from it, immune to the repercussions of overusing it. Yet with looming environmental catastrophe on a planetary scale, our circumstances are not all that different from the Saharans.

If their ethic of mutual sustainability is a survival strategy, then ours is a suicide strategy. If survival is the most hardwired biological impulse of all, we've got a short in our system. Our craving to consume, which in healthy amounts is critical to sustaining life, has hit pathological proportions, like a grossly obese person who not only can't stop eating, but justifies every bite. In other words, our culture is ill.

While gazing up at the celestial chandelier, rocking back and forth atop Lachmar's hump, I decided that the source of our collective malady was living lives ever less connected to or affected by the natural world. Barring extreme shows of force, such as tornadoes, tsunamis, earthquakes, and the like, we control our daily environment more than it controls us. If it's hot, we turn on the air-conditioning; if it's cold, we crank the heat. We humidify and dehumidify; we sit in bright light in the middle of the night. Most of us live apart from animals except for pets (and pests). As we have lost touch with nature, we have also lost touch with the instinctual intelligence that promotes survival through balance—the kind of balance so evident in the nomad culture. As Carl Jung once wrote about the human condition, "Too much civilization makes sick animals."

But what, I thought, of the environmental movement, the calls to conserve, to explore renewable sources of energy, to reduce pollution and greenhouse gases, to save animal and plant species from extinction, to preserve wildlands? It seems that there are still active vestiges of our archaic animal intelligence that know the need for balance. Really, it's like we're trying to save ourselves as we try to kill ourselves, as though Freud's Eros–Thanatos conflict has erupted on a collective scale.

Saharans don't have this problem. They have no misconceptions about their place in the order of things—not because they are "noble savages," but because with so few resources they reap immediate consequences if they abuse them. And they have learned from past mistakes, such as overgrazing and overhunting. By living as subjects of the natural world, their awareness of the need for balanced consumption has remained astute. Rather than viewing them as poverty-stricken semi-primitives, we might do well to appreciate them for what they really are—masters of survival, from whom we can learn to reconnect with our own instinctual intelligence simply by realizing we have it, and whose ethic of living in balance with the natural world we can emulate, not just for its sake, but for our own.

We rode on and on, late into the night. When we finally stopped and got the camels unloaded, Sali built a tea fire and Walid said he was leaving.

"Leaving?" I asked. "Where are you going?"

"My wife's family is camped near here, and she is there with my sons. I'm going to see them, but I'll be back in the morning."

He mounted L'beyya, reached behind himself and slapped the camel's rear with his stick, and shot off at a gallop into the darkness. Again, I was astounded. Not only were we in the midst of a featureless landscape, but it was nighttime; how could he possibly know exactly where we were, or how to find his wife's family, whose tent, when measured against the size of the desert, was proportionally smaller than the proverbial needle in a haystack? And, more important to me, how would he be able to find his way back?

Sali roused Anselm and I at first light. We finished our morning routine, and when the camels were loaded and up, we started walking. There was no sign of Walid. I was a little concerned.

"Where is he?" I asked Sali.

"He'll be here," he answered.

"But we won't be here," I pointed out.

"Don't worry," he said. "He'll find us."

We marched into a brilliant morning, the cool sand trickling between my toes, the sky a field of lavender. I imagined Walid sleeping in, loath to leave the comfort of his wife's side, and wondered what would happen if he didn't find us. Every few minutes I looked back over my shoulder to see if he was trailing us, and saw no one.

About an hour after we started, four figures appeared on the horizon directly ahead of us. Two were camels, two were humans. One was Walid.

The other was a man named Baba. He was short and slight of frame, with a black mustache, a beard that grew in a narrow swath along the bottom of his jawline and came to a point in a short goatee, and a prominent nose with a bulbed tip. Dressed in a loose, forest-green boubou and a meticulously wrapped black turban, he looked like an elf with a regal demeanor and a serious tan.

Sali and I greeted Walid and Baba as required by custom, though I dropped out of the redundant dialogue early while the three nomads kept it up. Walid seemed happy and refreshed, and I was glad he'd taken the opportunity to see his family.

We soon emerged from the monotonous flats into an area that was like a macrocosmic washboard road, crossing one long, rounded ridge of sand after another. Dunes rose against the horizon, cutting glowing ivory silhouettes against the gunmetal sky, looking like rends in the otherwise solid seam where heaven and earth met, through which streamed a noumenal light. I was transfixed by their sudden beauty after so much nothingness, and rode on in a meditative reverie.

This was abruptly shattered when a fennec—the desert fox—popped out of its hole and scampered away in front of us. Sali and Baba jumped off their camels and gave chase, Baba running with quick efficiency, Sali leaping and hooting like a madman. Like everything else in the desert, these men were opportunists, and weren't about to pass up the rare chance to hunt an animal that normally at midday would be sleeping in its den thirty feet below ground, where the temperature remains cool and constant. The little furry fox with tall pointy ears raced off like a turbocharged Muppet, and Baba and Sali kicked up a squall of sand trying to catch it but lost ground by the second. In a last-ditch effort to nail their prey, Sali hurled his camel stick at the fox; it flew end over end, and to my relief landed harmlessly in the sand.

I could hardly believe they had bothered to exert themselves like that. By this time the heat of the day was simply unbelievable—hotter, it seemed, than it had been since I'd left Timbuktu. Before long, Walid decided he'd had enough of it himself, and we parked atop a ridge of sand. Sali, however, wanted to keep going and make it all the way to Araouane, which was just four hours distant. Walid argued with him over the prudence of this course, urging him to get out of the sun, but Sali's mind was made up. They were leaving, and we were staying. Baba, Walid, and I said quick good-byes to Sali and Anselm, then got to work building our sunshade. Watching the two camels disappear to the north, Walid shook his head and declared that Sali was nuts.

While we waited for the tea to brew (it's never too hot for tea), I learned that Baba was Walid's cousin. He was thirty years old, had a wife and a child, and had been an azalai for half his life. He was coming along to join the caravan, so would be with us for the rest of the trip to Taoudenni. I immediately had a good feeling about him; his manner was relaxed, he laughed easily, and seemed surrounded by a halo of peacefulness.

We set off after a few hours of lounging, but stopped again just as it got dark. Except for the dorno and some peanuts and dates, we hadn't eaten all day, so Walid decided to break for dinner, then continue on the last hour or two to Araouane. After we ate, however, none of us was particularly motivated to load the camels and get moving again, so we stayed the night where we were.

It was the first chance I'd had to bask in the glory of the Sahara at night, neither trucking along on the back of a camel nor so exhausted that I wanted to pass out. And it was wonderful. The sky was enormous, and there was nothing to break the silence except the crackling of the fire and three stations competing against each other and a high-pitched squeal for dominance of the shortwave radio.

In my mind, we were as good as in Araouane, and making it that far felt like a major achievement. Though it was only one-third of the way to Taoudenni, and one-sixth of the entire journey, it was our first significant milestone. I had conquered my debilitating sinus infection, each day was getting easier, and I was finally beginning to enjoy myself, starting to thrive rather than merely survive. I thanked Allah that I hadn't been sick to my stomach, and prayed I would stay healthy.

I wondered what Araouane would look like, and imagined the three of us riding camels through the gates of a desert Xanadu, standing tall and gleaming among the dunes. I knew, naturally, that that wasn't what I would find, especially since this town supposedly didn't even have Coca-Cola. As the importance of caravan trade in the Sahara has diminished, so has the significance of this once major commercial center along the route from Timbuktu to both Taoudenni and Morocco.

The wells around Araouane—reputed to hold the best water in the region—have been a stopping point along this trail for some thousand years. The town itself was founded in 1575 by Ahmed ag-Adda, a famed religious scholar and renowned merchant of the Kel Es-Suq clan. His presence drew students—called *talamidh*—and disciples from far and wide, and Araouane, which was named for the length of rope it took to reach the bottom of the wells there, grew into a prosperous center of trade and Islamic learning.

The Kel Es-Suq belonged to the Qadiriyya, a Sufi order that became the predominant form of Islam in the western Sahara, including the Azawad—a wide swath of territory between Timbuktu and Araouane, which I had just traveled through. Their scholars were mystics who emphasized both prayer and meditation, balancing adherence to Koranic law with direct, personal contact with the divine. One of their guiding precepts was: "He who follows *fiqh* (Muslim jurisprudence) and does not possess mystic knowledge is a freethinker, while he who is a mystic and does not follow *fiqh* is in error and commits a sin. He who combines them arrives at the truth and is in true faith."

As part of their mystical legacy, the Kel Es-Suq shunned violence and conquest. They supported their pacifist convictions by referring to the Koranic Sura "The Table," in which the Cain and Abel story is retold. When Cain tells Abel he's going to kill him, Abel replies, "God accepts only from the pious. If you stretch forth your hand to slay me, I will not stretch forth my hand to slay thee; for I fear God, the Lord of all worlds. . . . You will become an inhabitant of the Fire." Better, the Kel Es-Suq thought, to avoid the Fire than to vanquish others, whether on an individual or tribal level. Instead, they devoted themselves to the peaceful pursuits of rhetoric, calligraphy, prayer, trade, and herding.

By the end of the eighteenth century, the Es-Suq had been displaced by the Kunta, an "Arab" tribe who also belonged to the Qadiriyya and adhered to similar principles of mysticism and nonviolence. Led by their great scholar-chief Sidi al-Mukhtar al-Kabir al-Kunti, the Kunta spread their influence throughout the western Sahara and assumed the religious leadership of Araouane.

Sidi al-Mukhtar had worked in the salt trade as a young man, then traveled through the desert solidifying his reputation as a teacher and holy man. His wisdom, generosity, and charisma drew "multitudes of disciples." The Kunta's spiritual hold over the Azawad became nearly absolute after they played mediator between the Tuareg and the settled people of Timbuktu, and once they could count the Berabish, as well as a number of Tuareg tribes, among their adherents. The association of the Berabish and the Tuareg through the Kunta was no doubt responsible for the eventual alliance between these two powerful hasani peoples.

Sidi al-Mukhtar asserted that it was appropriate for the Kunta to involve themselves in the political arena, since mediating treaties between warriors was a way to promote peace among the "people of the sword" while winning hasani allies for needed protection from rivals. His interest in expanding the Kunta's sphere of influence came less from a belief that theirs was the one true word and more for financial reasons. Based on the fact that "trade was the profession of the Prophet," Sidi al-

Mukhtar sanctioned the accumulation of wealth. And the talamidh were the foundation upon which the Kunta economic system was based. Aside from paying for their education and religious guidance with cows, sheep, millet, cloth, and the like, the talamidh served as a massive, usually wage-free workforce. They ran the trade caravans, oversaw the salt mines, worked date-palm plantations, herded livestock, bred camels, dug wells, and performed other forms of manual and clerical labor. Thus the Kunta's economic base grew in direct proportion to the number of talamidh they could attract. And they came not only to learn the Koran; once the talamidh had completed their work-study internships, they were positioned to join the ranks of the Kunta's wealthy traders.

At the center of this activity for more than three hundred years, Araouane had been the beating heart through which goods and spiritual teachings had flowed to all parts of the Azawad, south to Timbuktu, east to Niger, and west to Mauritania. Today it barely has a pulse at all.

When I first saw Araouane from a distance, it looked like an old fortress positioned atop the highest hill in the area, its dark, angular walls standing in ominous contrast to the curvaceous white landscape surrounding it. In truth, it is a crumbling village that is sinking into the huge swell of sand upon which it is built. Dunes break like waves against the dilapidated walls of the few mud-brick houses that are this desert outpost, some of which are almost completely buried. The streets, if that's what you call the space between buildings, are filled with deep, soft sand. Were it not for the few people walking around in vibrant, flowing clothing that billowed and snapped in the wind, it would've been easy to mistake the place for a partially excavated archaeological site.

There's no electricity, no shops, no television antennas on the flat rooftops. There is little activity except that of the livestock that gathers around its wells. But for a few trees that had been planted many years before, no plants grew. The only sign of modernity was the small concrete-block structure that housed a one-room medical clinic and a radio-telephone office. The entire town could've easily fit inside a football stadium.

We walked our camels to a house on the northernmost edge of town. As we unloaded, two girls and a boy emerged from the door, followed by a man in a white djellaba. After a hearty round of greetings, the man and the boy helped us unload our camels. We left our belongings in piles covered by blankets to protect them from the sun, then followed the man into the house.

Like many houses in this part of the world, this one was built around an inner courtyard that served as a kitchen, laundry room, and livestock pen. The northern "wing" of the house, which we had entered, consisted of two rooms divided by a partial wall, so it was possible to walk between them without passing through any doors. We were ushered into the smaller of the two rooms, which was lit by the open door to the courtyard, and were invited to sit on geometrically patterned mats of woven plastic fibers. The floor was made of the same loose, fine sand as the earth outside. The thick adobe walls that kept the house cool were rounded and plastered a soothing buff yellow. The ceiling of sticks and twigs was supported by aged wooden beams that must have been brought from more than 150 miles away.

The older of the two girls disappeared into the courtyard and came back carrying a small brazier topped with a teapot, then made a second trip for an aluminum tray with shot glasses, a box of tea, and a bag of sugar. While the water heated, the man, named Mohammed, exchanged news with Walid and Baba.

After the tea was finished, Walid, Baba, and Mohammed left to water the camels and take care of a few other things we'd need for the next leg of our journey. I was left alone in the room with the two girls, one of whom was nine, the other who was hardly more than a toddler. The nine-year-old, named Hannah, spoke French, which she said she had learned during the three years of schooling that children in Araouane receive. While we talked, her sister lay on the sandy floor, watching.

"Do you like living in Araouane?" I asked.

A look of disgust crossed her face. "No," she said. "I hate it."

"Why?"

"It's ugly here. There is nothing to do. There are no shops, no restaurants; we have nothing here."

"If there are no shops, where does your family buy food?"

"Three times a year we go to Timbuktu. There, we buy all of the rice, millet, flour, and everything else we need until the next trip."

"How do you like Timbuktu?"

"Oh I love Timbuktu! There is so much to see, so much to do! Timbuktu is rich and colorful. Araouane is poor and dead." In her mind, Timbuktu was still like the fabulous city of legend. "When I get older, I want to marry a man from there, someone who will take me away from here . . . ," she said, like a Saharan Cinderella.

Just then her mother called, needing her help in the courtyard. Hannah excused herself and I was alone again for a few minutes before Anselm came in and sat down. I was glad to see him, and asked him what was going on.

He said that Sali had wanted to get to Araouane the day before, but as the sun started to set, Anselm, with much gesturing, conveyed his desire to spend the night atop a dune just outside the village. They arrived in Araouane that morning, and Sali's intention was to take a quick look around, then head back the way we had come. Anselm, however, had found someone who spoke French to translate between the two of them. He asked about the possibility of returning to Timbuktu alongside a salt caravan, and asked why they hadn't come north through Bou J'beha.

It quickly became clear that Sali had no idea that Alkoye had promised Anselm that they'd take the Bou J'beha route, and they hadn't done so because it was longer. Moreover, there was no chance of him riding back to Timbuktu with a caravan, unless Anselm wanted to wait in Araouane for a few weeks. Feeling like he'd been screwed all around by the Timbuktu tour agent, he offered to pay Sali the hundred dollars he still owed to Alkoye if Sali would take him back through Bou J'beha. It was a tremendous sum in local terms, and Sali had instantly agreed. Anselm figured he'd claim a breach of contract if Alkoye gave him any trouble about it. They'd be heading out in a few minutes, and Anselm had just wanted to check in and say good-bye one more time. We wished each other well, and parted for the last time.

(Many weeks later, I learned that when Anselm got back to Timbuktu and explained the situation to Alkoye, Alkoye threw a fit and said the matter would have to be taken to the police, and could take weeks to get cleared up. If Anselm tried to leave town without paying, Alkoye said he'd have him arrested. Unable to spend the time to resolve the dispute, which he likely would have won, Anselm paid.)

Left alone with Anselm's story of frustration, my doubts about whether or not there'd be a caravan to meet surfaced afresh. Again, I suppressed them, and distracted myself by taking a walk around the village. Few people were out: Women were dressed in flamboyant colors that leapt out against the background of pale sand. Some, known as sand women, earned a few pennies by sweeping clear the ever-invading desert from the doorways of Araouane's houses. I looked down the hill where men were splashing water from a well into troughs, just as we had done, then passed by the mosque—a small wind-weathered box capped with a mud cone, from which a dark iron star and crescent moon protruded starkly against the colorless sky. As I'd just about completed my circuit of the town, I was approached by one boy whom I guessed was about eight, who greeted me with the traditional salutation offered by many Malian children: *"Toubab! Donnez-moi un cadeau!"* which translates into: "White guy! Give me a gift!"

I was surprised that this practice had made it out to Araouane. It's so annoyingly prevalent in "mainland" Malian cities (with the notable exception of Bamako), that it's practically impossible to walk down their streets without being accosted by throngs of kids demanding gifts, pens, and money. The funny thing was that even after I had been in

Mali for a few months, I never met any travelers who gave handouts to the children, since no one wanted to promote a culture of begging. I wondered why the kids kept at it, since it didn't appear to produce results. I began to imagine that sometime in the distant past, a foreigner once gave a kid the most wonderful cadeau imaginable, and the story spread across the land and was passed down through the generations— that at bedtime kids beg to be told the tale of the Toubab and the Fabulous Cadeau—so that even though none of them has ever received one, they live in hope for the day when they'll be just like the lucky boy or girl in the story. Then when they reach a certain age, they realize that, like Santa Claus, it doesn't exist, and they stop asking for it.

Rather than a cadeau, I gave the boy in Araouane a lecture on hospitality, telling him it was important that he leave the foreigners who came this way with a good impression of his village. He apologized, momentarily embarrassed, then asked me for a pen.

I got back to the house and read for a while, soaking up the luxury of resting indoors, before Walid, Baba, and Mohammed returned. Mohammed's wife, Barka, served lunch: a round loaf of freshly baked bread for each of us, smothered in a thin orange sauce that was mildly spicy and flavored with hints of meat. After eating the same boring food for the past week, the home cooking was downright ambrosial, and I devoured my portion like a starving man.

Mohammed's eleven-year-old son ate with us, and with him as a translator I posed a few questions to Baba and Walid that I didn't know how to phrase in Arabic. Most important, I asked whether the trucks that now ran the salt route would soon make camels obsolete. The three men chuckled. Some trucks did make the trip to Taoudenni, Walid said, but he claimed that camels were much more suited to the work and would never disappear from the salt trade. This took me by complete surprise. It contradicted all the assumptions with which I had embarked upon this trip, and I wanted to know why Walid thought the way he did.

His response was vague, and focused on the high cost of the gasoline that the trucks consume. Baba and Mohammed nodded in agreement. The camel caravans would only stop running, Walid said, if the nomads one day had the opportunity to do something else. He himself would much prefer to own a shop in Timbuktu than ride back and forth to Taoudenni, but he didn't have anywhere near the money to open one.

Though I imagined Walid knew what he was talking about, I had trouble letting go of the opposite conclusions drawn by the Western reports I had read about the situation—and I realized that these men were likely biased in favor of the camel. I wasn't sure what to believe, and knew I'd need more information before forming an accurate opinion. I'd have to wait until Taoudenni to get it.

When we finished with lunch, the men left again. I rose to go with them, but Walid told me to stay put. I didn't argue, knowing I'd soon be glad for whatever rest I could get, wishing I could store it up the way a camel stores fat in its hump. My own belly deliciously full, I drifted off to sleep, wondering what it would be like to finally meet up with the caravan, which Walid had said we were going to do this very night.

As the sun neared the western horizon, we prepared to leave. Walid had exchanged our inner tubes for bigger ones; we had new, thicker cargo pads; the camels' bellies were swollen to capacity with water. These small changes foreshadowed the increasing intensity of the terrain we were about to cross. While we loaded up, a crowd of about fifteen people gathered around.

"Where are you going?" one young man asked.

"To Taoudenni," I said.

"Taoudenni?! Eeeeee!" he exclaimed in surprise, shaking his head as though I had told him we were going to try to walk to the moon. "Good luck."

With our baggage slung, the camels stood. We thanked Mohammed and Barka, and said we'd see them in a few weeks, ensha'allah.

We turned north and the crowd followed us down to the bottom of the hill upon which Araouane sits. They stayed there and shouted blessings and good-byes while we waved back at them and kept on going.

The desert was awash in a magical light that had an almost tangible quality, as though the particles it was composed of had condensed into a vapor. Our shadows grew by the minute, falling to the right upon sand that had hours before been blindingly white, but appeared to have been recently touched by Midas. Soon the rippled earth was decked with sheaves of long, bent-over grasses. This, it seemed clear, was the "good grazing ground" north of Araouane where the caravan was supposed to gather. And before long, we passed a large herd of camels browsing among the bushes and a handful of men sitting by a fire. Though we kept our distance, we could easily hear the huffing and snorting and occasional groans of the animals. Walid shouted to the men, who answered back, but we didn't stop.

About twenty minutes later, just as it got dark, Walid dismounted. We unburdened our beasts and set them loose to feed. Baba, it seemed, was taking over most of the domestic duties, so he readied both the teapot and the dinner pot while Walid built a fire.

"Where is the caravan?" I wanted to know. "We should be with them tonight, right?"

"Oh, we passed it back there. Didn't you see it?" Walid said.

"Yes, I saw it. But why didn't we stop?"

Walid explained that it would be better for us to stay where we were. Lachmar and L'beyya wouldn't have to compete with the other camels for food; it would be quieter; and the caravan would have to come this way when it left, so we could join it then. I was a little disappointed, but I figured that one less night with the others was no great loss, and I trusted Walid to know what he was doing.

While we sat around eating, however, he suggested traveling to Taoudenni on our own, meeting up with the caravan there, then traveling back with it. He said the three of us would be able to move much faster by ourselves, which meant we'd have extra hours every night to sleep. And we could stop and let the camels graze in places that would be too sparse for an entire caravan. Overall, he said, it would be much easier.

I considered his proposal. *Easier* had an appealing ring to it, and I liked the friendly dynamic that was evolving among Walid, Baba, and me. But I had come here to immerse in caravan life, not just to take a camel ride to Taoudenni. So I said no, I wanted to hitch up with the caravan when they passed, and go with them to the mines. Walid said okay, and asked me to set my alarm for 1 AM.

I have never been a morning person. I naturally prefer to stay up late, then wake up late, and have always found that being dragged from dreamland by an alarm clock is a miserable way to start the day. So when, at one, Walid told me to reset my alarm for four and to go back to sleep, I didn't argue for a second. Besides, if he knew how to find his wife's family in the middle of the night in the middle of nowhere, I had faith that he'd know when a convoy of camels marched by.

At four, we did get up and, rather than waiting for the caravan to arrive, we started off into the darkness on our own.

"What's going on?" I asked. "Where is the caravan?"

"It passed us while we slept."

His words fell like a bomb upon my composure. I was speechless. The concerns I'd kept at bay about failing to meet the caravan had come to pass, after I was sure there was nothing left to fear. Stricken with angst, I felt an urgent need to catch up to it while we were still within its range, for fear of losing it for good. We were suddenly in a race against time, against the speed of the caravan. As light broke over the desert, I strained my eyes to the horizon, scanning for the herd, but saw nothing.

Our chase across the Sahara had begun.

Baba and the author.

CHAPTER FIVE

scending ridge after ridge of sand, my anticipation swelled, certain that from each crest the caravan would appear before us, marching in regimented rows across the undulating ivory earth. Upon spotting specks of brown in the distance, my heartbeat quickened, only for it to falter with disappointment when the "camels" proved to be nothing more than bushes. On and on we rode. My eyes grew tired from squinting, but I saw nothing.

We stopped for a break some eight hours after we'd left camp. I figured enough time had probably passed to allow us to catch the caravan, and was mystified as to why we hadn't. I asked Walid where it was.

"They're going a different way," Walid said.

"What?" I replied, completely bewildered.

"They are going the long way," he said, and drew a diagram in the sand that depicted the caravan's path as an arc, while we traveled in a straight line. "They need to pass places where there is enough food for all their camels. Since we only have three, we can graze where they can't, and can travel a more direct route."

"But I'm here to travel *with* the caravan, not just in the same desert."

"Don't worry," Walid said, without the slightest hint of apology. "We'll meet them up ahead at the well at Foum el-Alba."

I was torn by conflicting reactions to this news. Part of me was irate that my trusted guide, and now my friend, had changed the plan and was directly contradicting my wishes. But another part of me thought that maybe I hadn't been as clear about my desires as I'd believed, that my words might have been misinterpreted. Though disappointed, I gave Walid the benefit of the doubt and chalked it up to a misunderstanding. With nothing to do about it anyway, I chose to let it go, enjoy being with Walid and Baba, and look forward to our rendezvous at Foum el-Alba.

By the end of the day we had left the rolling ridges behind us. The earth had settled into an endless sheet of orange sand. In the evening, the pleasant breeze intensified into a blustery squall, buffeting my body and hurling plumes of grit through the air. When we camped for the night, I laid my blanket on the lee side of a grassy bush, thinking only of taking shelter from the wind; I'd forgotten that windblown sand accumulates in precisely such calm spots. By morning, it had worked its way inside my blanket, my ears, my clothing, and coated every inch of my skin as though I'd been in an explosion at a flour mill.

The gusts persisted for the next two days while we traversed terrain so changeless that we might have been walking on a treadmill for all the difference each mile made to our eyes. In the wind, the desert floor came alive; broad snakes of sand slithered swiftly over the ground in long, sinuous patterns. The sky hung low, aswirl with a hundred shades of gray. Rain fell one drop at a time, each drying before the next hit the ground, yet there was enough moisture to fill the air with that scent unique to wet desert—the pungent breath of parched soil sighing with relief. For hours at a time we crossed zones so barren that not a single plant grew. There weren't even any rocks. It seemed like we'd entered a two-dimensional world, in which the flat orange plane of the ground met the flat gray plane of the sky at the flat, hard line of the horizon. The cloudy sky appeared more substantial than the earth, creating the illusion that the ground hovered above us and we were treading upside down on air.

We had entered the Tanezrouft, the ancient "desert within a desert" some four times the size of England. Known as "The Land of Thirst" and "The Land of Terror," it is feared and respected by all who pass through it, a great dead zone that might have inspired the old nomad adage, "One does not live in the desert. One crosses it." From here on, we'd see no tents, no birds, no signs of animal life but for the rare beetle track. We traveled longer and longer hours, pushing through this comfortless land as fast as we could.

With sand whipping through the air, I wrapped my turban around my head and over my face, covering my nose and mouth. With my sunglasses on, I was completely concealed in my helmet of cloth. I looked down at myself and over at Walid and Baba. Our faces were mysteriously swaddled; each of us wore dirty boubous bulging with wind; we rode bizarre creatures through a mist of orange dust, occasionally passing creepy piles of camel bones—we could have been starring in a B-grade post-apocalyptic science-fiction movie. Cutting through the storm with no possible refuge and nowhere to go but deeper into the Sahara, it dawned on me that this was the real thing, and I was doing it. I smiled beneath my turban, aware that I was starting to appreciate my flight with the Rukh.

Out of nowhere, lyrics popped into my head. "Cosmic Charlie how do you do? Truckin' in style along the avenue. Dum de dum de doodeley doo. Go on home your mama's calling you." I ran through the entire Grateful Dead classic, fudging a few words here and there, then started again. And again. And again. The song stayed in my head for days, running as though the REPEAT button had been pressed in my brain. But I didn't mind too much—after all, even low-budget films need a soundtrack, and Lord knows I could have been cursed with something far worse.

One of the qualities that draws me to deserts is their sparseness. I go to be scoured by their winds, purged by their silence, humbled by their searing sunsets. The desert dirt, which accumulates in the chapped cracks of my fingers and the pores of my face, brings me solace. It somehow stills the subtle anxieties produced by living in a culture in which what you do is so often mistaken for who you are, where artificialities obscure essences. Immersing in the desert's simplicity is akin to a ritual purification. As the earth stands naked, so I am stripped to my unadorned self, with little to distract me from the truths of my life.

The glaring truth I confronted while riding for many a mute mile was that of my four-year-long relationship. I tried to tell myself that I didn't miss my girlfriend, Karen, because I knew she would have been miserable on this journey, that I was glad she wasn't with me for her own sake. But I knew that that was just a small part of the truth. As I assessed the many facets of our life together and searched my heart for its most honest feelings, every train of thought ultimately traveled in the same direction: It was over for me. Something as unnamable as it was essential was missing from what we had. Try as I did to rationalize my way out of this conclusion, the desert was like an opaque mirror reflecting the workings of my soul, and I could not deny what it showed me. Back home, I had tried for a while to evade this reality, in part because I dreaded hurting Karen, in part out of the hope that we could eventually find a way to return to the halcyon days we had once shared. I knew that Karen wanted to be married, and over the course of our relationship, even in the best of times, when I asked myself if I could marry her, the answer had always been "not yet." Now the quiet voice within, the one that ultimately demands to be heard, changed that answer to "no." While there were many reasons, there was also no reason at all, except that this is what that little voice said. Despite all the things that made us a good match for each other, I intuited, simply, deeply, in a way that defies logical explanation, that she was not my destiny. And it was this truth that I knew I'd have to obey.

After four years together, the thought of traveling through life alone once more was daunting. But, I figured, if I could endure the physical and mental hardships of this relentless journey into the heart of nothingness, I could survive a life alone without knowing if or when another woman would appear on my horizon.

My mind cycled in and out of its review of my relationship, and I finally forced myself to stop thinking about it. I didn't want to come to any irrevocable decisions before seeing Karen again, wondering if and hoping that the sight of her would remind me of why we had gotten together in the first place, renewing the passion for her that I had once felt. But deep down, I sensed that wasn't going to happen.

When we came upon a mass of camel tracks, my mind left the topic of my love life and returned to the task at hand: finding the caravan. Walid declared that the footprints were left by the very camels we were seeking. They were partially filled with sand and looked less than fresh, though with the wind it was possible that they'd been formed only an hour or two before.

I had no idea how Walid could tell that our caravan had made them, but if he was right, I thought, it was bad news. If they were now ahead of us, it meant that they had completed their long detour. And if that was true, they were making significantly better time than we were. Suddenly, it seemed like our chances of meeting them at Foum el-Alba were dashed. I wondered if we'd catch them at all before Taoudenni. With the speed at which they were obviously moving, it wasn't unreasonable to imagine that we'd arrive at the mines just as the caravan was about to return south—or worse, after they already had.

I was furious—at Walid, at Alkoye, but mostly at myself. Here I was, having taken myself into the middle of the Sahara the hard way, and I'd screwed up completely. I kicked myself for failing to urge Walid to return to the caravan's camp on the night we first passed it. I walked with a fast, angry pace, cursing myself and my stupidity. I envisioned returning home and telling people that I'd been inches from achieving my dream, and had blown it. I was convinced we'd lost the caravan for good, that I'd risked my life and forsaken all comfort and would have little to report on but some fool errand into the desert.

That night—the third since we'd passed the caravan—the clouds began to break, and my anger finally cleared along with them. Riding toward the tail of Cygnus the Swan, whose celestial body soared low in the heavens before us, I regained my emotional equilibrium. I decided to talk with Walid and, without blaming him for anything, explain how important it was that we catch the caravan—and that I was willing to travel as long and as fast as we had to in order to do so.

We surged deep into the night. The moon, which had been obscured for the past few evenings, was now a day past full. It slid across the sky, ever higher, as we continued on. Exhausted from the day's physical strain and the internal abuse I'd heaped upon myself, my mind was a weary void when we entered a field of dunes that rose abruptly from the flats. In the eerie moonlight, it looked as though we were wending our way among massive snowdrifts, the sheer lee sides of the dunes resembling glacial bergschrunds. It felt like we'd been transported to a place out of time, an ancient world of black and white before color was invented. Its pristine beauty seemed delicate, fragile, as if a sudden burst of noise could scatter the moonshadows and shatter the elegant, ice-like architecture.

We camped among the dunes. Awed by the otherworldly beauty that enveloped me, I forgot about my failed agenda; I brimmed with gratitude at being exactly where I was. So stirred, my weariness left me; I felt fresh again, as though I could travel many hours more. When I lay down, however, I fell asleep instantly.

We rose before the sun. As we were about to hit the nonexistent trail, Walid pointed to some nebulous place in the distance and said, "The well is right over there." This was good news, since we had less than one guerba of water remaining.

A pale, predawn light bled across the sky, erasing the stars one by one. The silvery moon still shimmered above. We wove our way through a labyrinth of dunes, around their curling tails and up soft slopes, to saddles between converging ridges. Our feet plunged deep into the cool, loose sand. As the glow from the east intensified, the dunes blushed with color, like life returning to the pallid cheeks of a waking Snow White. Long shadows fell from sharp, serpentine spines, accentuating the hard angles and voluptuous curves that flowed into one another.

I expected us to stumble upon the well at any moment but wasn't worried when we didn't, since I'd learned that Walid's "right over there" could mean a couple of hours distant. But a couple of hours later, we still weren't there. Walid looked puzzled, as though the trusty map in his head had a piece torn off it. He thought we should've reached the well by now, and was confused that we hadn't. Maybe we were off course; maybe it was farther than he'd predicted; he didn't know. For the first time, my confidence in him was shaken. Though Walid wasn't yet willing to concede that we were lost, the possibility loomed over us, unspoken, like a monster that we hoped would leave us alone if we ignored it.

Walid handed me command of our camels and pointed in the general direction toward which he wanted me to head. He and Baba split up, climbing different dunes and walking along their ridges, scoping the vistas for a familiar sign. I imagined that one of them would soon shout and wave, indicating that they'd found the well. But they didn't.

Minute after uncertain minute passed. My thoughts turned to our nearly depleted guerbas. We probably had enough water to last us the rest of the day, but no more. Suddenly, everything changed: My concerns about finding the caravan evaporated in the face of the much greater problem of finding the well. We had no way of calling in help, and it was hardly likely that anyone would randomly happen to rescue us; caravans steer clear of dune fields at all costs, due to the dangers of getting lost, the possibilities of injury to their animals, and the time it takes for long strings of camels to negotiate them. I remembered tales I'd heard of lost desert travelers forced to kill their camels, squeeze the juices from their stomachs, and drink their blood in an effort to buy themselves a few more days of life. Fending off visions of shriveling to death while the Saharan sun sucked the moisture out of me, I tried to convince myself that there was no need to panic until Walid did.

After about half an hour, Walid and Baba joined me again and paused for a minute to talk. Neither had seen anything recognizable; neither had any idea where we were. We were officially lost among the dunes. So, pursuing the only sensible course of action in one of the worst possible desert scenarios, we unloaded the camels and made a pot of tea.

When we'd finished the three rounds, Baba mounted his camel and shot off into the desert on a solo scouting mission. I lay down with my turban over my face, protecting me from the now blazing sun. For a few minutes, I wished I'd had a GPS and the well's coordinates, but I quickly banished this heretical thought. Nomads never travel with technological aid; they have to work their way out of difficult situations with nothing but themselves to rely upon. It was one aspect of their lives that I'd wanted to experience firsthand, and this was my opportunity, if an extreme one. Ultimately, my curiosity about how they'd manage our escape from the dunes overpowered my desire for an easy way out. As a result, I lay there, neither agitated nor optimistic, waiting for Baba's return—though some might attribute my odd sense of calm to that ever-helpful defense mechanism known as disassociation.

In fifteen minutes, Baba was back. He hadn't found the well itself, but said he'd spied the telltale tracks that led to it. Though there is no single trail that the caravans follow, their paths converge near wells, forming highways of trampled sand that eventually thin to invisibility the farther one gets from the watering holes.

We packed up quickly and continued through the dunes, trying for a shortcut to the well now that we supposedly knew in which direction it lay. Cascading crescents of sand formed a magnificent maze. Frequently, we worked our way down an alley between towering, sculpted fins, only to dead-end at a sheer, impassable wall. Forced to retrace our steps, we'd try another avenue, hunting for a navigable route. I felt like we were in a laboratory experiment, with humans instead of mice for subjects, and water instead of cheese as the prize at the end of the course. For more than two hours we wandered thus. I began to wonder whether Baba had, in fact, found the way, or if we were going ever-farther astray. Yet I was so entranced by the beguiling patterns formed by the sand—a breathtaking synthesis of chaos and order blown by the wind into perfect aesthetic harmony—that I relished every moment we were among these dunes, my worries about being lost mitigated by the realization that if we were, it'd allow us to spend more time there.

At last we emerged from the mouth of a narrow, winding gully onto a broad open plain. A freeway paved by countless camel prints ran directly past us, which we followed for a few minutes to our long-sought goal. The heaps of decomposing camel carcasses scattered around the well—their bones bleached and brittle, their hides withered and hard—underscored how fortunate we'd been to make it there.

It was nearly noon. The sun blasted from above. The sand scalded from below. We set up a blanket for shelter and crawled beneath it. We would wait to get water, Walid said, until the caravan arrived.

"The caravan?" I said, stunned. If the tracks we'd passed the day before were theirs, they should be long past us by now.

"Didn't you see them as we were coming through the dunes?" Walid asked.

See them? I wanted to say, *Everything I've thought might be a camel for the past three days has been either a bush or a rock, so I've given up on seeing the caravan until it's right in front of my eyes.* But all I said was, "No, I saw nothing."

"Well, they're on their way," Walid maintained, pointing in the direction we'd come from. "Give them half an hour."

I couldn't believe it. I checked my elation, though, knowing by this time that until we were with the caravan, we weren't with the caravan.

While we waited, Baba walked over to the bales of grasses cached by Taoudenni-bound caravans so their camels would have fodder on their southbound return. He snatched a handful from one after another so our camels could snack, and carried a sheaf back to our shelter, with which he made some repairs to his cargo pads. Though I wasn't sure if this unapproved appropriation counted as stealing, it seemed in line with the nomad ethic of sharing, and he took so little from each pile as to hardly deplete any one stash. When the camels finished eating, they stood motionless, heads high, facing straight into the sun. Though they do this to minimize the amount of direct sunlight on the bulk of their bodies, it looks as though they're receiving silent signals from outer space.

Sure enough, in half an hour, a dark stream of camels poured over the ridge to the south. Two of the azalai broke ranks and trotted ahead to meet us. The greetings were ardent and long, and when they were over the five of us filled guerbas and poured some water for the camels. Before we finished, the caravan, seventy-five camels strong, was upon us. They were loaded with food sacks, ropes, goatskin buckets, inner tubes, and many bundles of grasses—a few of which they dropped about a hundred yards from the well before marching on. The two azalai we'd hauled water with hurriedly left to join their convoy, while we loaded our camels and set out after them.

A deep sense of relief swept through me. My worries, my self-flagellation, had been premature. I would get to ride with the caravan after all.

The camels were strung in three rows that marched side by side, as though in a military parade. One azalai rode at the front of each train, one at the back. We hung toward the rear, and Walid bantered with the camel drivers, exchanging news.

I instantly understood why Walid preferred traveling on our own. Contrary to what I'd imagined, the caravan moved surprisingly slowly. Though I was glad to be riding alongside it, I felt constrained, like finding myself behind a slow-moving car after cruising along at high speed. The caravan compensated for its pace by traveling long hours with no breaks. Some of the camels were so big, so impassive, they bore a resemblance to the ships to which they're so often compared; their solid front flanks and stout chests looked as sturdy as any boat's hull, while their slight pitching mimicked the motion of a waterborne vessel steaming forward, gently rocked by waves. Other camels were young and irresistibly cute, just old enough to make the journey for the first time and begin learning the jobs for which they were bred; as with an adolescent azalai on his virgin voyage to Taoudenni, it seemed like a rite of passage for these camels, too, as they left the pasture and their mothers to set off into the world with other males.

Though females are more manageable, male camels are stronger and endowed with greater endurance, so they alone compose the caravan corps. The females are left behind to breed, nurse the young, and provide milk for nomad families. Similarly, no women accompany the caravans; they stay with the tents and tend to the herds and their children while the men strike out on the salt trail. Rather than the result of sexism, this tactical division of labor between the genders, both human and animal, is simply another strategy to promote survival.

We climbed atop a lifeless plateau, barren but for an occasional boulder that seemed to have dropped from above. Plodding forward through dizzying heat and overwhelming desolation, relief for body and soul came only with the sunset, which painted the cloudless sky in luminescent watercolors, all shades of the rainbow washing into one another. When we made camp at dusk, heaven and earth glowed in a purple light.

Since we'd run out of the cooking wood we'd carried from Araouane, Walid instructed me to collect dried camel dung, about the size and shape of robins' eggs, with which the ground was littered. Nearly dry when they drop, after a short time on the ground they are ready to burn and are so hard that they leave no stain upon your hands. They light easily and smolder well; all in all they're an excellent substitute for charcoal. I formed a basket with the front of my shirt and carried a pile of poop back to our camp.

Meanwhile, the azalai had unloaded their camels, working in fast motion to free them from their burdens. They threw bales of grass on the ground, which the camels huddled around, lowering their necks to grab a mouthful, then raising their heads and chewing contemplatively, as though in deep thought.

Rather than cooking all together, Walid, Baba, and I had a fire of our own, and the azalai had three separate fires among themselves. In fact, this large caravan was a coalition of three individual caravans that had linked up and were traveling together for safety. The leader of the camel train we had planned to accompany came over and joined us around our fire. Named Bakai, he was twenty-two years old and a cousin of Walid and Baba. His beardless face made him look younger than his years. Over his blue boubou, he wore a blue Nike sweatshirt. He greeted me enthusiastically, and was quick to laugh given the slightest cause.

While our rice was cooking, I asked my companions about their names for some of the constellations. Since we often seemed to be heading straight for it, I pointed first to Cygnus, then drew its pattern of stars in my notebook, which I lit with my headlamp. Baba said that, to them, it was a big bird. "Okay," I thought, "we're seeing basically the same images in the night sky." But then I asked them about Cassiopeia. Baba explained that it was a hand, and not just any hand, but that of the Prophet's daughter Fatima—a common symbol in the Muslim world that protects against the evil eye.

"For us it's different," I said. Along with telling them it was a woman in a chair, I sketched a rudimentary picture of a sitting woman, with a few long lines for hair and a pair of round breasts to emphasize her gender. When I showed it to them, Bakai chortled with laughter, pointing at her well-endowed torso, like a schoolboy seeing his first copy of *Playboy*. Walid and Baba cracked up, laughing more at Bakai than at my drawing.

The last time I'd talked about the stars had been at the port at Kourioume, while waiting for the taxi that took me to Timbuktu. I was sitting with a fifteen-year-old Ghanaian boy I'd befriended on the boat, whose name was Issifu. He'd asked me if I knew the constellations, so I pointed out Cygnus, Hercules, and Delphinius the Dolphin. When I came to Cassiopeia, I said that she'd been a great queen, who had once bragged she was more beautiful than the sea nymphs. Poseidon, the sea god and father of the nymphs, was offended by her boasts, so he loosed a sea monster to terrorize the coastline of Cassiopeia's country. The only way to sate the beast, according to an oracle, was with the flesh of Cassiopeia's daughter, Andromeda. She was chained to a rock at the edge of the sea and left to become monster food. Meanwhile, I told Issifu, a prince named Perseus was on a mission to slay the gorgon, Medusa, a woman with snakes coming out of her head who was so ugly that anyone who saw her face turned to stone on the spot.

Excited, Issifu jumped up and exclaimed, "I know that movie!"

"Movie?" I thought, puzzled for a moment. Then it dawned on me. "You've seen *Clash of the Titans*?"

"Yes, yes," he shouted. "He takes the flying horse, cuts off her head, and holds it up like this!" He lifted his clenched fist high in the air. "Then he flies over and saves the princess!"

I couldn't believe it. The ancient Greeks had made it to modern-day Africa by way of Hollywood.

After dinner I went to bed and read for a few minutes, escaping to Europe and the sinister world of occultism in Umberto Eco's *Foucault's Pendulum*, before fading off to sleep. When Walid woke me in the morning, it was still dark. But the caravan was already gone.

There was a change in the weather. A brisk, frigid wind blew steadily from the north, chilling me through my clothes. For the first time since arriving in Africa, I was cold. While we waited for the tea to brew, Walid, Baba, and I sat around the fire, our blankets draped over our shoulders. As we rode, the sun baked our backs, while our shadowed fronts froze, giving me newfound sympathy for the planet Mercury. The wind tossed loose grit into our faces. Streams of sand raced across the desert floor. We passed desiccated camel corpses with ever greater frequency. And the caravan was nowhere in sight.

I couldn't believe we'd lost it again. By this time, I knew that Walid understood my goal. Miscommunication was not the issue. Walid simply loved his sleep. I was frustrated and baffled, not sure what I had to do in order to have the experience I'd come for. The problem was that I felt fundamentally powerless, reliant on Walid for my very survival.

Though exacerbated by the fact that we'd caught them and lost them again, this kind of frustration was by now familiar territory and I was able to stop myself from repeatedly (and silently) cursing Walid after a few healthy rounds of internal ranting. I distracted myself with thoughts of food.

Normally, wherever I travel, I have no problem eating the same thing, day after day, if that's what the local people eat. For a time I grow tired of it, then I cross a threshold and feel as though I could go on eating it—

whether "it" is beans and rice, mutton stew, or eggs—forever. But not only was our food monotonous, it got worse every day. The goat butter, which had been hanging in a clear plastic bottle in direct Saharan sunlight for going on two weeks, became more rancid by the hour. Every bite of rice was gritty with sand, and though I was usually able to ignore it, it was like a form of slow torture that every so often made me want to scream.

Not to dwell too long on things I couldn't have, I'd allow myself to engage in food fantasies for ten minutes a day. Without fail, I'd imagine drinking a perfect cup of strong black coffee, vividly savoring the flavor of its rich, edgy brew, while being transported by its aroma to a far-off olfactory paradise. Then, nearly every day, I'd eat a burrito smothered in red chile from my favorite Santa Fe restaurant, slowly feasting on the hearty, spicy sauce, succulent roast beef, and melted cheddar. Occasionally, I caught myself moaning from a combination of pleasure and desire. It amused me that of all the tastes in the world I could've possibly conjured, a burrito was what I craved most, but I guess it's true that we don't choose our fantasies, they choose us.

To combat the monotony of hour upon hour of travel, I finally trained myself to read while swaying back and forth as I rode, after many nausea-inducing attempts. I took a small measure of pride in being able to do something on camelback that even Walid and Baba couldn't do—though only because they couldn't read at all. Not wanting to simply bury my head in a book all the time, I read for only a fraction of the day, just long enough to give myself a break from the numbing scenery and my own thoughts.

Despite the unbelievable physical demands and our loss of the caravan, I found it relatively easy to keep my sense of humor—after all, how seriously could I really take the scene of a Jewish guy raised in suburban Connecticut chasing a camel train across the Sahara with a couple of Muslim tribesmen just to pick up some salt? My sense of gratitude, too, remained intact, though sometimes only because my stomach was holding firm, for which I gave thanks frequently and fervently.

We rode through the day and deep into the darkness, seventeen hours in total, without seeing a trace of the caravan. When we finally made camp and sat around the dinner fire, I again talked with Walid about finding it and sticking with it all the time. He clucked with understanding, and again explained how much longer our days would be. I told him I was prepared for that, and wanted to do it. He said okay, and told me to set my alarm for 3 AM. To my great surprise, when it went off, he didn't tell me to reset it, but got up and started moving. Our conversation, it seemed, had had its desired effect.

For all practical purposes, when we started off again, it was still night. The clear sky glittered with stars; the Great Bear, which was usually below the horizon, as though hibernating in some astral cave, hovered toward the north. Orion stood in the southwest, leaning to the side, his Great Dog beside him. The wind persisted. It was cold but refreshing, and I felt like I could walk forever.

As the rim of the sun peeked over the edge of the earth, Walid handed me the camels' lead. He pointed in the direction we wanted to head, and I marched on while he and Baba stopped to pray. They had been inconsistent in their devotions, praying a few times a day when it was most convenient. Usually we broke camp just late enough to allow them to worship before we hit the trail, but on the mornings when we left before any light was in the sky, they always stopped at sunrise. Due to the lack of water and the sterility of the desert, they were allowed by Muslim law to use sand for their ablutions before kneeling in supplication to Allah.

The sand was littered with chunks of broken rock, and I had to look ahead and pick out a clear path so the camels could walk without stumbling. Seeing the camel carcasses along the way had impressed upon me how thin the line was between a successful desert crossing and a disaster, especially if traveling with few camels. On a large caravan, the death of a camel could be compensated for with only a small financial loss. For individuals or small parties, every camel counted. There is an old African saying, "You travel faster alone, but farther together."

We climbed a series of gentle rises, each capped with tables of fractured, worn rock. Here and there we passed shards of solid salt that had fallen from caravans on their way back south. It was the first sign that we were closing in on our goal, though it was still a few days away.

Around 10 AM, some seven hours into our day, we came across the smallest well I'd yet seen. We unloaded the camels and gathered some dung for a fire, then Walid and I went to fetch water while Baba made tea. To the north, west, and south, the desert stretched beyond the limits of our sight; to the east a small hill lent us a sense of having our backs covered. As at Foum el-Alba, heaps of grass had been left behind by mine-bound caravans. I wondered if any belonged to our caravan, which I was beginning to think of less and less as "ours."

The well was shallow and had no pulley supports, which was just as well since we had no pulley. Smooth grooves had been worn into the cement rim by years of friction with ropes. With no leather bucket, Walid tied our cooking pot to the end of a rope, lowered it, and pulled it up hand over hand, his bare feet pressed against the well for leverage. Metal drums, like those at Douaya, were placed here as troughs, which Walid filled. As he hauled the water, I used a bowl to fill our guerbas. I appealed to Walid to pour directly from the pot into the tubes to prevent the ubiquitous sand and cud particles that covered the bottom of the barrel from tainting our water supply, but he brushed me off, saying it would take longer. As far as I could tell, there was no reason to rush, but of course that was simply the azalai way.

When we were done, Walid and I went over to where Baba tended the teapot. Before the second round had been brewed and served, a dark mass appeared on the southern horizon, growing larger by the minute. While we sat there watching, our caravan trundled past slowly, methodically. The azalai waved and shouted greetings from their mounts, apparently glad to see us again. Walid yelled that we'd be right behind them. Though I was antsy to get going, with our superior speed I knew we could quickly close the small gap growing between us. Again, I was deeply relieved that our paths had crossed. I felt that Walid must have known what he doing to place us smack in the middle of the trail, and believed that now that we'd caught the caravan for a second time, we'd stay with it. Naturally we had to drink a third cup of tea before we could leave. When we finished, we loaded our camels quickly, as we always did. By this time, once the heaviest bags were slung atop Lachmar, Walid trusted me enough to secure the smaller items myself while he and Baba loaded the other two camels.

When we joined the caravan an hour later, we were in the midst of yet another great, featureless expanse. The desert floor was a hard mosaic of black and gray pebbles, a classic example of the vast, stony flats, called *reg*, that pervade the Sahara, making up over 50 percent of its surface—more than twice the area covered by dunes. Free from the effects of blowing sand, which quickly erase evidence of those who pass over it, the earth was marred by row after row of tire tracks, some faint, some deep, stretching into the distance side by side as though someone had run a giant rake over a gravel bed. As bleak as this place would have been in a purely natural state, the tire tracks made it look used, damaged, like even more of a forlorn wasteland.

As we trudged along, I was struck by the functional simplicity of the caravan. The system of carrying fodder—which balanced in unruly brown bundles over the camels' ribs—and caching it for the return trip captured the essence of ages' worth of cumulative knowledge for crossing the desert. The blankets upon which the azalai sat, under which they slept, and with which they made shade; the camel dung over which they cooked; the improvised ropes they used; their ragged, dirty robes and turbans—all these made a mockery of the expensive, high-tech gear promoted in outdoor magazines as must-haves for wilderness travel. And everything the azalai use is better suited to this environment than newfangled gadgetry would be: A dung fire will never clog with sand as a stove would, and fuel is free; blankets are more durable and serve many more purposes than a pricey sleeping bag; their clothing is cheap, easily repairable, superfunctional, and, most important, distinctively stylish.

To my surprise, the caravan pulled to stop with a couple of hours of daylight remaining. We unloaded our animals in a rare feature in this part of the desert—a wide, dry streambed cut three feet into the earth by water, which flowed here no more than a few times each century. They had chosen this as the night's camp because, thanks to the recent storms, just enough grass grew on the wadi's banks for the camels to graze upon. The grass was so short, so sparse, each blade hardly thicker than a strand of hair, that it was practically invisible; it looked like the camels were eating dirt. With too many animals to hobble, the azalai scampered around, trying to keep the camels from straying too far in too many different directions.

The floor of the wadi was a fine, rust-colored sand. Since the wind still blew fiercely, we built a wall from our bags and cargo pads to shield us from the clouds of dust it drove down the streambed. As on the gusty night when I slept behind the bush, sand slowly began to pile up around us and atop us.

Though, the cut walls of the wadi appeared to offer natural protection from the elements, this was illusory. I quickly noticed that the open, stony ground above the banks, though no less windy, kept the sand in its place. I took my blanket, my water bottle, and my day pack and left the arroyo for a spot on the plateau. Returning to Walid and Baba, I suggested we move all our stuff up there. At first they resisted, but after a particularly violent blast of sand, they gave in. Clearly a superior location, I swelled just a little at having shown them a better way to do something. It was another small step, I felt, toward earning their respect.

Once again, when we woke in the morning, the caravan was gone. I was speechless, but felt like letting loose a loud *AAARRRRGGGHHH*—like

Charlie Brown tricked into letting Lucy hold the football for the hundredth time. I complained bitterly to Walid, reminding him that he'd promised to stay with the caravan all the time. He told me we'd catch up to them soon. I hoped he was right: We only had one more night in the desert before we'd reach Taoudenni, ensha'allah, and I wanted to be there when the caravan arrived at the mines, to see what that moment of accomplishment was like for the azalai and share it with them.

After continuing for a few hours across the featureless gray landscape we'd begun traversing the day before, the trail descended a few hundred feet down a ravine. Like Dorothy leaving her colorless home in Kansas for the brilliant land of Oz, we were suddenly cast into a world of red, pink, and yellow. Mesas with flat tops and steep, creased slopes rose from the desert floor, hovering nearby and breaking the distant horizon.

I was filled with a mixture of anticipation and reservation at the thought of nearing the mines. I looked at our imminent arrival there the way I would view a successful ascent of a major peak: It would be a great achievement, worthy of celebration and a moment's pause to breathe deeply, but getting to the top of a mountain is only half the job—one still has to get back down safely, and things are even more likely to go wrong on the descent. This awareness kept any inclination toward cockiness or undue jubilation in check.

We didn't see our caravan all day. We did, however, cross paths with a small caravan returning from the mines: fifteen camels burdened with gleaming slabs of salt, tied with leather straps and balanced over the camels' humps, led by one man and a boy perched perfectly atop his mount, looking like he couldn't be older than ten. It seemed incredible that someone so young would make this journey, and I wondered at the power of the experience this father and son shared (assuming that's what they were), alone in the vastness together, confronting the elements, managing their animals, handling their precious, fragile cargo, one teaching the other about the ways of the desert.

Walid scouting for the route when lost among the dunes.

Walid and Baba preparing a meal on the trail.

Our meat supply, strapped to the side of a camel.

A Taoudenni salt mine.

Abdullai, the miner whose leg I repaired.

Walid at the Harseini well.

Baba binding a broken salt bar for transport.

Salt miners dancing at the end of a grueling day of labor.

Sidali.

A typical salt miner's dwelling among heaps of rubble.

Omar.

Hamid, dressed in a bathrobe, brewing tea on the portable brazier.

Marching south with the caravan in the early morning light.

Baker, cutting Sidali's hair.

Walid, his pregnant wife Feti, and their youngest son.

A typical house in Araouane.

The sands of the Tanezrouft.

Sali, with the goat he just slaughtered.

Abdi hacking out a slab of salt as he tunnels out from his main pit.

A train of camels carrying slabs of salt.

A tent at the camp of Walid's in-laws.

Camels at sunset on the plains Taoudenni.

Hannah, Abdi's nine-year-old sister, who was offered to me as a bride.

After some twelve hours on the march, we found ourselves amid a field of low ruby-red dunes with sharp contours, their sides streaked with mesmerizing ripples. Walid pointed to a lone butte that towered a couple of miles to the north. "That's Gara," he said. "We will find the caravan there." And sure enough, in a basin of sand at its base, we joined them at their camp. I was determined not to lose them again.

The alarm on my wristwatch went off at 2:45 AM. In the darkness behind me, the camels bellowed loudly as the azalai loaded them and strung them together with handmade ropes of twisted grass, joining the mouth of each to the tail of the animal in front of it. After a windless night, the sky was remarkably haze-free. Stars gleamed like diamonds spilled on a black velvet tray. As my eyes adjusted, the waning moon, still high above, cast enough light to create shadowy silhouettes. The humps of the seventy-five camels, standing together, looked like a mass of dark, restless dunes.

"Good," I thought. They hadn't left yet. At long last, Walid, Baba, and I would depart alongside the caravan rather than trailing it across the desert. We'd all arrive at the mines together, ensha'allah.

I rose, gathered some camel dung and a few strands of grass from the remnants of the fodder that our camels had eaten during the night, and lit a fire. I filled the teapot with water, set it on the smoldering pile, and packed up while it heated. Baba was helping the azalai load up; Walid had not yet stirred.

Within minutes, I was organized, my bag sheathed inside its protective rice sack, tied up and ready to be loaded. I went back to the fire to prepare the tea, having decided on a pot of Lipton because it would take less time than performing the green tea ritual.

"Yeh, Walid, Baba," I shouted, "kess," alerting them that there was something to drink. Walid groaned and rolled over. "Kess, kess," I repeated insistently, until he sat up and shuffled over to the fire, his blanket draped over his head to shield him from the chill in the air. He drank, gave the glass back to me, and slowly nibbled some peanuts from the bag I had opened.

The groans of the camels in the background were now accompanied by the inarticulate grunts of the azalai and the slapping of wood on flesh, as the men urged their beasts forward. They were leaving. Since we were probably no more than a few minutes behind, and would catch them quickly, I wasn't distressed. In fact, I felt great, surprisingly energized, and while Walid sat staring into the glowing dung pile, I tied up our guerbas, put away the teapot and our metal bowls, and suggested that we, meaning he, get moving. Then I walked away from camp, into the privacy of darkness, to go to the euphemistic bathroom.

When I got back, I saw that Walid had reignited the fire and had put the teapot back on to boil. The green tea box and the leather sugar bag were open beside him.

I couldn't believe it. Before we went to sleep, I had yet again impressed upon him how important it was for me to wake with, leave with, and travel with the caravan all day—especially on this day, since we were due to reach Taoudenni in the early afternoon, and I wanted to arrive there with the caravan. He clearly understood, and had promised me as much. Now, with the caravan already gone, he was just beginning the tea ritual. Then we'd have to load our camels, which together would put us close to forty-five minutes behind. Quickly doing the math based on estimates of our speed, I knew it would take about four hours to close the gap. My cheery mood was swept away by a tsunami of frustration.

"Y'allah!" I prodded, "let's go," motioning upward with my arms. "Forget the tea. Let's go!"

Walid waved me over and told me to sit, have some more tea, and then we'd leave. He was in no hurry to get anywhere. But I wasn't about to sit down.

"Come on," I said, "It's time to leave."

Walid didn't budge.

His indifference made me furious, pushing my normally well-balanced temper over the edge. "This is bullshit!" I yelled, switching from Arabic to English, "Fucking bullshit!"

I'd had enough. For two weeks, I'd handed control of my daily destiny over to Walid. My ignorance of camels, of nomad ways, of the Sahara and the route through it had made me completely dependent upon him for my survival. And though he didn't wield it authoritatively, he was obviously aware of his power. But in this moment, sick of the helplessness that had kept me from asserting myself, my anger urged me beyond it. I decided to leave Walid and Baba and strike out into the desert on my own.

From where we were camped, I knew the general direction in which we were traveling, and figured that the North Star would more or less point my way. I also imagined that the fresh tracks of the caravan would have been easy to follow across the sand. It was an undeniably rash course of action, but in the moment, it seemed better than sitting impotently while Walid and Baba drank the mandatory three glasses of tea.

Still cursing loudly in English, I stormed over to where our three camels were sitting. I picked up a lead, threw it over Lachmar's neck, slipped it smoothly over his snout, put the loop into his mouth and cinched it down over his lower jaw, surprising myself by how expertly I'd done it. Walid yelled at me to stop, but I paid no heed. I was going to catch the caravan with or without him. With the slurping/clucking command, I told the camel to stand, and he did. But when I began leading him toward my bags, he didn't move. I yanked on his rope, but he recoiled and let loose with a Chewbacca-like roar. I clucked and I slurped and I even spoke to him in words. But he wouldn't take a step. Was it possible that Lachmar understood what was going on and was in cahoots with Walid?

Walid shouted something at me that I didn't understand, and pointed in the direction of the camel stick that was lying on the ground. I thought he was telling me that Lachmar would shut up and move if I gave him a good whack. It seemed a little excessive but, as riled as I was, the thought of hitting something had some appeal. I went for the stick. Before I could raise it, Walid was at my side, still pointing. He had never meant to indicate the stick at all, but to show me why Lachmar wasn't following me. In my fury, I'd forgotten to un-hobble his legs.

Too worked up to be deflated by embarrassment, I quickly freed Lachmar's feet and led him to my bags; he followed me willingly, removing all suspicion that there'd been an interspecies conspiracy against me. I shushed him to sit and threw his cargo pad over his back. As Walid and Baba watched, I hefted the two large bags that Lachmar carried, which together weighed about a hundred pounds and were tied to each other such that they would hang on either side of his hump, and slung them over the pad. Once they were properly balanced, I lashed on the other items for which I was responsible. When I secured my blanket on top, my audience snapped from their trance; Walid slugged his glass of tea like he was doing a tequila shot and Baba hurried to the fire and kicked sand over it. They hastily loaded their camels while I began walking, and were just minutes behind me leaving camp. Even in the heat of my outburst, I suspected that they'd never let me take off ahead of them, partly because it would have been a shameful dereliction of duty, and partly because of their genuine concern for my safety.

Eager to catch the caravan as early in the day as possible, I marched rapidly, keeping Walid and Baba a couple of hundred yards behind me. Like most mornings, the predawn hours passed surprisingly quickly.

As a golden glow seeped from the eastern horizon and Walid and Baba stopped to pray, I was able to see that we were traversing a landscape of rose-colored dunes that swelled, crested gently, fell away, then swelled again, giving the impression that the earth was breathing peacefully while it slumbered. The air was still, the silence perfect, the earth and sky aflush with radiant dawn. Any residual frustration that I carried with me from camp instantly evaporated.

I paused to take off a layer of clothing and allow Walid and Baba to catch up. When they did, we mounted our camels and rode on without speaking, up a rounded hill and down the steep slope on the other side. As though we'd entered a different room in the desert, the scenery changed dramatically. Here, rows of red sand ridges poured like ribs from both sides of a spine of ancient black rock. A few flat-topped mesas abruptly broke the northern horizon line, jutting more than a thousand feet from the desert floor. And we could see the caravan in the distance—they were still quite a way ahead, but at least they were in sight.

As we rode up and down and up again, I wanted to break what felt like an uncomfortable silence to let Walid know that I was no longer angry. Without the language to really explain myself, I couldn't address the subject directly. Instead, I initiated a simple conversation. Since we were in the midst of the most stunning terrain we had yet crossed, I asked Walid and Baba if they, too, thought it was beautiful.

They each grimaced involuntarily, looked at me as if I were crazy, and simultaneously said "No."

I'm sure I looked at them as if *they* were crazy, and Walid asked, "Why? Do you?"

"Yes," I said, "it's very beautiful. It's my favorite place so far."

Walid shook his head in befuddlement and the three of us laughed in mutual disbelief at the vast discrepancy between our impressions. For them, the most beautiful places in the Sahara are those where enough vegetation grows to support herds of goats and sheep and camels. Everywhere else is the region of death, too terrible to be beautiful. This was as profound as any other cultural difference between us, for I thought that the landscape surrounding us made a powerful case for the objective nature of beauty, which nobody could deny. We grew to appreciate this difference in each other, and it became the source of a comedy routine we'd enact when Walid wanted to make other people laugh: He'd mention this place and ask me what I thought of it. Happy to play my part, I'd praise it in the most poetic terms I could muster.

Without fail, our audience would widen their eyes in surprise, then crack up at the fool ideas of a foreigner.

The tension between us lifted, and I thought back to the events of the morning. Aside from producing the desired effect of hastening our departure from camp, my tantrum had other unforeseen benefits. The entire episode proved to be nothing less than a rite of passage, in which I graduated from dependent neophyte to experienced Saharan traveler, in both my eyes and Walid's. For the first time, I had shown that I could load a camel by myself, a task so tricky that even the azalai help one another when possible. Moreover, by expressing my willingness to leave Walid behind and follow the caravan's tracks, I had seized the reins of responsibility for my own experience. Through my defiant self-assertion and my display of competency, I had finally earned his respect, which would soon prove key to the fate of the journey.

We caught up with the caravan in a valley between two of the red sand ribs. The azalai riding at the end of one of the camel trains gave a welcoming shout and a wave. Walid pulled up alongside him, and the two of them exchanged the traditional minutes-long greeting like they were reading from a script. As if to complete the ritual, the azalai passed his antelope-horn pipe to Walid, who packed it with tobacco, filling his own at the same time. They rode on side by side, trailing plumes of sweetly acrid smoke behind them while they talked.

The caravan, with ours now seventy-eight camels strong, was strung into three more or less equal lines. As we descended a sandy slope and wheeled in grand formation around the tail of a dune, we could have been a legion of desert cavalry riding proudly toward a battle choreographed by Cecil B. DeMille. I gasped with awe at the majesty of the scene, and at the fact that I was a part of it.

Now on the flats, heading toward a gap between two mesas known as Foum Alous, and just a few short hours from our final destination, the mood among the caravan turned giddy. The azalai were talking and shouting excitedly with one another. Baba slid off his camel and tied it to L'beyya. He took a handheld brazier, about the size of a small lantern, from one of the azalai, and scurried around filling it with camel dung, which he lit. Walid produced the teapot, filled it with water, and passed it to Baba, who placed it atop the burning pellets. Holding the smoking brazier by its wire handle, Baba looked like a Catholic priest swinging an odd-smelling censer.

Fortunately, this was one of the few times of the day when the light was good for taking photographs, so I grabbed my camera, slipped off Lachmar, tied him to Baba's camel, and walked among the caravan, taking shots. Eventually, I made it up to the head of the pack, where Bakai was leading one of the strings. He greeted me warmly, and I countered with the expected phrases.

"Taoudenni is that way," he said, pointing ahead. "We'll be there soon."

"Ensha'allah," I replied.

"Ensha'allah," he confirmed, laughing, amused that I had given him the appropriate response.

One of the other caravan leaders, named Najib, walked beside Bakai. Though I had met all the other azalai, for some reason we were still unacquainted. I had seen him from a distance—his posture expressed a certain aloofness, his manner was one of superiority. He was the only azalai on *any* of the salt caravans I saw who had a real leather riding saddle rather than a blanket folded atop a cargo pad.

I introduced myself in a friendly way, thinking there was probably a really nice guy hiding beneath his cloak of pride. Najib promptly asked me to give him my watch. I was taken aback by his brazenness, especially because it was the first time (but not the last) that any azalai had asked for anything other than my friendship. At first I thought he was kidding, but when I realized he was serious, I became uncomfortable. Najib was the most powerful figure on the caravan and I knew it would behoove me to be in his favor. To deny him this gift could be tantamount to an insult, and I was fully aware that, to him, I was nothing more than a dispensable hanger-on. I tried to play it off by acting dumb and pretending I thought he asked what time it was—since the words for "watch" and "hour" sound identical in Arabic—hoping he'd think it fruitless to pursue the issue with a moron. But he was undeterred. Finally, I had no choice but to give him a straight answer. No. He grew irritable, ordering me not to take any pictures of him or his camels. Making a mental note to steer clear of Najib in the future, I decided it was a good time to drift back toward my friends.

I reached them just in time to take the brazier from Baba as Walid passed a glassful of sugar down from atop his camel. Still keeping pace with the caravan, Baba mixed the sugar into the tea, then handed a glass up to the azalai riding beside him, who slugged it down and passed the glass back. Baba dashed between the camels to the other azalai, serving tea like a waiter in a mobile café, and when the pot was empty, another was brewed. I walked alongside Baba, handing him camel pellets and helping manage the brazier until teatime was over. Then, while Lachmar was still moving, I leapt atop his neck and slid tentatively onto his hump. Though I earned no points for style and few for technical merit, the azalai, who had never seen me do this and expected me to mount in typical tourist fashion by first couching the camel, gave a shout of approval and smiled their acceptance of me; with this successful if graceless maneuver, I'd shown that I was worthy of riding with them, if not with Najib.

*A Taoudenni miner hewing a raw salt slab
into a finished bar.*

CHAPTER SIX

efore long, the caravan traveled through a pass between two
burly, flat-topped buttes whose steep western walls were blan-
keted from top to bottom with sand. Their eastern sides were
practically bare. This was Foum Alous, the gateway to the plains of
Taoudenni; the Gates, I thought, of Hell. I remembered once seeing
Rodin's phantasmagoric sculpture of that name, in which he depicted
people in relief (an ironic term, in this case) agonized by various forms
of Underwordly torture. It was a deeply affecting work that captivated
me so completely, it seemed to possess an aesthetic force akin to gravity,
attracting my gaze like an apple to the earth and holding it there.

But here, approaching what I imagined would be the closest thing to Hell on earth I'd ever encounter, I grew uneasy. I wasn't sure I really wanted to see human beings enduring the kind of suffering I expected to witness at the mines. Rodin's work is so compelling in part because the viewer isn't looking at *real* people condemned to the Inferno, but an artistic envisioning of an archetypal realm. Likewise, the *idea* that men live and work the way they do at the salt mines is fascinating (humanitarian sentiments aside), but preparing to meet that reality face to face was unsettling; it seemed more than a bit perverted that Taoudenni was marketed as a tourist attraction—albeit a rarely visited one—to which foreigners in four-by-fours occasionally came to gawk at less fortunate men. The only mitigating factor in my favor, I thought, was what I had endured to get there.

When we arrived at the mines, we dismounted and unloaded the camels on an open, empty plain that had all the appeal of a giant parking lot. I felt a brief pang of triumph at having made it across the desert, but was quickly overwhelmed by the intensity of my surroundings.

Despite all I had seen thus far, and all I had imagined, I was unprepared for the untempered desolation of Taoudenni. It is situated on utterly lifeless desert flats; not a single leaf, or even thorn, grows from the parched, crusty dirt, which was so sharp it bit into the soles of my bare feet. The sun pounded the earth like a sledge on an anvil. Mound after mound of mined rubble receded to the eastern horizon. I was overcome with foreboding. I felt intuitively that I didn't belong there; that no one did. The severity of the Tanezrouft is easier to accept when it's just a place for passing through. Only when confronted by the reality of people actually living and working there was I struck by its overwhelming meanness. I could see why, until 1991, this place was used as desert gulag for Malian political prisoners; the threat of it surely stifled more than a few dissident voices.

Walid, Baba, and I piled our bags together and covered them with our blankets, a meager shield from the midday sun. Then we walked north a couple of hundred yards to where the miners lived, seeking shelter for ourselves and looking for Abdi Adurahman, Lamana's nephew, who spoke fluent French. Our path skirted the western edge of the mines, which were square pits hand-dug straight into the ground; each surrounded by hills of rubble, they looked like gigantic prairie dog burrows. A mile or two to the north, a throne-like bluff rose from the ground, providing a visual boundary for the area called Taoudenni. To the west, the barren, featureless plains rolled into dunes along the far horizon.

Two cargo trucks were parked at the opening of an alleyway into which we turned, which was bordered on both sides by heaps of broken rock. They were old, brawny ten-wheelers, with battered cabs and flatbeds walled with low metal gates. They looked like they could drive through just about anything—if they didn't break down trying. And though they could obviously carry more than a camel, they completely lacked the romance of the caravans; while they might replace camels in the desert, they would never be able to do the same in the human imagination. As when I first saw trucks at the well at Douaya, I was saddened by the thought that the imagination might soon be the only place where caravans would yet roam.

We wove our way among stony piles until we came to one of the miners' enclaves. Built of the same rubble that surrounded it, the miners' "village" was straight out of the Stone Age. The huts were built of ill-hewn rocks stacked atop one another and cemented with mud. Most of these shelters were built like row houses with four or five individual cells to each. Huge inner tubes swelling with water sat outside the scrap-tin doors.

Since it was near the peak of the midday heat, the place seemed deserted. Everyone was inside. Walid began knocking on doors, looking for someone who could direct us to Abdi. At the first house we stopped at, five miners emerged. They greeted Walid warmly, and looked me over with curiosity. One eagerly extended his hand to me, smiling with a genuine welcome that completely contradicted the message conveyed by his T-shirt, which depicted Osama Bin Laden riding out of the clouds on a white stallion, swinging a scimitar like a warrior-prophet.

As though word of our arrival had been broadcast by a silent PA system, other miners emerged from their dwellings to investigate. A few were clearly good friends of Walid; their reunion was celebrated with hugs and shouts of glee and, of course, the ritual greeting. One of the miners agreed to find Abdi and bring him to us, so a group of us retired across the lane to the hut of Walid's friend Mohammed.

We piled our sandals by the door and sat down in the cool darkness on thin blankets that covered the bare earth. Tea was promptly poured, and a big metal bowl of rice was placed among everyone. I, as usual, was given my own plate. I still found this strange; when I had been in Morocco, I was always invited by local people to join in the collective feeding frenzy, and plunged my hands into the same platters of couscous as everyone else. I initially suspected that these men believed I wouldn't want to eat with them—or that maybe they didn't want to eat with me. I subsequently learned that they merely thought I'd eat too slowly and wouldn't get my fill.

As they ate, the miners talked spiritedly, sharing and receiving news from Walid and Baba. With no telephones or mail service, miners rely on such word of mouth to keep in touch with their families. There didn't seem to be too much serious business; though they spoke too fast for me to understand most of what they were saying, they were obviously cracking jokes and teasing one another as they rollicked with laughter. At one point, they paused, and Walid asked me what I thought of our host, who had been particularly animated in his antics. Hoping I was judging the situation correctly, I answered, *"Mohammed? Howa majnoon,"* and shook my head. This broke them up, especially Mohammed, whom I had just declared insane. For the rest of my stay at Taoudenni, he was referred to as Mohammed Majnoon, to distinguish him from all the other Mohammeds. I was beginning to suspect that the impressions I'd gleaned from the articles I'd read about Taoudenni, which portrayed the miners as miserable souls, their spirits crushed by terrible living and working conditions, were less than accurate.

Mohammed's place was about eight feet wide by twelve feet long. There were no windows, no furniture, and no decoration but for half a rack of drying goat ribs hanging on the wall. The ceiling/roof was made of scraps from flattened fifty-gallon drums, and was supported by a spiderweb of twine laced over two truck axles that served as crossbeams. Mohammed's few belongings were kept in sacks around the edge of the room.

Aside from a simple lack of resources, the miners' cabins are so sparse because they are abandoned after a year or two of habitation. The mines of Taoudenni are perpetually spreading westward; each pit is worked for a month or two before its salt is depleted, then a new mine must be dug. Hence, before long, a hut that was once conveniently located becomes a long walk from a miner's quarry, so new, more accessible dwellings are built on a regular basis. The constant migration of the mines—and the mining community—explains why Taoudenni is rarely marked in the same spot on different maps of the Sahara.

The oldest salt mines in the region were dug at a place called Tegaza, some eighty miles northwest of Taoudenni, which were first excavated in the fourth or fifth century. The Taoudenni deposits were discovered around the year 1585. Due to harassment by Moroccan forces at Tegaza at about that same time, the mines there were abandoned in favor of Taoudenni, which quickly became the new quarry of choice for salt caravans from the Azawad.

Abdi arrived as I finished eating. He was dressed in his work clothes—a pair of light blue pants that had once been double-layered, though the outer material was so shredded it looked like it was made of cobwebs; a black Polo-style short-sleeved shirt powdered with salt dust; and a tattered army-green sun hat with a pink band that said TOMMY GEAR. His skin was a deep brown and his hands and feet were cracked like dried desert mudflats. He had perhaps the longest fingers and toes I had ever seen.

We spoke for a while about the camel journey, his family—who happened to be the people we'd visited in Araouane—and about what a relatively educated, French-speaking young man was doing in a place like this.

He was eighteen, and this was his third season at the mines. Like the other miners, Abdi had come to Taoudenni because work elsewhere was scarce. He learned French in Mauritania, where his family lived as refugees for five years during the Tuareg Rebellion. Since Araouane had become even more desolate in their absence, when Abdi turned sixteen he followed his father, and many other men from their village, up to the mines, where income was paltry but assured. His father taught him everything he needed to know about digging earth, cutting salt, building shelter, and preparing food for himself. Even with his father's help, Abdi said he found his first season at Taoudenni unbearably brutal. "The more you perfect your technique, the more accustomed you become to the heat, the easier it gets," he said. "But it never gets easy."

He dreamed of one day using his language skills to become a guide based out of Timbuktu, but felt like he couldn't yet trust his family's welfare to the whims of the tourist industry.

When Abdi asked what I wanted to know about the mines, I said, "Everything." But first, I asked him the question that had been nagging me since Araouane: "Do you think trucks are one day going to replace the camel caravans?"

Abdi broke into a wide grin and said, "Eeeeeee! No, no," in such a way that he might as well have added "You silly American" to the end of his exclamation.

"Ask them," I said, referring to the other miners. He did, and their answer, a collective laugh, needed no translation. The mere suggestion of it sounded ridiculous to their ears.

"Why?" I asked. "The trucks can carry more, and travel faster, right?"

"Sure," Abdi replied. "But most salt traders prefer camels."

He then explained the fundamentals of the caravan economy, checking in with Walid, Baba, and the other miners for verification.

Trucks, he said, were very expensive to run. First, the truck had to be purchased. Then more money had to be spent on repair and maintenance, and not a small sum, since these were ancient vehicles tackling a grueling route. Moreover, gas had to be paid for, and trucks carried an average of two thousand liters per trip. At about eighty cents per liter, the fuel alone cost somewhere around sixteen hundred dollars.

Camels, on the other hand, were virtually free. Any family involved in the caravan already had a herd of their own, and they reproduced naturally. Since they eat grass, it costs nothing for them to travel to and from the mines, and they can go for weeks without drinking water while carrying heavy loads. They rarely break down, and if they do, they don't jeopardize the entire enterprise—the lone sick camel is left to die, while the others continue on.

Since the nomad families who run the caravans view time from an African perspective, speed is only of the essence in crossing the desert quickly enough to survive. It's not a valuable asset in itself. Thus, the fact that trucks travel faster isn't such a compelling advantage when balanced out by their expense.

What's more, and is of equal importance to the equation, the caravans and the mines operate on an archaic, salt-based economy—one in which salt *is* cash.

The miners, Abdi said, earn their wage in the salt they harvest. The azalai act as middlemen, transporting the salt to Timbuktu, where they sell it. But they don't buy the salt outright from the miners; instead, they trade space on their camels, which allows the miners to get their own salt to market.

It works like this: Each camel carries four bars of salt, weighing approximately eighty pounds each. The azalai keeps three of these for himself, essentially as payment for transporting the fourth one, which is reserved for the miner. The miner's bar is marked with a unique symbol drawn with wet clay and is picked up at the end of the route by a member of his family. When the miners need new tools, they pay the Taoudenni blacksmith in salt—four bars for each pick or adze. Then the blacksmith makes a similar deal with the azalai. Moreover, since the nearest water is fifteen kilometers from the mines, the miners pay the azalai two bars of salt for each camel-load of water—usually four full truck-tire inner tubes. In none of these transactions does money change hands; only at the market in Timbuktu is the salt converted into cash, fetching about fifteen dollars per slab. Thus, because the camels cost nothing to drive and the azalai trade space—not money—for salt, the extent of each caravan's financial investment is the little it costs to supply a few men with five weeks' worth of rice and millet, meaning that nearly everything they haul back to Timbuktu translates into profit.

Truckers, however, don't participate in this system. They pay cash directly to the miners for the salt they take (about eight dollars per bar), and sell it for a profit in town—as though with modern means of transport comes a modern method of trade. But due to all their expenses, at the end of the day their profit margin is slim; they rely on sheer volume to make their work worthwhile. As a result, they often drive to the towns of Gao, Mopti, or Kidal, where the salt fetches slightly higher prices than in Timbuktu.

"So you see," Abdi concluded, "pound for pound of salt, camels are far more profitable than trucks."

With the resounding and unanimous verdict in favor of the caravans' survival expressed by the azalai and the miners, as well as the truckers, salt historians, and tribal leaders I spoke to later—and which the math of the caravan economy supports—I wondered why some American journalists had drawn the conclusion that the camels were doomed to obsolescence. My best guess is that they had been so influenced by an unconscious cultural perspective—one steeped in the myth of that steel-driving man who fell victim to the hubris of thinking he could outperform a machine, whose legend has been passed down in the most recorded song in the history of American music—that they naturally assumed no creature could successfully compete with machines in a head-to-head contest.

In fact, I later learned that the simple act of framing the relationship between camels and trucks as a contest is itself a culturally biased assumption. For in actuality, as a result of the Saharan worldview that values mutual sustainability, truckers and camel drivers do not compete against one another, but strive for balanced coexistence.

After his discourse, Abdi excused himself, since he had left his lunch uneaten when he learned that Walid and I had arrived. He promised to come to our camp in the morning, when he would take me to his mine to observe his work. I thanked him profusely for his introduction to the mining economy and bid him *"a tout a l'heure."*

As Abdi departed, it dawned on me that my entire journey had been based on a fallacy. I had traveled to Timbuktu and ventured across the desert, battling heat, hunger, and pain, to get a parting glimpse of a way of life that I believed was in its dying days, only to learn that it was alive and well. I laughed at my folly, yet was anything but disappointed. What I'd just discovered, I felt, was far more remarkable—and important—than what I set out to find. And that turned out to be only the first of the profound surprises in store for me at Taoudenni.

When the hottest hours had passed and the sun cast a bronze glow through a filter of haze, I told Walid I was going to take a walk and would meet him back at camp. After assuring him repeatedly that I wouldn't get lost, I meandered around the quarry, meeting some of the miners who had gone back for a late-afternoon shift at their picks. While most wore turbans, some wore brimmed sun hats, others baseball caps. While some wore boubous or other types of traditional robes, many wore jeans and T-shirts, or tank tops with the names and numbers of NBA or soccer stars—in one pit, Ronaldo was hacking away next to Shaquille O'Neal. Nearly all the miners were happy to take a few minutes to chat in Arabic and many invited me to take their pictures, erasing any fears I had of being viewed as an unwelcome voyeur.

With the sun nearly resting on the horizon, I headed toward our camp. I met Walid, Baba, and Mohammed Majnoon outside one of their friend's huts. A few of them had set up a fire line and were passing platters of dirt up to a guy on the roof who was finishing his new home on the prime real estate at the western edge of Taoudenni. Despite his beard, his broad, goofy grin reminded me so much of Horshack from *Welcome Back, Kotter* that I had trouble remembering his real name. I shook hands with those I hadn't yet met, including Abdullah, whose puffy beard opened to reveal a guilelessly kind smile; Abdullai, Walid's lean, clean-shaven brother-in-law; and another man named Baba, who was large and dark and wore a bright yellow turban wrapped around a face that, when revealed, expressed a mischievous but gentle nature.

Each wanted his picture taken, and after I'd snapped a few shots they began challenging one another to strike ever-more-humorous poses. All at once, the empty metal bowl heading back for another load of dirt was turned upside down and became a drum; Abdullah slapped the flat platter he was holding, and Horshack, still perched on the roof, started clapping. Big Baba began ululating and dancing in circles, weaving his hands through the air, then uncoiling his yellow turban and using it as a prop, stretching it and twirling it seductively; with the sensual swaying of his body and the expression of abandon on his face, he might have been performing a courtship ritual. Abdullai danced behind Baba, chanting with his arms raised skyward, hands aquiver. Soon, with the rhythm section pounding furiously and singing passionately, six other miners joined in the revelry, dancing together in a circle like a supercharged Arabic version of the Hora, whooping, chortling, and laughing—at one another, at themselves, and at life.

The festivities ended in breathless exultation as spontaneously as they began. The bowls and platters transformed back into vessels for carrying dirt; Horshack went back to his roof job; Big Baba rewrapped his yellow turban around his head. Walid asked if I would take a look at a wound on Abdullai's leg, and I said sure, but we had to go back to camp where I'd left my first-aid kit. I told my new friends I'd see them tomorrow, ensha'allah, and was bid a heartfelt good night.

The sinister aura I'd sensed upon arriving at Taoudenni had completely disappeared. Walking back to camp, I felt exhilarated. I could hardly believe what I had just witnessed, so completely had it defied my expectations. These men were not broken by hardship, but were as vibrant and alive as any I'd ever met. If this was Hell, they didn't know it. Sure, they would have preferred to be somewhere else, but they were proud to be supporting their families in a region where work is scarce, and where easy work is practically unheard of. So they made the best of it, stealing pleasure from every possible moment.

Back at our pile, Baba built a fire and Walid spread a blanket for us to sit on while I dug out my medical supplies. Word had traveled among the miners that the tourist was going to play doctor, and a small group of them waited for my attention. I imagined that this scene would repeat itself every evening we were here, and I quickly realized that I could exhaust my first-aid kit, leaving myself not a single Band-Aid for the trek back to Timbuktu. For the sake of conservation, I triaged my patients, employing what I thought of as "the futility test." In each case, I assessed whether using my precious supplies would have been truly beneficial, or basically a waste.

The majority of the miners were seeking treatment for deep cracks and cuts on their hands and feet. With continuing care, and rest, all could have been effectively healed. But since any bandages would have quickly fallen off while they worked, and none of these guys was going to take a few days off, there was little point in dressing them at all. They failed the test. Yet I couldn't just turn them away. I remembered

I was carrying a vial of New-Skin—an antiseptic that hardens to form a protective layer over minor wounds—which I could apply a hundred-odd times before the bottle ran dry. One after another, I swabbed their cuts with the stuff, which did no harm and which they thought did plenty of good.

Some of the "injuries" I was asked to treat were so insignificant I could hardly see them. I almost laughed. Here were these desert-hardened men making a big fuss over tiny boo-boos that I myself would have ignored. It occurred to me that perhaps they were truly seeking attention for something other, something deeper, than their hands. Or maybe, I thought less charitably, it was so ingrained in them to take whatever was offered by foreigners that if New-Skin was what the white guy was giving out, they'd get in line.

Abdullai was the only one who passed the futility test. He had accidentally jabbed his thigh with his pick. While the wound was just an inch long and half as deep, it was nasty and packed with dried dirt. Since he could easily work without shedding a bandage, I opted to give him the best of care. When I put on a latex glove, snapping it over my hand for dramatic effect, the other miners gathered around, hovering over us, sensing that some serious business was about to take place. As I pulled out a syringe, which I filled with a solution of water and iodine, a grave silence fell over the gallery. I irrigated the cut a few times, flushing out as much of the grime as I could. Ultimately, I had to scour it with an alcohol pad (as Abdullai winced) to loose the most stubborn particles, which I feared could cause an infection. At last it came clean, looking pink and fleshy. I applied some antibiotic ointment, covered it with two Band-Aids, then with tape, which I wrapped around his leg a few times. I promised to examine him again the following day. Through the care I'd provided, I succeeded in repaying the miners in some small way for the kindness with which they'd welcomed me into life at Taoudenni.

A Taoudenni salt miner.

CHAPTER SEVEN

In the morning, for the first time since the trek began, there was no reason to get up early. I lingered in my sleeping bag, dreaming of a leisurely big breakfast of pancakes, bacon, and coffee. The usual handful of peanuts and dates was a bit of a letdown.

When we were ready to head to the mines, we once again piled our belongings and covered them with our blankets. Then Walid led me to Abdi's quarry.

Abdi was glad to see me, and welcomed me down the cut stairs that led into his mine. He introduced me to his mining partner, Ali, a tall, lanky Saharan with a chiseled face and a goatee sprouting from his chin, who was wearing a T-shirt that said WWF SMACKDOWN and featured a faded image of "Stone Cold" Steve Austin flexing ferociously. Ali's pants were knockoffs with the letters NIKF on the side pockets. He was busy doing the finishing work on a block of salt, hewing a thick tombstone-like slab down to a width of about two inches so it would be ready for transport and sale.

Like all the mines, Abdi's was a pit about twenty feet square, hand-dug directly into the ground. I marveled at the care that had obviously been taken to make the walls, which were scarred with pick marks, so very straight. The colors of the cross section of exposed earth merged from rose to buff yellow before abruptly striking a hard, glassy layer of noncommercial salt—called *sel gemme*—that is the bane of the miners' job to cut through, and is discarded as garbage. Below that, the dirt is a deep brown, and below that, some six feet beneath the surface, is the salt that the miners prize, for which men and camels travel weeks across the desert to retrieve.

Three strata of rock-solid commercial-grade salt run horizontally beneath the entirety of Taoudenni. Once all the rubble is removed from above them, the top layer of valuable salt gleams from the floor of the mine like the surface of an icy pond. Using their hands, with spread fingers, as measuring rods, and calling the distance between the tip of the thumb and the tip of the middle finger 25 centimeters, the miners use picks to cut the salt into blocks 50 centimeters wide by 125 centimeters long. The thickness of each block is determined by the thickness of the strata, which is about 15 centimeters. Each weighs about three hundred pounds before being hewn down to its finished size. After the three layers of salt are harvested from the bottom of the mine, the miners tunnel out to the sides beneath the layer of sel gemme, which is dense enough to support all the dirt above it with no buttressing, even as the caverns grow into enormous underground rooms.

All the salt had already been extracted from the floor of Abdi's mine, and he was working on a new tunnel that, at this point, was only a meter—or two block widths—deep, and a meter and a quarter—or one block length—wide. He invited me to watch everything he did, so I stepped over chunks of broken salt and around a row of unfinished blocks that were propped on their sides and leaning against each other. With his hand, Abdi measured twenty-five centimeters from either side of the tunnel and etched vertical lines in the crumbly brown dirt on the wall in front of him to mark his place. His tool could hardly have been more primitive; it was a tapered wooden club, like those carried by cavemen, with a metal pick-head jammed into the fat end. He sat on a stump of salt covered with a folded rag, pressed his bare feet against the wall, and hacked away at the dirt to the outside of one of his marks—between it and the tunnel wall—grunting with each swing the way Jimmy Connors used to when he hit a tennis ball. When he'd cleared a narrow vertical space between the sel gemme and the good salt to the proper depth, he handed the pick to me, instructing me to do the same on the other side of the tunnel.

I sat down on the salt stump, grasped the rough handle of the pick, and went to work, grateful for the shade provided by the tunnel's roof. Though I was accustomed to chopping round after round of firewood back home, I felt like a weakling. I had to pause frequently to rest my arms and, by the time I'd cleared the gap to the proper depth, they felt like rubber. I was sufficiently humbled, and had gained the kind of respect for the miners that can only be acquired by laboring, if only for a short time, in their place. I remembered being told as a child that if I didn't do well in school I'd end up becoming a ditch digger; and here I was, momentarily sinking below my father's worst predictions.

When I breathlessly handed the pick back to Abdi, a pillar of earth stood between the spaces we had made. By hacking away at its base, just above the good salt, the entire pillar fell in one chunk, fully exposing the surface of the uppermost layer of commercial-grade salt.

The three layers of salt were of varying quality. The top, called Al-Beidha, was the middle grade; the middle, called Al-Bint, was the lowest grade; and the bottom, called Al-Kamra, was the highest grade and worth the most. Moreover, whereas one raw slab of Al-Beidha or Al-Bint could be trimmed down only to a single bar of finished salt, the Kamra could be split in half, yielding two bars from one raw block.

Though there were visible differences in their textures—the smoothest, finest-grained being the best—I was amazed by how quality-conscious Malians were about their salt, from the miners to the old women who sold small pieces of it at the market in Timbuktu. People spoke of Kamra with the same reverence with which a wine connoisseur might talk about a special vintage from a certain year. For a culture in which this now commonplace mineral has played such a central role for more than a thousand years, all salt is definitely not the same.

I sat and watched as Abdi worked to loose the salt from the grip of the earth. The mine was filled with the sounds of *grunt-thud-scrape*, *grunt-thud-scrape*, repeating itself in a steady, entrancing rhythm. Abdi sang as he swung—*"Pour le courage,"* he explained. When he had successfully cut around the edges of the top block of salt, he gave three powerful whacks into the thin line of sediment that separated it from the layer below it; the block popped free, and he used his pick-blade to lever it off and onto the ground. After another hour and a half, he had three hefty slabs to show for his morning's labor. Later, once he had a substantial stack of salt, he would begin the finishing work, trimming the salt with a simple adze-head pounded into a wooden baton, like his friend Ali was doing at that moment.

The miners work two shifts a day, one in the morning, one in the late afternoon, breaking during the hottest hours for lunch, tea, and rest. Abdi and I walked back to his hut, where the pot of rice he had set to simmer that morning was ready to eat. By this time, my clothes, hands, feet—and probably lungs—were coated with fine salt dust.

We sat on reed mats on the floor of his simple abode. Since there were only two of us, we ate from the same bowl. Abdi shared his quarters with another miner, who was reclining while listening to Arabic BBC on his shortwave. When he learned that I was from the United States, he informed me that an American helicopter had recently been downed by Iraqi insurgents. It was the first news I'd had in nearly three weeks.

Fearing I might be upset by the report, Abdi reprimanded his roommate for telling me about it, and a heated debate ensued. Abdi asserted that I had a right to my ignorance, while his roommate maintained that I had a right to know what was going on in the world. I personally didn't care that much either way; from this outpost in the midst of the Sahara, events in the rest of the world might as well have been happening on the planet Pluto. Fortunately for my sake, these sentiments were shared by virtually all the miners and nomads I met. The troubles of the Iraqi people—and even the Palestinians—seemed too remote to upset these West African Muslims, especially when they had their own immediate difficulties to deal with. Even so, Iraq was a topic upon which I preferred not to dwell, so I steered the conversation back to life at the mines.

Since there was no form of civil government or law enforcement at Taoudenni, I asked Abdi about the crime rate in this community of a couple of hundred poverty-stricken men. Judging by his expression, I might as well have inquired about Internet access. There was no crime at all, he said, no robbery, no violence, nor was there any alcohol. When the rare disagreement arose between miners, they took their complaints before the acknowledged chief of the mines for arbitration. A religious leader respected for his wisdom and fairness, the decisions made by this Solomon of Taoudenni were accepted by all as final, without complaint. The ethics of Islam clearly served to create a stable society in conditions where lawlessness could have easily reigned. Peaceful and crime-free, Taoudenni seemed like the most unlikely of utopias.

When I asked why there were no women at the mines, I was given two answers: that the miners would get less work done if there were women to distract them, and that, because of the severity of conditions and the poor quality of the brackish drinking water, women would become sick. There seems to be some truth to the latter explanation, since prior to 1968, women and children did live at Taoudenni with their husbands and fathers. Illness was such a problem, particularly among the kids, that a collective decision was made to keep women away from the mines for the greater welfare of the families. Since then, men have performed the household tasks normally assigned to their wives, mothers, and sisters, such as cooking and cleaning.

The only all-male society I could think of in the United States was within our prison system. Based on what I knew of that, I asked Abdi directly if the miners ever had sex with one another. He laughed, vigorously shaking his head, assuring me that they didn't. It was the only thing he told me that I had trouble believing.

During this lunchtime conversation, Abdi debunked a number of the misconceptions I had about life at the mines, which I'd acquired from the preparatory reading I had done. I'd expected Taoudenni to be filled with debt-slaves, toiling for meager wages in an impossible effort to repay loans made by mining financiers. While this was once true, Abdi said, times had changed over the past decade, and most miners now worked for themselves.

The critical development in liberating the miners from their debt-masters was the introduction of trucks into the salt trade. Before, transportation of miners and the supplies they needed to survive was difficult to arrange and terribly expensive; the financiers fronted miners the money for transport, and for months' worth of victuals, at a steep interest rate. Now that trucks come and go from Taoudenni with relative frequency, miners pay the truckers reasonable fees—in cash or salt—to take them to and from Timbuktu, and they can have supplies brought to them as needed, rather than buying and stockpiling huge stores in advance.

Thus, thanks to the trucks, most miners are now self-employed, enjoying both the financial and emotional rewards of working as free men. Their average salaries have more than doubled, to a whopping $150 or so for the six-month-long mining season. Since trucks are not going to displace camels, I realized that the Caravan of White Gold is that rare instance in which the introduction of modern technology into an age-old commercial system has yielded great benefits without destroying the traditional way of life.

As Abdi was explaining this, Walid entered the hut and sat down. He was wearing a new army jacket that he had just bought from one of the few merchants who drive across the desert from Morocco in old Land Rovers to sell clothing, blankets, and green tea at the mines. Though Walid said he paid only one thousand CFA (West African Francs) for it, he could have meant ten thousand; because he didn't understand numbers, he thought that anything he paid for with a single bill cost a thousand CFA, regardless of the bill's denomination.

Through Abdi, Walid told me that we might have to return to Timbuktu without the caravan. Feeling my hackles start to rise at what would be the complete frustration of my mission to really experience caravan life, I checked my emotions and calmly asked what was going on. Walid explained that the caravan we arrived with might have to wait at Taoudenni for a week before it could leave with a full load of salt.

This, I learned, was the one major complication posed by the introduction of trucks—since they can carry hundreds of bars of salt, if a few arrive at the same time they can virtually buy out the mine, requiring the caravans (and other trucks) to wait until the miners dig more. Waiting is no problem for truckers, since their vehicles use no fuel while sitting. But the camels must eat in order to maintain their strength for the return journey and, since nothing grows at Taoudenni, the only food they have is the grass they bring with them. Once this is depleted, the caravans can only linger a short while longer. On very rare occasions, caravans have been forced to turn back empty-handed.

The situation is exacerbated by the fact that the miners no longer work year-round, as they did in the days of debt-slavery. Back then, vast surpluses of salt accumulated during the summer months, since the miners kept digging even though the caravans only ran from October to March, as they do still. Now that they are free of their debt-masters and earn more money in less time than before, the miners, too, break during the hottest months of the year. Between the capacity of the trucks and the shortened digging season, salt shortages are a growing problem.

After I returned to Timbuktu, I spoke about this issue with Sidi Mohammed Ould Youbba, a historian who is an authority on the salt trade. He said that soon an agreement would have to be forged among the truckers, the azalai, and the miners to resolve the matter. Wondering whether the truckers would concede to tinker with a system that currently works to their advantage, I asked if he thought it was likely that the three groups could come to mutually acceptable terms. "Of course," he replied, without a drop of doubt. Such pacts are commonplace, he said, and no one wants to drive anyone else out of business— which was a shock to my American ears. The truckers, miners, and azalai recognize the importance of the system as whole, he continued, and, as long as their own survival isn't threatened, will make agreements and even sacrifices to promote the welfare of the others. This is due in part to the familial ties among all three groups, as well as to the ethic of mutual sustainability that permeates Saharan culture. Again, it seemed like a perspective plucked directly from the desert ecosystem, in which resources are shared such that no one gets fat but the whole is able to survive, which in turn supports the survival of its members.

At that moment in Abdi's hut, I was concerned only about the survival of my dreams to travel with a working caravan. I had accepted the inconsistency with which we'd done so on the way to Taoudenni by telling myself I'd get my fill on the return trip. Still coolheaded, I firmly told Walid that heading back to Timbuktu by ourselves was not an option. I didn't care if it took a week or more, I would wait for the caravan. After the incident two mornings earlier, when I'd threatened to leave Walid behind, he knew I meant it.

Walid then said there might be another possibility: We might be able to join a different caravan, led by one of his friends, that he believed would be departing in a day or two. I asked him to find out, and he said he'd let me know that evening.

After a few hours' rest, Abdi and I went back to his mine. While he dug, I carried rubble up the stairs in a wooden crate, dumping it on the piles that ringed the mine's perimeter. Abdi urged me to leave the dirt where it lay, trying to convince me that it was an insult to him for a guest to perform such menial labor. But his protests seemed perfunctory. I wanted to help him out as well as show him and the other miners that I was willing to get dirty right alongside them.

As afternoon turned to evening, I decided to head back to camp. On the way, I ran into Walid, Mohammed Majnoon, Horshack, Abdullai, Baba, and Big Baba standing at the edge of one of their mines. They greeted me enthusiastically, inviting me to join in their horseplay while they hoisted finished salt bars to the surface. Like the evening before, their animated mood proved irresistible; I was soon laughing with them and feeling as though I'd truly been accepted into their clique.

Horshack motioned for me to follow him, and led me down into an abandoned mine. A hole about two feet deep had been dug in the corner, into which he plunged an empty jug. When he lifted it, it was full of water. I dipped my finger in, then licked it; even the Dead Sea was less salty. We went back to the mine where his friends were, and Horshack poured the water over the salt bars. With its high saline content, it acted as a hardening agent, making the slabs more durable for the long journey to market. Meanwhile, Walid and Abdullai secured strips of damp goatskin around the bars—one lengthwise, two widthwise—which also helped keep them intact, like taping windows during a hurricane. Then they joined the bars into pairs, fastening the widthwise straps one to another by inserting wooden cotter pins into loops at the ends of the straps. Just enough slack was left between the salt slabs so they could be slung over each side of a camel's hump, balancing each other out. The salt was now ready for shipping.

Before returning to our camp, Walid and Baba took me to see the Taoudenni blacksmith. A dozen miners surrounded him, watching as he sharpened old tools and forged new ones. The forge itself was a primitive yet effective contraption, which lay on the ground. Two goatskin sacks, which looked like a pair of brown lungs, served as bellows. Their mouths—or really necks—were fitted into the hollowed prongs of a forked piece of wood. This was joined—at the foot of the Y—to two metal pipes about eighteen inches long that led to a heap of coals. As the blacksmith's assistant squeezed the bellows, alternating between them in a rapid, panting rhythm, the coals glowed then faded, glowed then faded. Upon this beating heart of fire rested eight pick-blades, arranged in a circle like iron flower petals. The blacksmith hammered away, then plunged his finished work into a can of water to cool it.

We couldn't linger long; the sun was setting behind a swirling sheet of cirrus, casting a smoky orange light. And I had patients to tend to.

Abdullai walked back to camp with us, where we found a group of injured miners already waiting for treatment. I arranged myself on the blanket, unwrapped the tape from Abdullai's thigh, and lifted the Band-Aids I'd applied the previous evening. The bandage had remained intact all day and his wound looked remarkably good. I covered it with fresh supplies and told him to leave it alone, promising to examine him one more time before leaving Taoudenni. The other miners got a few dabs of New-Skin before I sent them on their way.

Abdi joined us for dinner and, through him, Walid laid out the options for our return. We could wait about a week and head south with the same caravan with which we'd arrived, or we could join his friend's caravan and leave two nights hence. His friend, he explained, was driving twenty-five camels with one young assistant, and would be grateful for our help. Though I was somewhat hesitant to trade the glory of riding with an armada of camels for a string so small, I also saw the possibilities for a more intimate experience, and the chance to be more involved with the operations of the caravan. I told Walid I'd be willing to do so on one condition: that he teach me everything about being an azalai along the way, so I could play an active, useful role on the caravan, which I already knew would be impossible with the larger one. And, I reminded him, I wanted to travel with the caravan all the time, waking, sleeping, riding, and eating on their schedule, never leaving them. Walid agreed, and made sure I knew what that meant—that we'd be traveling even longer hours than on the way to the mines, never eating more than one meal a day. Was I sure I wanted to do that?

Given the chance to change my mind, I paused for a moment, taking stock of myself. The trip to the mines had been hard enough as it was. Riding more and eating less would up the challenge significantly. But I had come here to experience caravan life, and there was no other way to do it. Though I'd surely be hungry, it was a sacrifice worth making. It's not like the food was all that appetizing anyway. I told Walid not to worry, that I could handle it, and he said he'd finalize the arrangements the next day.

I spent most of the following day in Mohammed Majnoon's hut, along with Walid and a rotating crew of miners who came and went. One of these, a young man also named Mohammed, spoke French well, and with him as a translator I talked with the others. Until this point, I'd been so absorbed with learning everything I could about Taoudenni, and the miners had been so generous with their answers, that we had rarely talked about life in the United States, about which I imagined they were probably curious. This felt like the perfect time to field their questions, so I asked if there was anything they wanted to know. Expecting queries about the number of cars people owned or what the average yearly salary was, I was taken by surprise when one of them asked what kind of animals inhabited our deserts; were there cows and sheep and camels?

There were cows, I said, and some sheep, as well as snakes, lizards, antelopes, and raptors. But there were no camels.

They could hardly believe that a desert without camels could exist, and reacted as though something was fundamentally out of order in my part of the world. They urged me to export some and begin breeding and herding them back home. Aside from being an infallibly profitable venture, eating their meat and drinking their milk, the miners all agreed, could cure any sickness; camels were, they said, like a walking hospital.

"If you were traveling in the desert there," Walid wondered, "and you came across a cow, would you kill it and eat it?"   •

I laughed, realizing that these guys had no conception of the way Americans obtain meat. To them, meat was alive until they slaughtered it, then it was skinned and hung up to dry. They only ate fresh meat immediately following a slaughter. I told them about supermarkets, and they nodded soberly as I explained the concept of refrigerated steaks wrapped in plastic. Even to my ears, in this context, the practice sounded bizarre and exotic.

Still stuck on the subject, they then wanted to know if I would kill and eat the big birds and the antelopes that lived in the desert. No, I said, telling them that, normally, Americans eat only cows, chickens, and pigs.

This proved more difficult to explain than the meat department in the grocery store. Since eating pig is forbidden by Muslim law, none of these men had ever seen one, and Mohammed, who was translating, looked at me blankly when I repeated the word *cochon*. Quite reasonably, he'd never had occasion to learn it, as I'd never learned the word in Arabic, though I could name most other barnyard animals. I drew a picture of a pig, which obviously didn't help, but at last, by telling them it was an animal banned for consumption by the Koran, I was able to achieve an abstract kind of comprehension.

For me, it was a lazy, uneventful day of napping and reading. Everything was set for Walid and me to leave the day after next, so I relished the opportunity to do nothing but rest.

. . .

The following day, my last at the mines, was busier. Baba had made a somewhat unusual decision to stay, dig salt for a few weeks, and return with another caravan. (Usually miners and azalai stick to their roles.) Walid and I helped Baba move into a partially finished room adjacent to Mohammed Majnoon's, running rope above the space and scrounging for scraps of metal with which to make a ceiling. Since he wouldn't be there long, Baba didn't want to spend the time excavating a mine of his own, so we scouted out old, abandoned pits, looking for any whose tunnels could be dug a little deeper, some of which were used as makeshift outhouses. Then, in the afternoon, as if in response to the conversation I'd had the previous day, I saw how the miners purchased *their* meat.

Since we had finished the goat carcass we'd been eating for the previous two weeks, Walid suggested we buy some camel meat for the return trip. I had eaten camel a number of times in Egypt, and found it succulent and flavorful, so I thought it was a great idea.

There is no regular meat market in Taoudenni, but when enough miners get together and pool their money to buy an aged camel, the butcher brings out his knives. Walid and I arrived too late to witness the slaughter, which I had believed I wanted to watch, but after seeing the severed head of the camel lying on the ground with glazed, lifeless eyes, next to a dagger and a bowl full of blood, I was glad we had missed it. Unlike the killing of a goat, which I can watch with little emotion, I felt that witnessing the murder of an animal for which I had fondness and respect would have been upsetting. I had no problem eating camel; I just didn't want to see one suffer and die.

The animal had already been skinned by the time we showed up. The hide was laid flat on the ground, hairy-side down, serving as a drop cloth on which the disassembled body parts were heaped. The bearded butcher—the only fat man I'd seen at Taoudenni—and his helpers carved away, stripping muscle from the camel's legs, which were as tall as many of the miners who stood around watching, waiting for their portions.

The meat men, dressed in turbans and blood-soaked boubous, crouched around the edge of the hide, working quickly and methodically, grasping the slippery flesh with bare hands as they sliced it from the bone while bantering with one another and the miners. The cut meat was divided into fourteen piles, which, for fairness' sake, were equal in both size and contents, so each stakeholder would receive the same amount of red meat, intestine, stomach lining, and vital organs. When the job was finished, the butcher filled the bowls and rice sacks that the miners brought with them, and the meat was carried away. To my great relief, the share we bought included no guts or organs, since they would rot while we traveled.

From the meat market, Walid and I went over to Abdi's mine, where, in preparation for our departure, Walid collected from the floor shards of salt too small for sale but perfect for cooking with; he filled a rice sack to bring back to his family. Abdi gave me a fragment about as big as his huge hand, which looked remarkably like a representation of the African continent. Though it caused some confusion when going through airport security in Europe and the United States, since none of the inspectors had ever seen anything like it, I got it home in one piece, where it's displayed as one of the most cherished mementos I've returned with from any of my travels.

When Walid and I returned to our camp, a group of wounded miners had already lined up on what everyone knew was the last night the medical clinic would be open for service. After doling out another round of New-Skin, I examined Abdullai. Removing his bandage, I saw that the wound on his thigh was still clean, but that it really needed to be stitched. I had heard that Krazy Glue was an effective substitute for needle and thread, and though I had never before used it as a surgical tool, it was something I'd always wanted to try. With the little tube I carried in my repair kit, I drew a thin line of glue around the edges of the laceration, careful not to get any of it inside. I pinched the skin together and held it closed until the glue dried. I don't know whether Abdullai or I was more surprised when I let go and we saw that his wound was so perfectly sealed it seemed to have vanished. I spread a thin layer of glue over the seam, for extra protection, told Abdullai to stay still until it hardened, then pronounced him cured. Abdullai, Walid, and the other miners reacted as if I'd performed a small miracle, praising and thanking me effusively.

As night cloaked the desert in darkness, the miners with whom I'd become most friendly came to say good-bye. While we sat around the fire, talking and joking, a miner whom I'd never met approached, carrying a tube of something in his hand. He had bought it believing it was nasal medication, but said that when he'd applied it inside his nostrils, it had felt funny. He wanted to know if he was using it correctly. Abdi glanced at it, then handed it to me, the doctor, for inspection. The label read SENSODYNE.

"*C'est dentifrice!*" I declared, and Abdi burst into hysterical laughter. He translated for everyone else, and they literally rolled on the ground with glee, pointing at and mocking the poor fellow who had tried to cure his cold by squirting toothpaste up his nose.

After about half an hour, Abdullai, Abdullah, Baba, Horshack, and Mohammed Majnoon rose to go back to their village of salt and rock. I shook their hands in warm farewell, promised to send photos to them through Walid, and gave them a pound of the tobacco I'd purchased in Timbuktu to share with one another. Walid nodded his approval of my gesture, and said he was going to leave me with Abdi while he said good-bye to his other friends. He told me pack up as much as I could before going to sleep, since we'd be rising at 2 AM to leave with the caravan.

Abdi asked if I'd deliver two letters for him, taking one to his mother in Araouane and another to his uncle Lamana. I gave him my notebook and a pen, then asked if he wanted to sit in my Crazy Creek camping chair while he wrote. He had never before seen this marvel of American ingenuity, which is essentially a flat pad that folds in half and clips into an L shape, providing a thin posterior cushion and some back support. All the nomads I have ever met have been impressed by this simple form of portable furniture and, as Abdi sat down in it, he started giggling. "I feel like the president!" he said, and launched into a speech, imitating Mali's leader, Amadou Toumani Touré, in a deep, aristocratic voice, extending his hands in sweeping gestures of benevolent authority. He welcomed all foreigners, especially me, to his country, extolled the virtues of peace among men, and promised to give cars to every Malian citizen. With a total lack of inhibition, this impoverished salt miner momentarily assumed the presidency from a throne of foam in one of the most desolate places in the world.

I stoked the fire under the cooking pot as Abdi settled into writing his letters. When he was done, perhaps because his mind was filled with home, he looked at me and asked if I would accept his sister's hand in marriage.

"What is she like?" I asked.

"You know what she is like," he said. "You told me you met her at my house."

I thought back to the afternoon I'd spent in Araouane, realized he was talking about Hannah, and started laughing, getting the joke.

"What's so funny?" he asked, not laughing with me.

"She's nine!" I said.

"So?"

"I'm thirty-three!"

"So? Did you like her?"

"Sure I liked her, but I can't marry a nine-year-old!"

"Don't be silly," Abdi scoffed. "You'll just make the contract now, but you won't marry her until she turns thirteen."

It was no joke. I learned then that Abdi himself was engaged to the nine-year-old daughter of his mother's cousin. The union had been arranged by their parents, and Abdi had approved, since he found the girl to be smart enough and cute enough. They would wed soon after her thirteenth birthday, when he'd be twenty-two. His uncle Lamana, he said, had married a fifteen-year-old when he was thirty-six. From the sound of things, that girl's family may have feared she'd end up as an old maid.

There have been moments in my travels when I've met young women so beautiful that I've been seized with the fantasy of marrying them and moving into a Berber village or a Kazakh tent. But no matter how cute Hannah might have been, even my unleashed id would not be drawn to a girl who hadn't yet hit double digits. For Abdi and his people, however, marriage has little to do with desire.

Too sensible to leave the perpetuation of families and tribes to the whims of romantic love, the Saharans, like many others in the world, marry for purely practical purposes. In context, the age discrepancy between husbands and wives makes some sense: In order to fulfill their roles as husbands and fathers, men must be old enough to provide for their families; in order to fulfill their role as wives and mothers, women must be old enough to bear children. And given the startlingly high infant mortality rate (Mali's is the highest in all of Africa), it's no wonder they start as early as they can. Though completely contrary to Western ideas about love and partnership, not to mention statutory rape, I find it hard to criticize, especially when considering the questionable success rate of marriages based on romantic love.

"This is how things are done here," Abdi said, "so if you want to marry my sister and become part of my family, it's no problem."

"Maybe not here," I said, "but back home, I'd be thrown in jail." I explained that each state has laws defining at what age men and women can legally marry, adding that in most it was sixteen or eighteen. Abdi said that by those standards, most men he knew would be criminals.

When we finished eating, I readied my bedroll, hoping to get as much sleep as I could before my departure. I gave Abdi ten dollars worth of Malian francs to thank him for the time he spent with me, but he refused to say good-bye. He'd sleep out at our camp, he said, waiting until we walked out of Taoudenni to say farewell.

Wrapped in my blanket, gazing up at Orion and the Big Dog, I was inundated with a mixture of emotions, eager to be on the move once more, yet saddened at the thought of leaving Taoudenni. I'd been deeply affected by my contact with the miners, not only because of their kindness, but because they'd taken this potentially hellish place and made it, if not heaven, at least human; through their simple rituals of eating, drinking tea, smoking tobacco, praying, playing, and talking, they'd created civilization in one of the most impossible places to imagine it. And what seemed like a miracle to me was, to them, just another day at work.

*The caravan on the move, with Ali
in the background*

CHAPTER EIGHT

My alarm woke me at 2 AM. I roused Walid and, to my surprise, he rose without resisting. With help from Baba and Abdi, we loaded Lachmar and L'beyya quickly. Since it felt like we'd said our real good-byes the night before, our final farewells were brief. I promised Abdi I'd deliver the letters he wrote and thanked him again for everything, then shook Baba's hand and said, "May Allah watch over you."

"Safe travels," he replied. "Peace be upon you."

"And upon you, too," I answered.

Walid grunted, slapped L'beyya lightly with his stick, and we set off toward the south. I'd thought we were going to rendezvous with our new caravan before departing, but something about Walid's manner implied that we were hitting the trail for real, not casually sauntering to a meeting place. I wanted to know what was going on.

"Where's the caravan?" I asked.

"Just up ahead," Walid said. "We'll catch it in a minute."

Too reminiscent of what I'd heard so many times on the way to the mines, Walid's words conjured a dread-filled premonition that we were in for a replay of the trip north, ever chasing the caravan and mostly traveling without it. Should I stop and refuse to leave Taoudenni until we were *with* a caravan, I asked myself, even if it meant waiting a few more days? But what if Walid was right this time? My head spun as I weighed the possible options and outcomes, knowing this was a crucial decision, feeling pressured to make it quickly, and having no actionable intelligence, just hopes and fears.

Before I could make up my mind, a man who was seeing off another caravan came walking in our direction. He told Walid that ours hadn't left yet, and if we waited it'd probably pass by in a few minutes. So we stopped where we were and, true to the man's word, a shadowy string of twenty-six camels soon shuffled up in the darkness. At its head was an azalai named (what else?) Baba; taking up the rear was his helper, a young boy named Ali. We all exchanged greetings as Walid and I fell in alongside them, I awash with relief.

The waning moon hovered in the east, the constellations shimmered brightly against the inky blackness of a perfectly clear sky. My turban was wrapped around my face for warmth; walking took the chill from my body. As we moved through the night, Baba sang lilting Koranic chants, one after the next, to keep the evil spirits at bay.

Images of the past few days flashed through my mind. What I'd discovered at Taoudenni was as unexpected as it had been profound. Each memory was a jewel without price and, like a beggar who stumbles upon a treasure chest, admiring them one after another made me drunk with exuberance. I had to deliberately slow my strides if I didn't want to leave the caravan behind.

After a couple of hours, we mounted up and rode into the morning. At dawn, by silent agreement, everyone slid from their animals and took to their feet once again. It was time to pray. Walid handed me our camels' rope and, to my astonishment, Baba asked me to lead his caravan as well. While the three nomads knelt in the sand, I marched on with a grass rope over each of my shoulders, pulling twenty-eight camels behind me.

Now that it was light out, I was able to get my first glimpse of my new companions. With a patchy beard over his sunken cheeks, eyes bulging from deep sockets, and a nearly shaved scalp, Baba looked like a well-tanned Hare Krishna on a hunger strike. A shredded blue sweater covered his ragged blue boubou. I guessed he was in his mid-fifties, but later learned he was thirty-three, the same age as me. Ali, on the other hand, was fifteen but looked no older than eight. His face was full, his ears stuck out to the side, and his gleaming, squarish teeth were a little too big for his mouth. Over his boubou, he wore a navy-blue hooded sweatshirt with a zipper in the front. It was his second season working on a salt caravan. Walid teased that he was the littlest azalai in the Sahara, and Ali scowled silently at the gibe. He could be playful and credulous—like the child he resembled—but turned touchy and spiteful when his inferiority complex got the best of him.

With the night behind us and prayers out of the way, it was teatime. Baba untied the portable brazier that was lashed to his camel; Walid leapt atop L'beyya, fished the teapot out of his bag, and filled it with water and tea leaves. I traded Baba the caravan for the brazier, which Ali and I packed with camel dung we picked up on the trail. The two of us worked as a team, heating the water, brewing the tea, mixing the sugar, and passing glasses to everyone else, careful not to spill a drop while we strode over the sand. Though of course the azalai could have managed just fine without me, I was already feeling more useful than I had at virtually any point on the trip to Taoudenni. Having led the caravan during prayer and contributed to our morning's caffeine fix, I was making their lives just a little bit easier and was glad to prove myself an asset—however small—so early in our journey south. Traveling with twenty-eight camels lacked some of the majesty of traveling with seventy-five, but the large caravan had an impersonal, almost corporate feel to it. This was like a family-run operation and gave me a chance to have a more hands-on experience. I was happy with the trade. And, soon enough, I'd have the best of both.

Traversing a plain of red sand, we followed a trail trampled by countless camels, crisscrossed by the textured ruts left by truck tires. Before, I might have seen this juxtaposition as symbolic of the coming death of the caravans; with what I now knew, it seemed like an apt metaphor for the harmonious coexistence of camels and trucks, and the system that worked for their mutual survival. Up ahead, another caravan came into view, snaking up a rounded ridge, the slabs of salt slung over the camels' backs reflecting the light of the rising sun like pieces of moon. Seeing us, the caravan slowed, allowing us to catch up to it.

It was a little smaller than ours—twenty camels led by two azalai. One of them was dressed in a dark blue bathrobe that hung below his knees, as though he'd just stepped outside to grab the morning paper. It was cinched around his waist with a wide leather ammunition belt, like an empty bandolier. His name was Hamid. His cousin, Dah, dressed more traditionally, wearing a dark sweater over his boubou. Both were twenty-one years old, and each had just a faint trace of a mustache with no beard to speak of. After the greetings finally came to an end, Dah pulled out a bag of peanuts and offered everyone a handful. To reciprocate, I passed some biscuits around. The food sealed a tacit agreement that we'd stick together from here on.

As the morning wore on and we neared our tenth hour on the trail, a heavy languor settled over the caravan. Unlike the trip north when the sun was often at our backs, it now blazed directly into our faces, persuading me to close my eyes. We rode in weary silence, smothered by heat, swayed into semi-consciousness by the hypnotic motion of the camels, until a sudden burst of chaos jarred us to attention.

With no warning or cause, two camels went berserk, jerking their leads away from the camels in front of them, breaking the ranks, bucking and rearing like broncos stung by bees. Cargo pads, bags, and bars of salt flew from their backs and crashed to the ground. In an instant the five azalai and I were off our mounts. Walid ordered me to the front of the caravan and told me to hold the ropes of all the lead camels to prevent a general mutiny, while he and the others surrounded the renegades. Walid darted in front of the bigger of the two beasts, reaching for the rope that was still attached to its mouth. The camel leapt and flailed, kicked and roared—towering tall on its hind legs, its front feet thrashing the air, it was terrifying and ridiculous, looking like some bizarre creature out of a fairy tale that might shoot flames from its mouth. With its strength and clumsiness it could surely do some serious damage to a man whether or not it intended to.

Walid, however, was unflapped. Once he seized the camel's rope, he didn't let go. Trying not to spook it further, he waited patiently for his moment, then pulled its head toward the ground. The others then rushed in like wolves and forced the camel to its knees while Walid pressed its head pressed against the sand. He held it there until the camel calmed down, while the others went to wrestle with the second animal. Seeing its cohort subdued, it lost heart for the struggle and offered little resistance. I continued to hold the caravan in place while the azalai loaded the fallen goods back atop the camels that had flung them off. A couple of the salt bars had split upon impact, and had to be bound together with rope before they could be carried.

While watching the azalai quell the camel rebellion, I'd desperately wanted to take photographs of these coolheaded nomads—one of them in a bathrobe—wrangling with crazed camels like they were in some kind of Saharan rodeo. But I'd been given a job, and couldn't do it and take pictures at the same time. Torn between my roles as an observer of the caravan and a participant in it, the temptation to leave my post and pick up my camera was tremendous. In my gut, however, I knew my duty to the caravan had to come first; aside from enhancing our overall welfare, it was the only way I could hope to be accepted as anything more than a total outsider.

Before starting out again, Baba took the big camel, the one that started all the trouble, and moved it to the front of the line, tying it to the tail of his own camel on a very short lead, like the caravan version of sending a kid to the principal's office. Though there were occasional outbursts among the ranks in the days that followed, they were very rare and very minor. Contrary to their reputations for nastiness and ob-stinance, for spitting and other forms of rudeness, the camels were gen-erally compliant and well behaved, especially considering what was demanded of them day after day.

We continued on across the sand, now orange in the full glare of the sun. Mirages flowed like cool, sparkling streams. I realized that this was the last time in my life I'd ever see this place; I had no illusions about returning someday in the future.

We reached camp—a flat hollow among low, sharply cut dunes of rose-colored sand flecked with black—a little after 3 PM. The azalai couched their camels and began unloading salt immediately. When Walid and I had our bags off Lachmar and L'beyya, we went over to help. If I'd been expecting Walid to patiently demonstrate the proper technique for taking salt off a camel's back, I'd have been disap-pointed. There was simply no time for instruction. The azalai worked as though unloading the camels quickly was a matter of saving lives, so I just jumped in and lent a hand, observing, learning, and doing simultaneously, hoping I didn't screw anything up. At first the oth-ers tried to shoo me away, afraid I'd break the precious bars, and I understood. After all, this was their income, and they'd risked their lives for it. But unloading salt was definitely not rocket science, or even cooking. With the camels prone, one man took hold of a bar on one side of a camel while another man grabbed its sister bar; they were lifted off simultaneously and carried a few feet behind the camel, where they were propped against each other at an angle, so they stood up forming an A-frame. The same was done with the second set of bars, which were rested up against the first set. It had to be done with care, especially since each weighed more than eighty pounds, but it was pretty simple. I knew that if I stayed on the sidelines, it'd only create the perception that I was useless and establish a routine in which I was left out. Walid, remembering his promise to include me in all things azalai, worked with me. By the time the last camel had been freed from its burden, the azalai conceded that I was fit to help, and even congratulated me on doing a good job. The camels were set to graze upon the fodder cached here days earlier.

Shortly before sunset, I wandered off to take some pictures of the dunes. After about ten minutes of meandering around the sand, it occurred to me that even though I spent much of my days in silence, this was the longest I'd been alone since leaving Timbuktu. It was profoundly liberating; for the first time in weeks, I could fly around that internal space that only expands when no one else is around; a place where I need to spend time regularly in order to stay sane. Loath to leave it before I had to, I stayed out until it was nearly dark.

By the time I returned, Walid had started dinner. Another caravan had arrived during my absence, with thirty-four camels and three azalai. Though I didn't meet them then, we would all depart and travel together from then on.

After eating, Walid told me to set my alarm for 2 AM. I lay down at 7:30 PM and fell asleep quickly. The next thing I knew, I was being shaken awake and told to get moving. It was 9:30 PM. As usual, Walid's estimates of time were a little less than precise.

• • •

Due to the time it took to load all the camels, it was nearly two hours before we actually left camp. When we did, we made a number of false starts. Baba and the leader of the new caravan, named Sidali, struggled in the total darkness to find the channel that would take us through the dunes in the right direction. The camels were led one way, then the opposite way, so the camel train doubled back on itself in a U. Baba swept the weak beam of his flashlight across the sand, with inconclusive results. At last Walid, who had kept his counsel to himself until this point, strode to the head of the line and kept on going, with a clipped, confident pace. I was right behind him and, even though the others had the benefit of the light, I trusted Walid's instincts more than anyone else's eyes. Apparently they did, too, for they followed along behind us. Aside from not needing a light, I believed it would be beneath Walid to use one.

Just as I finished that thought, as though to deliberately shatter my idealization of him, he asked Baba if he could borrow the flashlight. But he only needed to see in order to fix his flip-flop; the piece that ran between his toes had broken. Once he assessed the damage, he clicked the light off and put it in his pocket, took a handful of grass, lit it on fire, then melted the severed plastic back together.

About five minutes later, Baba questioned Walid's route, pointing to Sidali, who was beginning to set out on a different angle. "Look," Walid said, snapping the light on and pointing it at the ground for a few seconds, just long enough to prove his point. We were walking directly atop a trail of camel prints left by the last caravan to pass this way.

Emerging from the dunes onto the open flats, we were met with a blast of frigid wind. Walking kept me just warm enough, but when I mounted Lachmar and sat motionless and high, the breeze drilled through my clothes and my body. My bones felt brittle, my flesh frozen. For a few moments, I weighed the merits of putting on my sweater, which I'd been using as extra saddle padding, but there was little to debate—only whether or not I'd gone nuts, since I couldn't believe it could be this cold in the Sahara. Even the sweater wasn't enough. Reluctantly accepting whatever price my ass would pay, I unfolded the blanket I was sitting on and wrapped it around myself, as the other azalai had done. My legs, however, unlike theirs, were too long to tuck under the folds of the blanket. My bare feet dangled, fully exposed, going numb. I pressed them into the soft fur on Lachmar's chest and neck, trying to warm them. I periodically checked my watch—after weeks of praying for the moment the sun would go down, I couldn't believe I was desperate to see it rise! By the time it did, my water bottle had iced over.

Confronted with a new form of suffering, my thoughts turned to death. I no longer feared it as I had when embarking on the caravan, not because I was any more confident I'd make it back alive, but because I felt that if I did die, I'd have no regrets. My experiences at the mines had made everything I'd endured thus far, and almost anything I could endure, worth it. Since there were few ways in which I'd die instantly, I imagined that if I became injured or ill I'd have at least a few hours in which to bring some closure to my life. I would first write a letter to my parents, then I'd write about Taoudenni, so others could glimpse what I had seen there. I'd leave instructions for it to be read at my funeral as my last farewell, as the last thing I had brought back from the world to family and friends. Thinking about this scenario, which was admittedly a little grandiose, I saw that greater than my fear of death was my fear of dying for something stupid—now that I didn't have to worry about that, I could accept a hypothetical demise more readily.

I slipped off Lachmar about an hour before sunrise to get the blood moving in my feet. As on the previous morning, the others paused to pray when light began to fill the sky, and I became captain of the caravan—only this time, with our additional companions having hitched their animals to ours, I single-handedly led a train of eighty-two camels into the dawn. I looked at myself as if from above, and starting laughing, touched by the image, as beautiful as it was absurd, of a man living out his farthest-fetched dreams.

When the azalai caught up to me, the morning tea was started and I met the members of the new caravan. Sidali, its leader, was forty-two, with a shock of wild black hair, a heavy black beard and mustache, a prominent nose, and creased mahogany skin. Over a soiled tan djellaba, he wore a long, dark plaid trench coat that might have been from London Fog's mid-1970s line. His twenty-year-old son, Bakar, was equally fashionable, sporting a gray wool suit jacket over a brown, blue, and beige djellaba, plus yellow pants and a teal turban. Omar, the third member of their team, was Sidali's twenty-one-year-old nephew; judging by his outfit, he was like their poor relation—his standard blue boubou was torn and frayed around the edges. While Sidali and Bakar welcomed me with warmth and respect, Omar immediately demanded that I give him my lighter, which Ali had used to start the tea. When I laughed at his brashness and said no, he asked me to give him some food.

Since it was teatime, I conceded, passing some biscuits around to everyone, and setting a problematic precedent. Aside from millet and rice, which were only eaten at camp, the azalai carried virtually no other food (though Dah had some peanuts, he didn't have many), meaning they had nothing to eat during the long hours on the trail. Walid and I, of course, had biscuits, peanuts, and dates, but just enough for us to indulge a little bit every day; if we regularly shared with seven other people, our supplies would've been quickly exhausted.

As Walid had promised, we only had time to eat one plate of rice a day. It felt like one plate too many. Since the camel meat we'd bought at the mines had to be carried in a bag, it hadn't dried thoroughly and had gone foul, though it was hard to tell when doused with our rancid, sun-aged goat butter—now going on four weeks old. And as always, the rice was sprinkled with generous helpings of sand. It reminded me of the joke Woody Allen recounts in *Annie Hall*, the one in which two women complain about a restaurant: "This food is terrible." "And such small portions!" Though I'd force myself to eat my entire serving purely to keep up my strength, it only sated my hunger for a short time; I relied on our snack food to quell the gnawing in my belly during the long nights and days on the march and didn't want to give it all away.

My instincts for self-preservation conflicted with my ethical ideals, especially in a Muslim context, where food is treated as communal property. After all, I was traveling with these people and felt like there was a moral imperative to share what I had. But driven by hunger and the fear of future hunger, I tried to rationalize my way around it. These men, I told myself, were accustomed to their Spartan ways, and if I wasn't there they'd be fine surviving on their meager diet with no extras. Moreover, by sharing with everyone, the food would be spread so thinly among us that no one would ever get enough to even dent his hunger. Still, a part of me was unconvinced, so that evening I asked Walid what he thought about this dilemma. His answer was unequivocal.

"It's your food," he said, "and you need it. They know it, but will ask for it anyway. You don't have to give them anything."

Even with Walid's blessing, I felt uncomfortable about eating in front of the others and not offering to share. At night this was no problem, thanks to the darkness; when I got hungry during the day, I'd hide a small bag of peanuts and dates in my lap and shuttle them to my mouth a few at a time, as discreetly as possible. Every so often I'd share with everyone else.

For the most part the others obeyed an unwritten code: Since I didn't flaunt it, they didn't ask for it. Baba and Omar, however, were the exceptions, and they didn't limit their requests to food. Over the next week, they demanded everything from peanuts to my sunglasses to my shirt. Sometimes they cajoled, other times they pouted. At camp each afternoon, when Walid dished up a couple handfuls of peanuts and dates to eat along with our dorno, Baba inevitably appeared, knowing he wouldn't be turned away; finally Walid, of his own volition, pretended we had eaten the last of them—fooling even me into believing him—so Baba would stop expecting to be fed. But he still expected me to supply him with black tea. Every afternoon, without fail, he'd approach, imploring, "Michael, Lipton? Lipton?" Since I had plenty, I gave it to him freely, and it turned into a joke; I'd pull out a tea bag and hand it to him before he even said a word. Omar so persistently asked me for my lighter that I finally gave it to him, just to shut him up. I had a spare one anyway.

I felt I had to deal delicately with Omar. He was energetic and charismatic and could be quite charming. But he was capricious and would turn suddenly, becoming obnoxiously dismissive or mildly menacing. He reminded me of one of those classic teenage types, one of whom I imagine everyone knew back in high school: They're popular, athletic, and good looking, usually in a Nordic kind of way. They treat you like a buddy one day and a loser the next, drawing you in then putting you down. This was similar to the game Omar played, keeping me ever off balance—such as the time he asked me to take his picture, then aggressively demanded that I pay him for the privilege after I did (he calmed down only when I reminded him about the lighter I gave him). But there was one big difference between Omar and those high school kids, and it was me—back in high school, as an insecure teenager, I'd really wanted those jerks to like me. In the desert, I wanted to be able to like Omar but didn't really care how he felt about me—though I figured it was important that he not *dislike* me too much.

For the most part, though, I felt very much at ease among the azalai. Sidali and Bakar were funny and kind. Dah and Hamid were quiet and usually kept to themselves in camp. Of the two, I became particularly friendly with Hamid, who came to me every day for medical treatment for his hands, which were covered with lacerations he'd acquired when harvesting the bales of tall desert grasses carried and cached for camel fodder; the edges of the grasses were so sharp, they'd cut into his skin like razors when he yanked them from the ground. Seeing me apply New-Skin to Hamid, Baba, naturally, wanted some for his own cracked fingers. Since I had plenty of the stuff to spare, I happily doled it out, but convinced him that his wounds weren't bad enough to require the Band-Aids I gave Hamid. Though his perpetual pleas for tea and food were occasionally annoying, Baba, too, was easy to get along with, and I had a sense that, in a pinch, he'd have my back. He gracefully tolerated my imitations of him: I'd mimic the call he often uttered while driving his caravan—which was a wordless chant similar to Tarzan's trademark cry—and I'd ape the way he shouted to his partner, a high-pitched "Yeh, Aliiiiiiiiiiiiiiiii!" The other azalai loved these impersonations, and would ask me repeatedly to "do Baba, do Baba," after which they'd break into hysterical laughter.

We arrived at our second camp in the full heat of midafternoon after fifteen hours on the trail. We unloaded the camels, made tea and dorno, then I collapsed for an hour or so under the shade of our blanket shelter. After dinner, I passed out again, getting in about three hours of sleep before being woken around 10 PM to start packing for the evening march. This time I kept my socks handy.

Though it was easier on the camels to march through the cold nights than to face the afternoon heat, I found it even more demanding than traveling during the day. With a late-rising moon near the end of its cycle, the desert was usually pitch dark. Unable to see the ground before me, I slammed my feet into countless rocks, which would've resulted in many broken toes had my sandal soles been a few millimeters shorter. If I had to go to the bathroom while riding, I'd slide off Lachmar and step to the side as the caravan continued on, all sight of it quickly absorbed by the night. At times, when it would get far ahead, I feared I'd wander off course, completely alone, while trying to catch up to it. I'd only find it again thanks to the call-and-response system Walid and I had practiced since our first day on the trail; I would shout, an azalai at the back of the caravan would shout back, and I would follow the sound, moving as quickly as I could, until I could hear the soft shuffling of hundreds of camel feet and the exotic melody of Baba's chants. Fortunately I'd become deft at mounting a moving camel, and could do so in the dark without disrupting the camel train.

Most challenging of all, by 2 or 3 AM, having snuck in only a few hours of sleep at camp, it was nearly impossible to stay awake. Exhaustion posed no problems for the azalai; having grown up in the saddle, they could slumber for hours at a time while we rode. Often they slept sitting upright; other times, they'd lie down and curl up on their blankets; the only ones who had to stay partially alert were those at the front of the line. But every time I'd start to drift off, I'd wake with the terrifying jolt of my body righting itself just as I was about to topple off my camel. The scare would be enough to keep me awake for a few minutes, but I was so tired that sleep soon seduced me back into its sweet caress. Again, I'd be jarred awake moments before tumbling from my perch. I tried lying down like the azalai did, but couldn't; my head and feet hung down over the slopes of Lachmar's hump, and the camel rocked like a rowboat on rough seas. Aware that falling would result in serious injury, I had no choice but to fend off sleep with all my will. After flirting seriously with it for a while, as with a woman I found irresistible but knew I'd best keep away from, I'd muster my resolve and renounce it.

I devised activities, physical and mental, to help me stay awake. I took the loose rope dangling in front of me and challenged myself to tie different kinds of knots in total darkness, pretending I'd gone blind. I bit my dirty nails and the cuticles around them. I sang. I made lists: the best meals I ever ate, letting my mind travel from Cairo to the Loire Valley to Houston Street; the worst meals I ever ate: the festival of guts on the way to Araouane; the dinner I'd had a few hours earlier. I tried to run through Descartes's ontological argument for the existence of God, which, as a college philosophy student, I would review in my head while I was having sex, since I didn't know any baseball statistics. (In the desert, I couldn't remember it all—obviously I hadn't gone over it enough times back in school.) Sometimes I would remember particular scenes from my past, trying to recall them in supersharp detail, down to textures, smells, and shadows, unsure how many of those details my mind was inventing. One night, in groggy delirium, my mind wandered back to the night of a concert I'd seen when I was a teenager, and I made the terrible mistake of listing all the Billy Joel songs I could think of—for days afterward, I was cursed with verses of "Scenes from an Italian Restaurant" playing in my head, and came to rue the day I ever heard the names *Brenda* and *Eddie*.

When nothing worked and sleep seeped through me like a drug, I would get off and walk. At least if I fell over then, I'd be much closer to the ground.

Between camps we never, ever stopped and hardly ever slowed, moving anywhere from fifteen to nineteen hours at a stretch. That men did this was impressive; what the camels did was astonishing. Many of them carried more than four hundred pounds. None of them drank a single drop of water for twelve days.

We reached our next camp in midafternoon. It was at the small well called Ounane, the one at the base of a low hill at which Walid, Baba, and I had briefly stopped on our way north. Our arrival was followed by a frenzy of action—unloading the camels, then rushing to fill our guerbas. Since it would take hours to water all the camels and they could survive without it, we only drew enough for ourselves. My job was to scoop water from the trough into the inner tubes, and as usual, I didn't do it fast enough to meet azalai standards. As Walid and Baba hauled up the water, Ali knelt by the side of the trough, "coaching" me with all the compassion of a drill sergeant. For the first time in his camel-driving career, Ali wasn't the low man on the totem pole. Finally there was someone he could boss around, and he never missed an opportunity to do so. At first, thinking he was trying to tell me how I could best help out with whatever job was at hand, I followed his instructions. But after a day or two, when I realized he was simply exercising the little bit of power that he had and that what he told me to do was sometimes ill advised, I felt free to ignore him. As I poured water into the guerbas at the well, Ali peppered me with criticism and finally, to demonstrate what a poor job I was doing, took the metal bowl from my hands. I bristled, then after a minute of standing dumbly, stalked back to where Walid and I had left our bags and started a fire and a pot of green tea.

Meanwhile, Sidali, Bakar, and Omar were busy branding some of their younger camels. The camels seemed to sense something unpleasant was about to happen to them and resisted couching on command. Together, the three azalai would muscle one to the ground and lash its front feet close together so it couldn't get back up. Omar held the camel in as much of a headlock as can be managed on a creature with a yard-long neck. Bakar pressed the weight of his body against the front of the camel's hump. Sidali drew his knife and cut into the camel's hide on its front flank, deeply enough to draw blood and, ultimately, create a scar.

Massive gray clouds swept in from the west, like an armada of war-ships steaming across open ocean. The leading edge sprayed us with a gentle drizzle, which suddenly exploded into a raging deluge. Rain poured in torrents. Gusts of wind ripped through camp, battering us with waves of airborne sand. Hail the size of grapes fell like shrapnel, chasing us under our blankets to protect us from their stinging, bruising impact. Lightning shot from the clouds. Thunder echoed across the sky. Parked as we were in a vast, open plain, we were in one of worst possible places to sit out an electrical storm. Of the many ways I'd imagined dying in the Sahara, being struck by lightning wasn't one. I was glad that the camels were so tall, thinking they might act as lightning rods.

In fifteen minutes, the heart of the storm had passed, though rain fell intermittently into the night. The azalai decided we would lay over the next day to make sure the salt bars and the leather tie straps had a chance to dry completely and regain their integrity before being transported. I greeted the news gladly.

Our things had been so thoroughly drenched that nothing had dried by the time dinner was over. Wearing my damp clothing, I headed for a clammy night's sleep, slipping between the folds of my dirty, soggy blanket that reeked like wet camel—an odor not unlike wet dog, but much more gamey.

By morning the clouds were gone. Blankets and clothing and salt all dried quickly. With nowhere to go, we enjoyed a day of leisure. I took out my map of Mali, which actually showed the main wells between Timbuktu and Taoudenni, and upon which I'd been marking the general location of our camps each night. Omar and Sidali were intrigued, so I showed them the route we were following. Since they couldn't read, I listed off and pointed to the wells, while they nodded in excited recognition, thrilled that the features of their isolated world had been published on a map. I explained how to estimate distances using the kilometer scale, then gave them the map; they spread their fingers between Timbuktu and Araouane and Taoudenni, then compared it with the scale, then debated how many kilometers actually lay between each place.

When they tired of that, Sidali decided it was time for some personal grooming. He lay on his stomach in the sand, still dressed in his trench coat. Bakar pulled out a pair of old metal scissors, crouched by his father's head, and proceeded to crop Sidali's hair nearly down to the scalp. Walid criticized the unevenness of the cut, so took the scissors and finished the job. He then asked to borrow my Swiss army knife and used its small scissors to prune Sidali's beard. When Sidali was cleaned up to everyone's satisfaction, Walid trimmed his own beard, then used a razor blade to shave his cheeks—no water, no soap, just steel on skin. Omar borrowed the blade afterward, and shaved himself. I felt like I was hanging out with a bunch of guys playing beauty parlor in the middle of the desert.

The late-morning heat rose quickly, so I set up a blanket for shelter, which Walid and I crawled under for a midday nap. We woke after a couple of hours and I read for a while, now Kipling's *Kim*. I restitched my shirt, which had split along the seams between the sleeves and the shoulders, and sewed up a few tears in my pants, then helped Walid with dinner and tea. I was able to sneak in another two hours of sleep before being wakened and told to start packing. It was only 8 PM.

The next five days and nights were a grueling exercise in endurance. Each evening we broke camp between eight and nine, meaning that every day I was only able to get an hour or two of sleep in the afternoon and an hour or two after an increasingly disgusting dinner. We walked and rode and walked and rode for what seemed like forever, through freezing nights, into blistering days. Though I had many years of wilderness experience behind me and had often pushed myself beyond my perceived limitations, nothing I had ever done came close to comparing to the endless rigors of traveling with the caravan. Walid had been right—it was far more challenging than traveling on our own schedule. When not on the move, I closed my eyes at every opportunity and, regardless of how hot it was, who was talking around me, or whether or not I was even feeling tired at that moment, I could throw my internal circuit breaker and shut myself down as fast as if I'd injected sodium pentathol.

There were times when thinking about the rest of the day, the rest of the journey, became overwhelming. As I fought to put one weary foot in front of the other, to bear the sun staring me in the face, or to stay seated atop Lachmar when ready to drop from exhaustion, it was impossible to imagine making it to the next camp, let alone all the way back to Timbuktu. In order to slip from beneath the crushing weight of future thoughts, I adopted a technique of focusing solely on the moment I was living. In itself, removed from the time line that stretched forward and backward from the present, no single moment was that bad. Perhaps I was walking under a starry sky at 2 AM; forgetting that we'd already been on the move for five hours, and probably had another twelve to go, I could find pleasure in being exactly where I was, right then. Maybe because I was so tired it was easy to achieve an altered state of consciousness; with a little focus I was able to travel through the desert as though in a temporal bubble, totally immersed in the present, as though past and future no longer existed. It became something of a spiritual practice—the transcendence of suffering by meditating on "the now"—and I nearly signed on wholeheartedly to the clichéd mantra of "Live the moment." Then I realized that, while I spent half my time doing just that, I spent the other half of the time *escaping* the moment—distracting myself with mind games, reading while I rode—and that that was just as crucial to maintaining my sanity.

At times, when all else failed and I felt myself succumbing to exhaustion, doubting that I had it in me to reach the next camp, I'd gain strength by thinking about my grandmother.

She had grown up in Romania, and was sixteen years old when that country's fascist regime, complicit with the Nazis, ordered the deportation—or death—of the entire Jewish populations of Bessarabia and Bukovina in 1941. In many ways a trial run for the mass exterminations that followed in other parts of Europe, Jews were rounded up in towns and villages and sent east on forced marches into an area of Ukraine between the Dniester and Bug Rivers, known as Transnistria. Rather than leading the deportees directly to the Transnistrian camps, German and Romanian soldiers herded them in circuitous routes. My grandmother and her family marched, at the prodding of Nazi rifles, every day for more than two months. The roads were knee-deep in mud. Typhus raged unchecked through the convoys. No food was provided, so the Jews scavenged what they could from fields they passed or traded diamonds for onions with local peasants. Regardless of the weather, they slept in the open—and they were walking straight into the Ukrainian winter with little more than the summer clothes they had on their backs when they first left their homes. My grandmother's group only stopped when waist-high snowdrifts made further travel impossible. While some deportees were shot by the soldiers for lagging behind, most were simply left to die. Of the estimated 190,000 Jews who lived in the provinces of Bessarabia and Bukovina in the spring of 1941, some 65,000 died before ever crossing the River Dniester—some in orchestrated massacres, many more while in transit. Another seventy-five thousand perished on the roads and in the camps of Transnistria. If my grandmother could survive such a nightmarish trek as a teenage girl, I thought, surely I could meet any challenges this caravan posed.

Surprisingly, I wasn't always miserable. Though the tough times were barely bearable, at other times I felt energetic, even inspired. Without fail, sunrise filled me with new life, with relief, with humor. As the morning tea was made and we could see each other again, the azalai and I reveled in one another's company like men who'd been separated and spent a lonely night traversing some mythic Underworld. We talked and joked—once, spying a piece of wood that had fallen from another caravan, I went to pick it up. It would burn hotter and longer than dung. But little Ali snuck up behind me, trying to steal the prize for himself. We raced, and when I beat him, I held the fat stick over my head in triumph while everyone else hooted with laugher—except Ali.

Our eighth day out from Taoudenni was first day of the Muslim month of Shawwal—the holiday of Eid-al-Fitr, which marks the end of Ramadan. Being a time of great celebration across the Islamic world, during which prayers are offered, charity is given, families visit one another, and feasts are held, I wondered if the azalai would do anything special for it. Just because they hadn't observed the fast, I thought, was no reason not to take advantage of a good excuse to party. But the day passed just like all the others, as though there was nothing special about it.

Two nights later, we left camp at nine. After about four hours, Walid and I, whose camels were hitched together, veered away from the caravan, striking off from it an angle. At first I thought he wanted to give us a little bit more space, but the distance between us kept growing, so I asked what was going on.

"Araouane is this way," he said.

"Well, why are they going the other way? Don't they know the route?"

"Sure they do, but they aren't going through Araouane."

"What do you mean? Aren't we all traveling back to Timbuktu together?"

"No. They're not going to Timbuktu. They're going home first, and Araouane is out of their way." I wouldn't learn exactly why this was for two more days.

I was speechless. Parting ways with the caravan so suddenly, with no warning, was like having something stolen out of my hands. I couldn't believe that Walid hadn't mentioned anything about it in advance, and I prickled inside. But worst of all, I hadn't even had a chance to say good-bye to any of the azalai. I felt like something important had been left incomplete.

I was so thrown by the abrupt shift in my reality that I hardly realized how incredible it was that, in the middle of a pitch-dark featureless plain with even the stars obscured by haze, Walid had known when and in which direction to turn in order to lead us to Araouane.

After an hour or so of juggling a jumble of emotions, from anger to loss to anxiety, I let them all drop and left them behind me in the sand. I'd had an incredible experience with the azalai, and this shining truth easily burned off the disappointment of leaving them sooner than I'd expected. Besides, thanks to what the trials of caravan life had taught me, I knew in my bones, not just my brain, that there was little worth getting upset about as long as I was alive and well. And, though I didn't know it then, leaving the others would allow us to enter an entirely different, even more exotic kind of nomadic world.

Walid and I rode on and on, into what would be our longest day on the trail of the entire journey.

Dawn broke beautifully. The sun poured like molten brass between platinum-fingered clouds. The ivory sand was drenched with pinks and blues and yellows absorbed from the sky. I heard the twitter of a bird-song for the first time in weeks. The entire world seemed at peace with itself. And I was no exception. I felt clean inside, utterly content, and gave heartfelt thanks for all that I had in that moment, and in my life. It was an appropriate time to do so, since it was Thanksgiving morning.

Though I was half a world away from family and friends, nibbling on peanuts rather than gorging on turkey, riding forever on a camel rather than resting on a couch, I found myself in a more natural state of gratitude than I ever have when celebrating the holiday at home. With nothing but the essentials for survival, surrounded by nothing but desert, I felt like a rich man. I had my memories of Taoudenni, and of the azalai. I had a trusty camel beneath me. I was sharing the day with a man whose life and language were so different than my own, yet with whom the seeds of friendship had blossomed in the common ground of our humanity. Most of all, I was grateful that my body and mind had been able to adapt to the insane regimen of caravan life.

This attitude stayed with me throughout the day. I felt strong, like I'd crossed a threshold into a new level of endurance, where no amount of strain could break my body or my spirit. And it served me well: except for two brief stops for tea and dorno, we traveled on until sunset, a total of twenty-two hours on the march.

For the effort, we earned ourselves a full night of sleep, though for the reward I was really looking forward to, I'd have to wait one more day.

*Walid's brother-in-law pouring tea
at his family's camp.*

CHAPTER NINE

From a distance, it was so small it could have easily been over-looked, dwarfed into invisibility by the immensity of the desert that surrounded it. But its dark, blocky features stood out unnaturally against the rounded, rolling rhythm of the pale landscape, drawing the eye in its direction. Riding side by side, Walid and I aimed our camels straight for it.

It was just past noon when we arrived. We'd traveled for six hours that morning, over washboard ridges speckled with the very bushes that I'd mistaken for camels when we first began pursuing the northbound caravan, and on through the "good grazing grounds" where we'd first lost it. We ascended the slope that Walid, Baba, and I had once walked down to the clamor of blessings offered by the people of Araouane. Exactly three weeks had passed since then.

I reentered Araouane with a sense of quiet triumph. I felt like a knight returning successfully from a quest that had taken me deep into the fabled "Land of Terror." Weathered and dirty, the naïveté with which I'd left this place had long since been scoured from my face. Though I fantasized we might be welcomed by cheering crowds, there was no fanfare. Since it was midday, and hot, the town seemed empty. Walid and I slid from our camels and walked the last fifty yards to the same house where we'd rested on our way north.

As we couched Lachmar and L'beyya, the wooden door swung open and the children ran out to greet us, followed by their mother, Barka, and their uncle, Lamana, whom I'd last seen when he'd bid Walid and me a concerned farewell on the outskirts of Timbuktu. He hurried over to me, clamped both his hands over my right hand, and shook it vigorously. Relief radiated from his smiling face as he asked, *"Ça va?"*

"Ça va bien!" I answered, grinning back. *"Al-humdulillah!"* (Praise be to God!)

"Humdulillah," he replied. "All month long I've been worried about you. I've been waiting here in Araouane for the past few days, thinking you might have made it back a little earlier, and when you didn't come I thought maybe something was wrong. I'm very glad to see you."

I assured Lamana that I was glad to be there. He then went to Walid and welcomed him with equal enthusiasm, while I turned my attention to Barka and the kids. But we didn't waste much time on hellos. We had to unload the camels and water them before we could have tea.

Down at the well, Lachmar hauled water for L'beyya, then L'beyya for Lachmar, while Walid, Lamana, and I dumped the water from the goatskin buckets into the cement troughs. Lamana and Walid talked to each other rapidly in Arabic, most of which I couldn't understand. I watched in awe as the camels drank unbelievable amounts unbelievably quickly. Their sides swelled like they were sucking on an air hose. What would it be like, I wondered, to have your first drink of water in twelve days? In my own way, I was about to find out.

When Lachmar and L'beyya were so full I thought I'd be able to hear the water sloshing around inside them, we filled our inner tubes, and I gave my hands and face their first good rinsing in weeks.

Back at the house, Barka invited us to sit on the mats that covered the floor of fine, soft sand. The yellow walls brightened the diffuse light in the room that was cool as a cave. Hannah, the nine-year-old, carried in the charcoal-filled brazier, then the tea tray. I no longer felt like a stranger, as I had the first time I'd been here, less because I'd been here before than because I knew that this was Abdi's home, Abdi's family. And if he'd had his way, it would have been mine, too; all I would've had to do was accept the girl who brought the tea fixings as my prepubescent bride. Though nothing had been lacking from Barka's welcome three weeks ago, this time she was even warmer, for I'd spent time with—and had news from—her son. I gave her the letter Abdi had written to her, and handed Lamana his. They received them gratefully. Barka took hers back out to the inner courtyard, while Lamana read his in silence where we sat.

The tea was served, and while we drank I began peppering Lamana with questions about the caravan. I wanted to make sure I'd understood the things Walid had told me, and to ask questions that had been too complex for me to pose in Arabic. Sensing my urgency, he smiled and told me to relax—he'd be traveling back to Timbuktu with Walid and me, and there'd be plenty of time to talk on the trail. Even so, he couldn't wait to find out how I'd fared in the desert and how I'd liked the mines. He let out a loud "Eeeeeeee!" and broke into a chuckle when I told him about the bloody sores I'd acquired on the first few days of the trip; he seemed to expect as much. He translated what we were saying for Walid, and he, too, started laughing. "That was a long time ago," he said, sparking his pipe.

We talked like this for a few minutes, Walid telling Lamana about our experiences in Arabic and Lamana asking me about them in French. In the meantime, Abdi's father came in, offered a hearty welcome, and sat down to listen with interest. But our conversation was cut short when Barka and Hannah entered the room, each carrying a bowl of food.

Barka placed a large metal bowl amid the three men, while Hannah handed me a small one. Many times on the trail, as I'd suffered through meal after barely edible meal, I wistfully recalled the lunch that Barka had served when Walid, Baba, and I had rested at her house on our way north. The closer we got to Araouane on our return, the more vivid those memories became. I'd been looking forward to this moment for days.

This time Barka had prepared rice, topped with a slab of camel meat smothered in thick red gravy. Unlike what we'd bought at the mines, which was tough and foul, this camel meat was fresh, succulent, and plentiful. It fell apart at the gentlest touch and practically melted in my mouth. The rice itself seemed to be an altogether different grain than what I'd eaten for weeks on end, fluffier, lighter, and, best of all, sand-free. And tasting the gravy, I can say without exaggeration, was like falling head over heels in love after having given up all hope of ever loving again. It sent my mouth straight to Paradise after weeks of torment in gastronomic Hell. I praised Allah as my hands quickly traveled between the bowl and my mouth and back again. It was so good, so beautiful, tears welled in the corners of my eyes. I was too overwhelmed with emotion to care if the others saw me getting misty.

After lunch, Lamana said we'd leave in a couple of hours, and that he and Walid were going to visit friends in the meantime. He suggested I stay where I was, so I lay down on my mat, still in a state of bliss, and fell asleep.

. . .

When it was time to leave and Lachmar, L'beyya, and Lamana's two camels were loaded and ready to go, Lamana told me to take our animals and go with Abdi's younger brother, Salim, who would escort me to the edge of town. Lamana and Walid would catch up to us in a few minutes.

I placed the camels' lead over my shoulder and headed south with Salim, past the eroded adobe houses half submerged in sand. Walking by my side, his curly-haired head no higher than my chest, the hem of his white djellaba swaying just above his bare feet, Salim started in on me immediately.

"Give me your watch," he said in French.

"What?" I exclaimed, surprised and offended that a member of Abdi's family would demand things like Omar, or Najib before him.

"Give me your watch," he repeated. "I don't have one and I need one."

"You must be kidding," I said. "I'm not going to give you my watch."

"Then give me money."

"I'm not going to give you that, either."

"But you owe me."

"What are you talking about?"

"My brother showed you the mines at Taoudenni. You owe me money for that."

"I gave Abdi money before I left."

"How much?"

"Ten dollars."

"So give me ten dollars!"

"Forget it."

"Okay, give me five."

"No."

"But you ate at my house. You can't just eat and not pay."

"Walid has all the money for food," I said, fully aware that Barka wasn't running a restaurant anyway.

We plunged down the slope of soft sand that descended toward the open desert.

"What about the tourist tax?" Salim continued.

"What are you talking about?" I answered, beginning to get annoyed.

Salim pulled a few of what looked like small raffle tickets out of his pocket. "All tourists who come to Araouane have to pay a tax. You can pay me and I'll give you this receipt."

I didn't go for it. If there was a tourist tax, Walid should've had the money for that, too, but no one had said anything about it. Besides, I felt, perhaps a little egotistically, that I was no tourist. If tourists did have to pay a tax, let Salim collect it from someone who'd driven here in a Land Cruiser.

"I'm not going to give you any money," I said firmly, as though once and for all.

"Okay, then give me your watch."

I started laughing and Salim let loose with a rapid stream of invective in Arabic.

"Two can play that game," I said in English. "I can talk just as long in English as you talk in Arabic, and I don't even have to say anything bad about you because you wouldn't understand it even if I did."

Salim paused, taken off guard by the English. Then, with nothing to lose, he cursed me again.

When Walid scurried up from behind, Salim fell silent and pretended that he and I had been walking together amiably. Since he didn't ask for another thing, I knew that he knew he'd be in trouble if anyone heard him harassing a family friend. When Lamana joined us, we said good-bye to Salim. He turned back toward town, throwing a parting pout in my direction. The three of us, with our four camels, aimed for a saddle between two massive ramparts of sand in the distance.

In the basin below the saddle, we passed between clumps of tall grasses so large they could've covered a pitcher's mound. The eastern flanks of the dunes, lightly shrouded in shadows, looked like they were made of silver dust, while their sunny western sides glittered bright and white, like grains of opals. Long, thin ripples slithered up the slopes in rows, like an army of snakes carved in relief. Coming through the pass, an impressive camel caravan—easily as big as the one I'd traveled with—wended through the S-curve formed by the dunes' overlapping tails. It was led, among others, by Walid's brother. We said a quick hello, nothing more, since even though these were two brothers meeting in the desert after at least a month apart, the rules still applied to their caravan: No stopping.

We traveled on for another hour or so, under periwinkle skies flecked with small puffs of clouds flushed with sunset. Just before dark, we made camp, gathered dung, and lit a fire.

While dinner cooked, Lamana invited me to pose some of the questions I'd started to ask back in Araouane.

"Why did we split from the caravan north of Araouane? How come they didn't go with us to Timbuktu like I thought they would?" I asked.

"Ah, yes," Lamana began, doodling in the sand with his right index finger, as was his habit. "The caravan didn't go to Timbuktu because it was their first trip to the mines this season. After the first trip, the azalai go back to their camps or their home villages and drop their salt there, so they don't have to go so far south before going north again. They let their camels rest and graze for a month, then head back to Taoudenni. They carry the salt from the second trip all the way to Timbuktu, then head home and let their camels rest and graze again. If the rainy season is good and enough grass has grown, they'll go back to Taoudenni a third time; if it's a dry year, the caravans only make two trips. But in either case, the salt from the first trip is only brought to Timbuktu at the end of the season, once the caravans are done traveling to the mines."

Lamana translated what he'd said for Walid, who confirmed its accuracy with a single cluck from the back of his throat.

"And after the caravan season, the azalai return from the desert to tend their animals, yes?" I asked, to confirm what I'd gotten from Walid.

"Well, mostly," Lamana said. Then he clarified.

"Most azalai work the caravans, sell their salt in Timbuktu, then spend the rest of the year with their herds. Walid, however, now sells only some of his salt in Timbuktu. When the caravan season is over, he makes a few trips to Mopti, where salt prices are higher. He travels upriver by boat with his salt and some goats, and trades them for things like sacks of millet and rice, cases of tea, cloth, and other things that his family needs, then sails back with them to Timbuktu."

"He doesn't sell the salt for money?"

"Not Walid, not usually. Remember, he doesn't understand numbers well and can't grasp the difference between a thousand-CFA note and a ten-thousand-CFA note. It's all paper to him. But he understands well the size of a bag of millet and knows what it's worth in salt."

Of course he had to use cash for some things, and sometimes sold salt for money. Fortunately for Walid, most salt buyers were honest and wouldn't take advantage of his ignorance. Often, other people in his family took care of selling the salt for cash.

I told Lamana about the assumptions with which I had embarked on this journey, how I'd believed the caravans would soon become extinct, and wondered where that idea could have come from. Lamana shook his head and smiled. "Some journalists come here and drive around the desert in a four-by-four for a few days, ask a few people a few questions, and think they understand us. Most of them are nice people, very nice, but they don't understand. They want to get their story or their pictures, but they don't want to truly face the desert or don't have the time. And all we have out here is desert and time. Maybe they hear a little of this or a little of that . . . who knows where they get some of their ideas."

Walid spooned some rice, with slivers of dried goat meat he'd picked up in Araouane, onto my plate. I took a bite and said in Arabic, "Sorry, Walid, but you're no Barka."

"Eeeeee!" Lamana exclaimed, while Walid laughed. "It's true! But no one in the whole Sahara cooks like Barka!"

We woke just before sunrise and ate a leisurely Tuareg breakfast as the growing light erased the last traces of darkness from the western sky. Compared with traveling with the caravan, we were living the easy life. While we drank our tea, Lamana said that this day we would aim for the camp of Walid's nomadic in-laws, with whom Walid's wife and sons were staying. This was a completely unexpected bonus, and I was excited. On the trip north I'd itched to see what was going on inside the tents we'd passed, but never expected to have the opportunity; if we'd ridden with a caravan all the way to Timbuktu, we wouldn't have had the time.

Throughout the morning, we walked and rode up low ridges and down shallow valleys, as uniform as a stable wave pattern. White whale-backs of sand breached and plunged back into the earth. The camels deftly dipped their heads toward every bush we passed, grabbing what they could with their lips as we went by, as though they feared we'd soon be back in a land where nothing grew.

Despite all the sleep I'd had, I struggled to find the groove I'd perpetually been in, as though relaxing a little had thrown me out of it. Without the driving urgency of the caravan, I felt lazy, like my transmission was stuck in neutral and I couldn't get into gear. Lachmar, too, seemed to be working harder than usual; I had to constantly goad him into moving fast enough so L'beyya wasn't pulling him forward by his lower jaw, as foam oozed from his mouth and covered his lips before being peeled off by the breeze.

By noon, the terrain had flattened out into familiar monotony. Then, around three, I spotted the white peaks of three tents in the distance.

We rode along a sandy wash, a slight crease in the otherwise level ground. As we neared the tents, two young men came running from their direction, shouting and leaping in a jubilant welcome. Chattering excitedly, they ran alongside us until Walid and Lamana dismounted and I copied them. Still in the wash, Walid couched our camels and Lamana couched his, and they started unloading. We were about a hundred yards from the tents.

Maybe this wasn't Walid's in-laws' camp, I thought. Maybe these young men were friends of theirs, with whom we were going to stop and rest for an hour or so, before traveling on to our destination. The four nomads were talking without pause and I didn't feel like interrupting, so it wasn't until our blankets were spread in the sand and a tea fire was smoldering that I had the chance to ask Lamana, "What's going on?"

"We're here," Lamana said.

"How come we stopped so far away from the tents?" I asked, for this was clearly where we were camping.

"This is the way we do things," Lamana said. "It's a sign of respect. None of us, not even Walid, is allowed to approach the tents until after night falls. We have to wait here until it's dark before we can say hello."

"You mean Walid can't even see his wife now?"

"No, and she can't come see us. The same goes for her parents. Only his brothers-in-law and young children are allowed to visit with us now."

I couldn't believe that after weeks of absence, Walid would have to wait for hours, sitting out in the sand, before he could say hello to his wife or visit her family at their tents. In fact, everything about our arrival flew in the face of my prior experiences with nomadic peoples. Anytime I neared an encampment when I'd walked through Bedouin territory in Jordan, barefoot children scampered out into the desert to take my hands and lead me back to their tents, where tea had already been started for the arrival of a stranger. While trekking in Mongolia, there were days when I had to deliberately swing wide of the tents I encountered if I intended to cover any ground at all, since every time I approached one, its owners urged me to come in and rest, share salty-milky tea with them, and eat the many kinds of snacks they were always ready to serve. Here, however, not only was I close to a nomad tent but was with a member of the family, and protocol demanded that we keep our distance.

While we drank our tea, one of Walid's brothers-in-law, who had run back to the camp, now returned carrying a small child. Walid beamed as he took the boy in his arms and smothered his cheeks with gentle kisses. It was his youngest son, fifteen-month-old Ali. The little one smiled sweetly, soaking up his father's affection. His face was smooth and pudgy. Gobs of snot dribbled from his nostrils. The corners of his eyes were crusted with dried mucus. He wore a filthy green T-shirt and was bare-bottomed; a sensible alternative, it seemed, to putting him in diapers, when that would have simply created more work and it didn't really matter where he relieved himself. Ali's skin was a sickly-looking blue-gray color, making me wonder if something was wrong with him until I realized that it had simply absorbed some of the dark indigo dye from the robes his mother wore. The right half of his head was shaved down to the scalp, while the other half was lightly covered in wisps of brown hair. All of the little boys I'd meet at the camp had similarly bizarre hairstyles—one even had a Mohawk. Such haircuts are meant to fend off the evil eye, based on the reasoning that since the evil eye is drawn toward ruining things that are perfect, it would take one look at these kids' heads, decide they were already marred, and leave them alone. Parents hoped that this would keep their children healthy, and some continued to shave parts of their kids' heads until the age of twelve. Though it could, of course, be written off as primitive superstition, I understood why they did it; aside from having a grandmother from Romania who is always on alert against the evil eye, I could plainly see that there were no medical facilities for these nomads and I knew that the infant mortality rate was staggeringly high. They would try anything, even a haircut, to give their children an edge over death. More than I'd ever felt with the caravan, I sensed that I'd just slipped into a world of ritualized manners and mystical superstition, ruled by invisible forces.

Walid put Ali down on the ground, then dug around in his bag and pulled out a present that he'd carried all the way from Timbuktu. (I'm not sure why he didn't give it to Ali when he stopped at the camp for a night on the way north.) It was a new T-shirt and a pair of shorts, bright yellow with green trim. Walid stripped off Ali's dirty old shirt and pulled the new one over his head.

"Ah, Ronaldo!" Lamana exclaimed, recognizing the trademark colors of the Brazilian national soccer team.

"No, no, it's not Ronaldo," I said, pointing at the front of the shirt. What Lamana had failed to recognize was the patch that said THE HERO—SPIDERMAN, below an image of the friendly neighborhood web-slinger swinging into action.

I tried to explain who Spiderman was; remembering the conversation I had with Walid on one of our first days on the trail, I said he was a djinn, a good djinn, who had the powers of a spider and helped protect people from evil.

"That is good!" said Lamana. "Maybe he will protect Ali." Walid, too, was glad to hear it when Lamana translated what I'd told him.

Distressed over Ali's oozing eyes and knowing that I had eyedrops, Walid asked if he could borrow them. Since they were the kind that are supposed to be like natural tears, I figured they wouldn't hurt the kid, so I gave Walid the bottle. He rubbed the crust from his son's eyes, held the baby's head back, and squeezed in some drops. Ali, surprised, writhed and screamed. Walid comforted him for a minute, then passed him to his brother-in-law, who took the boy back to the camp.

The tea box that Lamana took from his bag was printed with a cartoon-like picture of three turbaned Arabs sitting happily around a fire in the desert, with two camels standing behind them. I picked it up and pointed at it, saying, "This one's Lamana, this is Walid, this is me, and here's Lachmar and L'beyya!" My friends laughed, and we spent the rest of the afternoon just like the guys on the box, brewing pot after pot of tea, simply enjoying being with each other. I felt completely at home.

Lamana told me that Walid wanted to stay here one more day, and asked how I felt about it. I remembered the regrets I'd had about my adventure in Mongolia, how I felt in hindsight that I'd hurried too quickly out of the Altai Mountains when I could've spent more time with its nomads. I didn't want to make the same mistake again, and realized I wasn't in a rush to get anywhere. There was nothing to gain by racing to Timbuktu, and there could be much to gain by spending another day here. I told him that I'd gladly stay.

We didn't have to cook dinner; a large pot of food was brought to us from the tents. It was filled with plain rice, without even the morsels of meat Walid and I usually ate on the trail, but I didn't mind. It was no worse than usual. Walid, however, seemed a little embarrassed by the humble offerings and said he thought that the next day we would eat like we were at Barka's house. His prediction was overly optimistic.

When darkness fell, Walid left to visit his family, his turban wound meticulously around his head and pulled high over his mouth and nose as a sign of respect. He returned in about half an hour and asked if I wanted to go with him up to the tents.

"Of course," I said, and asked if I, too, needed to cover my face.

"No," he said, "it's not so important," and, since his face was now exposed, I simply tied my turban over my head and under my chin, so I could pull it up over my mouth if it proved necessary.

I walked beside Walid, filled with curiosity and a touch of anxiety. Lamana had said that this family wasn't used to seeing foreigners, and I wondered how I'd be received.

The walls of the tent, each about twenty feet long, were pulled to the ground on three sides. The fourth was propped up with two sticks that were placed about a third of the way in from either of the corners, creating an opening about a yard high, like a gaping mouth. A heap of camel dung burned in a giant brazier just outside the tent. Its glow cast the only light by which to see; inside the tent it was almost completely dark, impossible to discern anything more than shadows.

As I ducked beneath the lip of the tent and offered a *"Salaam w'aleikum,"* the five women who were sitting inside instantly scattered toward the wall to my right, like a school of spooked fish darting for cover. Walid ushered me to the middle of the tent, and I sat down on a small mat that was laid over the sand. There was silence, pregnant with tension. Walid and I were the only men under the tent. I hoped he hadn't transgressed any taboos by inviting me in. Then one of the women started giggling. The others joined in, barely visible in their dark robes and head scarves in the darkness of the tent; it was like being laughed at by a chorus of tittering ghosts. I breathed with relief. Rather than making me uncomfortable, it helped me relax, for laughter is often the first sign of acceptance when stepping into the lives of very foreign people. And I'd been laughed at plenty of times before.

Gradually the women migrated back toward the center of the tent. After we exchanged the ritual greeting, they talked among themselves, and I listened, enjoying their soft, rolling phrases without trying to understand what they were saying, as though their voices were musical instruments. One of the women came over and sat right beside Walid. The two of them talked in intimate tones, and the woman's voice was beautiful. Obviously, I thought, this had to be his wife. I strained to see what she looked like, but it was futile, until one of the other women dumped more dung on the fire, causing it to flare up for a minute. Gazing upon her in the dancing orange light, I could hardly believe my eyes. Her skin was shriveled like a raisin, her nose was long and hooked, her teeth were ajumble—the front two hung down over her lower lip even when her mouth was closed. Knowing that Walid's wife was in her early twenties, I thought she'd perhaps been stricken with some kind of premature aging disease. Though I knew it was unkind, I couldn't help feeling a bit horrified that Walid—young, strong, and good looking—was married to such a hag. Maybe the light was playing tricks on my eyes, I allowed, or maybe he was so kindhearted that he loved her despite her looks. It wasn't until the next morning that I learned this was actually his mother-in-law, and not his wife at all.

After we drank tea, Walid rose and said it was time for us to return to our camp. We said good night and walked back to the sandy wash. Though I hadn't really interacted much with the women, they'd become accustomed to my presence, which was accomplishment enough for one evening.

By the time Lamana, Walid, and I had finished our morning tea and wandered over to the tents, a goat had been slaughtered. It was lying, skinned and beheaded, on a pile of long dried grasses that had been spread in a modest attempt to keep the meat off the sand, which would stick to it the way the diamonds stuck to the carcasses thrown into the Valley of Serpents in the Sindbad story. The older of Walid's two brothers-in-law, named Mohammed, had the sleeves of his green boubou rolled up to his elbows as he deftly gutted the animal, slicing out the organs and placing them neatly to the side. A big metal cauldron filled with water was sitting atop a mountain of smoldering dung.

I said hello to everyone and was quickly put at ease by the casual manner in which I was welcomed. The women met my eyes with no trace of timidity, and Mohammed happily let me take pictures of him butchering the goat. Aside from Lamana, Walid, and myself, there were fifteen people at the camp: Walid's two brothers-in-law, his two sons and four nephews, his mother-in-law and father-in-law, his wife, and her four sisters. Only one of Walid's little nephews, who was about a year and a half old, seemed unduly perplexed by me. He'd been crawling around in the sand in just a red-and-white-striped T-shirt and a necklace strung with three protective amulets slung across his chest, when he first noticed me. He froze and stared, his mouth agape, unsure whether I was friend or foe. He had never seen a foreigner before. Trying to assuage his confusion and convince him I was a normal human being, I knelt down a few feet from him, said hi, and smiled. He screamed and started crying, scrambling toward his mother who knelt ten yards away, where she'd begun to pray. He grabbed at her arms, pulling little fistfuls of cloth, then threw himself down beside her, wailing. She would not be distracted from her devotions, however, and continued to pray, her eyes fixed to an invisible point in the distance as her child writhed in the sand and clutched at her robe. When she was finished she picked him up and, not the least bit perturbed, sat him on her lap and held him. He quieted quickly and she gave me an amused smile, wordlessly communicating that kids would be kids.

Looking at pictures of myself that were taken that day, I could see why—aside from just being a Stranger—I might have scared him. My beard was overgrown and unkempt, my forehead and cheeks were browned from sun and dirt, while the area around my eyes—which my sunglasses normally covered—was starkly white in contrast. My lips were chapped, my fingers, and especially my toes, were riddled with cracks and calluses. I looked like the human expression of the wilderness in which I'd been immersed for a solid month.

Walid introduced me to his wife, whose name was Feti. Her intense eyes were as black as ravens, her demeanor friendly but meek. The resemblance she bore to all the women in her family resided in her mouth—well-defined lips and large, widely spaced teeth. Like her sisters and her mother, Feti's indigo head scarf covered her hair, but none of her face. By her side was Walid's other son, Karim, who was nearly three. He was a beautiful child with bronze skin, long eyelashes, and a habit of pursing his lips into an angelic little smile.

In the light, I was able to get my first good look at the tent. The fabric was composed of many long, narrow strips of heavy, woven cotton cloth, stitched together. Patches of the same material were sewn over numerous holes. The peaked center was propped up by two long wooden poles, pitched at steep opposing angles, sheathed in metal sleeves, and held in place by the pressure of the roof. Along one side was stacked a wall of rice sacks, oil jugs, pots, bowls, gourds, and a battered metal tool box. These were partially covered by a wool blanket and a sky-blue sheet embroidered with pink and yellow flowers. The corners and sides of the tent were staked out with handmade grass ropes tied to wooden rods that had been pounded into the sand. There was no floor, just a few mats, rugs, and pillows.

When it was time to move to a new pasture, I learned, a couple of the men would take off into the desert and scout out a camp, then return to get the rest of the family. The tents would be broken down and all the family's belongings would be loaded onto camels and taken to the new site. They might stay in one place for as little as a week or for longer than a month, depending on the amount of grass in the area. I asked Lamana if there were ever any disputes between families, if one felt that another had camped too close and encroached upon their territory.

"Not really," he said. "Everyone knows that the herds need a certain amount of space to graze, so no one wants to camp too close to anyone else. It's like an unwritten law enforced by the desert, because only so much grass grows in one place. If it turns out that a family mistakenly camps too near to another one, the problem is resolved peacefully and the newer family moves on."

"Do families go to the same places year after year?" I asked.

"It depends on the year. You travel as little as you have to, but some years that's farther than others. And you never camp in exactly the same place twice."

"Why?"

"Because the djinn know that you have been there, and will wait for you to come back."

I remembered that the Tuareg call certain evil spirits the Kel Essuf, one meaning of which is "the people of nostalgia," and I thought I understood why they wouldn't camp in the same place twice.

. . .

The goat's organs were rinsed and dumped into the pot of boiling water, and the carcass was dismembered. Some of the meat was added to the pot, some would be roasted over the fire, and some was hung up to dry. The head was thrown directly into the coals, where it started smoking as the hair began to singe.

Though the sky was overcast, the air chilly, it felt like a lazy Sunday morning, with the whole family hanging around, waiting for the goat to cook. The morning's work was finished: The women had already led the goats out to pasture, the men had taken out the camels. Nothing else had to be done until the afternoon.

When the stew was nearly finished, Lamana and Walid told me we should go back to our own camp. Walid's younger brother-in-law, Hasan, who was eighteen, with short curly brown hair and faint traces of a mustache, came with us. When we were settled on our blankets, we were joined by Walid's father-in-law, whom I hadn't yet met. He appeared to be a few years older than Lamana, and carried himself with the distinction befitting a patriarch.

He took a seat beside me and pulled his antelope-horn pipe from within the folds of his boubou. Walid passed over the knotted cloth in which he carried his tobacco, his father-in-law packed the pipe and asked for a lighter. I handed him mine; he sparked up and moved to pass it back, but I told him he could keep it. He thanked me, and examined the lighter, asking where the opening was to refill it.

"There is none," I said. "When it's finished you throw it away."

He looked at me like this was the dumbest thing he'd ever heard of.

"It's American," I said, as though this would exonerate the lighter's deficiency. He shook his head. If he'd been under the illusion that American culture was something to aspire to, the lighter gave him second thoughts.

He asked me about the trip to Taoudenni, which he said he'd made many times as a young man. I felt like he accepted me easily, and though he thought it was a little crazy that I rode with a caravan when I didn't have to, he respected the fact that I did.

Mohammed walked over to us, a large, steaming bowl of offal in his hands. My companions perked up, poised to pounce upon the parts. Once a plate was dished out for me, they plunged their hands into the bowl. I'd been given a smattering of everything—some heart, some lung, a healthy portion of intestine, and a few pieces of the dreaded stomach lining. I was also given what was either the prize or the joke of the meal—I couldn't tell—but as I chewed it, no amount of pretending it was something else could erase the knowledge that I was eating boiled goat's penis. For propriety's sake, I acted like I enjoyed it and felt compelled to clean my plate.

While we drank tea afterward, I asked Lamana why we were eating separately from the women.

"Oh, they have something that they need to do," he said.

"What?" I asked.

Lamana cracked a smile.

"Do you know why they killed this goat today?" he asked.

"Well, I figured it was to celebrate Walid's safe return from the mines, or maybe because I'm here."

"No, no, it's neither of those things," Lamana said. "Feti is pregnant, and is almost ready to have the baby. Eating the goat will make her give birth. When we do something like this, the women eat alone."

"Oh," was all I could say. I never would have guessed that Feti was pregnant, though it was hard to tell how big she really was under her loose-fitting gown. I wondered how eating fresh goat could possibly induce the birth of a child. Though I felt certain it was an old wives' tale, I wanted to believe it and wondered if maybe, just maybe, it would work.

Once the meal was done, we were all free to mingle together again, and Walid and I went back over to the tents. Lamana saddled up one of his camels and left to visit a relative who was camped about an hour away. Mohammed and Walid's father-in-law slung some empty guerbas over one of their camels, and led it and a few others off to a well a few miles distant. They'd asked if I wanted to join them but, figuring I'd get enough riding in over the next few days, I opted to stay at the camp.

A midday lull fell over those of us who remained. Walid and I lay down in the tent. He fell asleep instantly, while I watched Hasan fiddle around with a broken cassette player, trying to fix it with the same knife that had been used to eviscerate the goat. The faint bleating of goats floated in from the distance, sounding remarkably like a nursery of crying babies. One white goat with a black spot over its left eye foraged around the inside of the tent, nibbling on its walls. It seemed like the family pet, at least temporarily. I asked myself how I'd like to live as this family did, and surprised myself with my answer. When I'd spent time in Bedouin tents around Wadi Rumm, where Lawrence of Arabia had trod some eighty years earlier, I was tempted to move there and adopt their ways as my own, certain I'd find contentment in herding goats and camels, traveling from watering hole to watering hole, fathering a tentful of rambunctious children. A simple existence, lived outdoors, on the move. Though there were many similarities between their lifestyles, I felt no attraction to the vision of living like a Saharan nomad. Something about their situation seemed harder, sparser than that of the Bedouin of Rumm. Maybe, I thought, I had this perspective because I'd already spent a month in the sand, in the wind, eating terrible food, and moving daily with no comforts but tea. Maybe the Bedouin life would've looked the same had I been among them longer. But the truth, I thought, lay somewhere else. Wadi Rumm was one of the most spectacular places I'd ever been—a sandstone wonderland of massive multicolored cliffs, delicately carved by the wind, bursting skyward from salmon-colored dunes. I wandered through it agasp, in a mind-altered state of awe. Every vista inspired feelings nothing short of religious, seemingly confirming the existence not just of a God, but of God as an artist. The tent in which I reflected upon this, in contrast, was pitched in an aesthetic black hole, surrounded by nothingness. I think it was the absence of beauty that made life here appear so much harder than life in Rumm.

Walid's mother-in-law was a model of nomad hospitality, gracious and kind, yet tough, and easily able to hold her own against any matriarch in the world when it came to making sure you ate your fill. Moments after I awoke from my nap, she brought me a bowl of camel's milk and urged me to drink it "for strength." When I finished it, she served me a bowl of bread soaked in milk and sprinkled with sugar. Its soggy sweetness reminded me a little bit of the matzah brai—essentially French toast made with matzah—that my grandmother used to make during Passover, but I refrained from mentioning this, figuring the reference would be lost and still not daring to reveal to anyone that I was Jewish. While with the caravan, it wasn't such a stretch to imagine that Omar might have spouted some anti-Semitic invective in the moments when he tried to make me uncomfortable, but I had little fear of that happening among Walid's family. I just didn't want to take any chances. In hindsight, I realize I may have missed an opportunity to bridge a perceived cultural gap, and I regret it, but in the moment it felt wiser not to invite the risk, however small.

I admired the small goatskin pouch that the sugar was kept in. Softened from years of use, it was shaped like the bottom half of an hourglass and decorated with leather fringes and a faded geometric design. Walid saw me looking at it and, with a nod to his mother-in-law, said, "She made it."

"It's beautiful," I told her.

"It's yours," she said.

I protested weakly, mostly to let her know that I hadn't been asking for it and certainly didn't expect her to give it to me. With a dismissive wave of her gnarled hand, she said it was nothing, that I should take it. I thanked her and felt lucky. Along with the salt Abdi had given me, the little bag would be another prized memento from a place where there were no souvenirs to buy.

By late afternoon, the men had returned from the well. The clouds began to fray and sunlight rushed between them as though being released from a dam. Tea was brewed, and everyone sat together by the tent's opening. Men and women joked and argued with each other as intensely as only family can. Walid's older son, Karim, busied himself mashing buttons on the broken tape player. One of the other kids toddled over with the charred goat's head in his hands and plopped down in the sand to play with it. His younger cousin—my friend in the red-and-white shirt—wanted to get in on the action. They batted the blackened head around, pulled on its nose and ears, and rolled it back and forth between them like a ball. When the little one decided he'd had enough of sharing, he tried to claim it for himself. The older one protested loudly and the two tussled over their toy, shoving each other while the head lay between them in the sand. The adults watched and laughed. I laughed, too, but only partly at the kids; I couldn't help imagining the expressions on the faces of people I knew back home who had young children, had they seen these two babies playing with a severed goat's head. Somehow I doubted this toy would make its way into the Fisher-Price catalog anytime soon.

As the sun began to set, everyone rose. The women, except for one of Feti's sisters, who stayed with the children, walked into the desert to round up the goats they'd set out to pasture that morning. The men went out to bring in the camels. Walid and I went back to our camp, where we stayed for the rest of the night. On our way back, I watched Feti seemingly glide over the sand in a long flowing robe that billowed in the breeze. I wondered how long it would take for the goat meat to do its job, or if it would at all.

Feti gave birth to a baby girl that very night. When I heard the news the next morning, I could hardly believe it. I began to imagine hospitals back home offering plates of goat guts as a natural alternative to labor-inducing drugs. Though I would have liked to see how babies were delivered by these desert people, not even Walid was invited into the tent. It was strictly a women's affair, which was the way Walid liked it. When I told him that American husbands were often with their wives when they gave birth, his face cringed in disgust. He couldn't believe that any man would want to witness such an event, or that any woman would want a man around.

"Today I'm glad I'm not American!" he exclaimed, and he was only half joking.

Nearly as astonishing to me as the fact that the goat meat had worked was what I saw while we prepared the morning tea, just before sunrise. Walking across the sand, leading her goats out to pasture, was Feti. It was no more than four hours after she'd given birth.

A camel scratching himself on a bar of salt

CHAPTER TEN

magining that any father would be reluctant to leave a newborn daughter and the mother who'd just birthed her, I told Walid it was okay with me if he stayed with them. I could go back to Timbuktu with Lamana. Walid, however, dismissed my offer without hesitation, saying he wanted to go with us. Lamana explained that, according to custom, Walid wasn't permitted to hold the baby for two weeks, until the naming ceremony took place. Newborns, he said, weren't thought of as real people until they'd survived their tenuous first days, and prohibiting fathers from holding them made an early death easier for them to accept. What's more, though Walid could talk to Feti during the day, he couldn't sleep in the same tent as her for forty days after the birth. By going to Timbuktu, Lamana continued, Walid wouldn't be missing much, and it would give him a chance to pick up a few things in town.

After tea, we packed up and moseyed through the camp on our way south. Our good-byes with the family were brief and casual, little more than a handshake and a "thank you," as though we'd be returning in a few hours. For nomads, saying good-bye was too commonplace an event to make a fuss over.

I felt rested and somehow more complete, as though getting an unexpected glimpse into the life of a nomadic family filled a gap in my experience that I didn't realize existed until after I'd done so. I was recharged and ready to take on the last leg to Timbuktu, which seemed like it'd be a quick jaunt across the sand, not counting on the illness and injury that awaited me.

The morning was cloudy once again. A brisk wind swept across the desert. Before long, the sparse pasturelands dotted with clumps of grass gave way to bare, lifeless sand. As we traversed the open flats, I asked Lamana and Walid more questions about Saharan life. Since it seemed that families spent so much time isolated with their herds, I wondered how men and women met, and marriages were formed. There obviously wasn't much of a Saharan singles scene.

Though they usually lived far apart, Lamana said, nomadic families often knew one another, if not personally then at least by reputation. It was unusual, he said, to run into a complete stranger—if you didn't know them, then you knew someone who knew them. In this part of the Sahara, there were far fewer than six degrees of separation. Matches were made through these family connections, with parents negotiating on behalf of their children. As often as not, future husbands and wives became engaged before they'd ever met each other in person.

The parents of the eligible bachelor, who is often a teenager at the time, suggest a bride to him, touting her beauty, her ability to cook, or the number of livestock her family owns. If he agrees to the match, his parents then make a marriage offer to the girl's parents, explaining why the union of their children would benefit the couple as well as the families. If her parents approve, they present the choice to their daughter, who has ultimate veto power over the whole affair—and, if she lived in the United States, would most likely be in elementary school.

Assuming the girl consents, Lamana continued, an engagement contract is drawn up setting the wedding for sometime after the girl turns thirteen. The boy's father seals the deal by giving a token offering of about two dollars to the girl's father. The betrothed children might not see each other until the wedding day.

When the time comes, the groom's family goes to the camp of the bride's family for the wedding feast, where people sing, drum, dance, and eat. The groom presents the bride with an even number of blankets, scarves, dresses, and the like; for example, depending on his wealth, he might give her two or four or ten blankets. At the end of the evening, the newlyweds retire to a tent to consummate the marriage. In the morning, their bedsheet is checked for bloodstains, though, Lamana said, a couple will sometimes take a cup of goat's blood to their tent to ensure they pass the ritual test. For the first month of their married life, the couple stays at the wife's family's camp; she sleeps in the husband's tent at night, then returns to her parents in the morning. When the month is over, the couple heads to the husband's family's camp, where they spend the next four weeks. When they get there, the husband sends a young female camel—or, if he's poor, a goat—back to his wife's father. In the days before the Great Drought of 1973–74, Lamana said, many more camels and goats were exchanged, but when families lost their herds, expectations were lowered.

When the second month of marriage is over, there are no hard-and-fast rules; often the couple returns to the wife's family, though sometimes they remain with the husband's. The wife is given a dowry of goats, sheep, and a tent—her share of her inheritance—by her father, which becomes her property.

Little of what Lamana told me—except the part about the cup of goat's blood—surprised me, since it was similar to what I'd learned about marriage in other parts of the Muslim world. Unlike other places I'd been, however, the Saharan system survives uncomplicated by some of the dilemmas that arise when traditional customs conflict with contemporary conventions.

One of the brothers in the family I had lived with in Cairo, named Yehieh, was engaged to a woman he had met only once. He was excited about his upcoming wedding, but before the day arrived, problems arose. Yehieh, though no Islamic extremist, was a man of traditional sensibilities, best illustrated by the startling fact that, though he was in his early thirties, attractive, and successful, he had never kissed a woman in his life, so strongly did he feel about staying sexually pure for marriage. His fiancée, while no radical secularist, was a student at a university. As the wedding approached, Yehieh urged his fiancée to drop out of school—for, he argued, how could she tend to her wifely duties if she was in school, and what purpose would graduating serve if she was going to get married? It's not like she would ever put her education to use. To his dismay, his fiancée insisted on completing her degree.

The families negotiated, and Yehieh finally agreed to allow his fiancée to attend classes twice a week. She wanted to continue her studies full time, however, and refused to compromise. Finally, the engagement was annulled, and the ten-thousand-Egyptian-pound bride price (about three thousand dollars at that time) that Yehieh had paid to his fiancée's father was refunded—because *she* was to blame.

Initially, I judged Yehieh to be a small-minded chauvinist, but I came to see the wisdom of his decision. He was a traditional guy who wanted a traditional wife. A union with his ex-fiancée would have produced unhappiness for both. Yehieh didn't condemn her as being immoral, just as a poor fit for himself. Better, he thought, to begin a new search for a more suitable partner.

Such dilemmas, which are becoming ever more common in the modern Muslim world, have hardly touched the nomads of the Sahara, since there are so few alternatives to life as it's always been lived. The closest comparison I could imagine would be if Abdi's sister Hannah, who so desperately wanted out of Araouane, insisted on only marrying a man who would whisk her away to the good life in Timbuktu.

Walid and Lamana wanted to know what marriage was like in America, so I explained some of the biggest differences, such as how men and women in the States usually get to know each other very well, often living together for a long period of time, before deciding to wed. I told them that most people had quite a few boyfriends and girlfriends before settling on the one with whom they'd spend the rest of their lives, which usually didn't happen until people were well into their twenties, thirties, or later. And, of course, we could only have one spouse at a time.

"So you can have many girlfriends, but we can have up to four wives," Lamana said, his tone implying that he thought they had the better of the deals. Having been married and divorced while in my twenties, I respectfully disagreed. One wife at one time, lovely as she was, had been plenty.

Walid and Lamana absorbed what I told them about American courtship habits without passing judgment, even when we talked about the potentially touchy subject of premarital sex. Though at other times, in other Islamic places, I'd been scolded about the immorality of our more liberal ways (even while I sensed a touch of envy behind it), Walid and Lamana were curious without being critical.

When it was time to mount up, I was urged to ride Lamana's spare camel instead of Lachmar, who was visibly tired. I hesitated. I'd bonded deeply with Lachmar, at least in my own mind, if not in his. We'd been through a lot together; I trusted him and knew his idiosynchracies. But, despite any fantasies I might have had about us being like the Lone Ranger and Silver, I knew that Lachmar himself would be more grateful than insulted if I got off his back for a while. I put my exaggerated sense of attachment aside and went over to Lamana's extra camel.

"What's his name?" I asked.

"Mabrouk."

"What does that mean?"

"Something like 'good journey.'"

Mabrouk was taller and stockier than Lachmar, though somewhat less attractive, with cruder features and a grayish coat. He was powerful and sure-footed, and his larger hump made a roomier seat. I could tell the difference between the two camels after only a few steps; it was like trading in an old VW bus for a brand-new SUV.

We rode through the day at a good pace, without stopping, and made camp just before sunset. Traveling a mere eleven hours was like being on vacation. As I gathered dung, the broken clouds of the mackerel sky blazed with fiery reds and pinks while the streaks of cirrus farther to the west looked like a golden horse's mane blowing in the wind. The sky behind the clouds was a penetrating, incandescent blue that faded to indigo and black before my eyes. The light show more than compensated for a day of scenic ennui. Dinner was fortified with a hearty helping of the goat that had been killed the day before.

Since we'd talked about birth and marriage, I asked Lamana what nomads do when someone dies. He said that Koranic prayers are recited, then the corpse perfumed, covered in a shroud, and buried in the sand.

"Is the place marked with a stone or anything?" I asked.

"No. But we remember. And that's not so important anyway, since once someone dies, if they've been righteous, they join Allah in Paradise and leave their body behind. We know where *they* are even after the body disintegrates."

Their ritual struck me as elegant in its simplicity and lack of sentimentality.

My companions asked if our practices were the same in America, and I laughed and shook my head. I explained that, typically, a dead person was buried in an expensive, cushioned box, dressed in his or her finest clothes. Sometimes, I said, the corpses were made up to look like they were still alive. Lamana and Walid couldn't comprehend the reasoning behind any of this. They thought that putting cosmetics on a corpse was ridiculous, and were flabbergasted that people would spend more money on a fancy box than many Malians earn in years, only to bury it in the ground.

"Can you dig the box up and use it again, once the body decomposes?" Walid asked. This, he suggested, would make a little more sense.

I was wakened in the dark by an urgency in my stomach. I got up, fast, and hustled barefoot across the cold sand as far from camp as I could before dropping my pants and squatting. Back in my blanket, just as I was about to fall asleep, I felt it coming on again. Again, I hurried off, clenching, until I could clench no longer. Time after time, into the dawn, long after I believed my body must've expelled every last bit of food that was in it, I was forced to rise and relieve myself without delay. By the time Walid and Lamana got up, I was dizzy and lethargic, and still making trips away from camp.

I packed my bag slowly, putting each item in with effort. Determined to do my share of the work, I went to load the camels. Seeing I was struggling, Lamana came over to help me lift the heaviest bag. While we hefted it together, he slipped and quickly moved to regain his balance, smashing his heel down, hard, on two of my middle toes. I yanked my foot back and stumbled away in agony. As I recovered my composure, I tested my foot. I couldn't put any weight on it at all without buckling from the pain. I was sure the toes were broken. Lamana was profusely apologetic, and I told him it was okay, that I was fine, but it'd probably be better for me to ride than to walk out of camp as we usually did. Then, just before mounting up, I felt that telltale watering in my mouth and hopped a few feet away. I knelt in the sand and vomited up two chunks of solid goat fat, each about the size of a marshmallow. Unable to chew them, I'd managed to swallow them whole the night before, and had obviously been unable to digest them. I hoped that with the poison out of my system, I'd start to recover.

I was weak and light-headed. Timbuktu, which just hours before seemed to be only a few quick days down the trail, now felt very, very far away. Remembering how Gordon Laing had been strapped to his camel after being attacked his Tuareg assailants, I felt I had little to complain about in comparison; I also realized that he was about as extreme a baseline as I could possibly refer to. I rode on in a daze, watching the desert pass as though through a steamy window, grateful, at least, that the Imodium had started to work.

Before long, we came upon the first tree, where Walid, Sali, Anselm, and I had stopped to gather one last bundle of firewood on the way north. Ahead of us loomed the edge of the illusory forest—the miles' worth of sparsely scattered trees that looked like a dense wood, thanks to a total lack of depth perception.

We rode until we reached the well at Harseini, where the boy had been sent down after the lost bucket weeks earlier. Since we didn't have a bucket of our own, we had to wait about half an hour for someone else to arrive. I was thankful for the rest, and forced myself to drink some of the dorno Lamana mixed up, trying to rehydrate myself. I inspected my toes, which were swollen and tender, then lay down in the sand, my face covered by my turban, hoping to gather some strength for the rest of the ride. I was nudged awake by Walid once our guerbas were full and it was time to move on. I wobbled as I climbed atop Mabrouk, and braced myself to face the miles ahead.

As we traveled on under a seething sun, the hours melted into one another. Having practiced it countless times before on this trip, I disconnected my brain from my body and rode as though outside of myself. We camped a few hundred yards past the big well at Douaya, just after dark. As though triggering an ingrained Pavlovian response, when the sun went down, my energy level and optimism suddenly rose. I felt my pluck returning, not fully, but enough so I knew that I was conclusively on the mend. Though still a little shaky, I could think straight and laugh again.

By morning, I felt like myself, except for my toes. I taped the injured two together, using them to splint each other and buffer them somewhat from impact, which allowed me to walk without hobbling too much. I'd years ago trained myself to ignore severe foot pain, so I used that ability to push through and forget about it.

We were south of Douaya. Timbuktu was in striking range. If we traveled as many hours as we did on a typical day with the caravan, we could sleep in town this very night.

The thought stunned me. I can't say it made me happy, or even relieved. I didn't really know how to feel about it. Rather than thinking about *how* my life would be different once we arrived in Timbuktu, I was swamped only with a deeply emotional recognition that my reality was about to drastically change. Though I'd only been in the desert for five weeks, they were some of the most intense weeks of my life. The daily experience of facing the Sahara had been so completely consuming, had demanded the total investment of all my physical and mental resources, that leaving it would be like leaving the self I'd become, and become familiar with. Contemplating this impending, radical shift left me disoriented and a touch nostalgic—less for the specifics of the life I'd led than with the vague but overpowering sense that I was leaving what had become home, even if it had been a hard place to live.

Traveling back across the landscape I had first traversed on only my second day in the desert, I realized just how accustomed I'd grown to life in the Sahara. The gently sloped landscape, lightly dusted with grass, speckled with thorn trees, seemed downright lush after the sheer desolation my eyes had grown used to. Herds of camels and goats browsed their way slowly across the range that now appeared rich with fodder. Tents were pitched in shallow basins and on open plains, still widely spaced but with greater frequency, giving me the feeling that this was a densely populated place. And why wouldn't it be? I now knew that this particular piece of desert was a relatively easy one in which to dwell.

I recalled how I felt the first time I'd crossed this terrain. I was battling that sinus infection, had an aching back and raw sores on my ass, thought the heat might drive me insane, and was dismissed as useless by Walid. I smiled with knowing empathy at the vision of myself struggling along, as though that greenhorn I remembered wasn't even me.

I thought back to why I had come to the Sahara in the first place: to get a glimpse of an age-old culture reported to be on the brink of extinction. What I had gotten instead was something that felt far more valuable: a glimpse into an age-old culture that had successfully assimilated some features of the modern world—most notably, trucks—without sacrificing its traditional way of life.

Though I couldn't deny being glad that the salt caravans were alive and well, this feeling was accompanied by a twinge of compunction. In order for the caravans to survive, there have to be men to drive the camels and dig the salt. I had the uneasy sense that cheering the caravan's survival implied, by logical necessity, that I was glad that men have to endure the hardship inseparable from it. But that wasn't the case.

It would have been one thing if the azalai and the miners loved their jobs despite their superhuman demands, and while I imagine that some azalai are fiercely attached to their lifestyles, most of the ones I met didn't seem to be. Walid was actively trying to work less as an azalai and more as a guide, and if he had his way, he'd be sitting in Timbuktu behind the counter of a boutique. He dreamed of sending his son to me, in the United States, so he could learn English and live an easier life. Lamana had already traded his career as an azalai for that of a full-time guide. Abdi certainly didn't want to return to the salt mines year after arduous year. Even his sister Hannah, who didn't have to trek to Taoudenni or cut salt, craved a change, praying she could one day escape the isolation of Araouane. None of them was sentimental over the prospect of leaving behind the lives they've known. The latent threat to the salt trade is not the introduction of trucks, but future possibilities for education, economic development, and social mobility in the Sahara.

I wanted Walid to have his boutique, for his sons to have opportunities, for Abdi to leave the mines and become a guide, for Hannah to move to Timbuktu. How could I ask other people to live lives that I would never choose for myself, nor they for themselves? Yet at the same time, I wanted the caravans to continue operating forever. I felt that their ultimate demise would be a tragic loss to the world.

As the tentacles of globalization creep toward the ends of the civilized earth, the life is being squeezed out of traditional cultures with startling speed. In many regions, environmental devastation—whether the razing of rain forests in South America and Sumatra or the flooding of farmland behind dams in China—has bulldozed cultures dependent upon their land into oblivion. In other places, people have been understandably lured from indigenous ways by the conveniences and comforts of the modern world, as could become the case in the Sahara. One way to gauge the pace of cultural dissolution is to look at trends in language; since a culture's essential ideas are inextricably bound to the language that expresses them—through story, prayer, or the naming of things in the natural world—the death of a language often heralds the death of a culture. Today half of the nearly six thousand languages spoken around the world are no longer taught to children; they'll die along with the elders who speak them. Only 10 percent of the world's languages are said to be "stable and secure." Though there may not be an exact correlation between loss of language and loss of culture, the overwhelming trend toward more people speaking the same tongues is a powerful example of one way in which humanity is becoming undeniably more homogeneous.

Thinking about this as I rode, I was torn about declaring outright that the loss of cultural diversity is an objectively bad thing (though I have an easier time saying that about the environmental destruction that often contributes to it). Perhaps, my mind said, the disappearance of civilizations and the trajectory toward homogeneity are part of the natural course of human evolution. If so, I wondered, what is the nature of that evolution? Is there an inherent telos, a subconscious wisdom, maybe even a divine plan, to the path we're on? Is there something good for humanity in becoming less diverse? Might speaking fewer languages help increase cross-cultural understanding? Are we fulfilling our role in some bigger drama by rushing toward the edge of the cliff of total environmental catastrophe—and will we plunge over that edge, taking plenty of other species with us, or will we save ourselves, and the planet, in the nick of time, catapulting ourselves to a new level of awareness? It's all possible. Of course it's just as likely, I reasoned, that our current course toward ecological devastation and cultural eradication is inspired by something far less grand: the collective illness of the modernized world that, so far removed from nature, has lost the innate instinct for survival and is swallowing everything up as it gorges itself to death. I didn't know.

What I did know is that when I imagined the world without camel caravans and all the other age-old practices, rituals, styles of dress, music and dance, as well as forms of housing, fishing, hunting, traveling, and planting that still exist in the less modernized nooks of the globe, the planet looked like a much poorer, more boring place. Each civilization is like a unique color woven into the complex tapestry of human expression and ingenuity that dazzles with its variety of belief, knowledge, and possibility. Many of them inspire wonder and awe, not just because people *could* or *did* live and think in ways so foreign from our own, but because they *do* live in those ways, now, in the twenty-first century—and because they are not aliens from another world, but humans who live on ours. In other words, as different as their cultures are, they are like us. This allows us to imagine *ourselves* in hues and textures that transcend the limited palette offered by our own culture, to recognize that there is more to being human than buying precut meat at the grocery store, marrying someone over the age of eighteen, and using electrical appliances. As these to-our-eyes-exotic civilizations vanish one by one, the human tapestry becomes more monochromatic, more bland. Humanity as a whole becomes less beautiful. It's the loss of this beauty that saddens me.

Though I know well that the skin-cracking, sand-eating, sleep-deprived, undernourished, unwashed, painful reality on the trail has little in common with the romantic fantasy of riding camels across the desert, there is yet much beauty to be found in the salt trade. There is Walid, antelope pipe fixed in his mouth, setting an unwavering course across the desert with no technological devices or even landmarks to aid him, referring only to the map imprinted in his soul. There is Baba, chanting away in the darkness, defending us from the djinn. There is Hamid, brewing a pot of tea, swinging a dung-filled brazier as he scampers across the sand in a bathrobe. There are the miners, playing, dancing, and laughing after a day of Herculean labor. There is sunset, and sunrise, and turbaned men kneeling in the sand to pray, hundreds of miles from anywhere. There is Cygnus the Swan, soaring low, glittering in the night sky. And there are the camels, swaying one behind the other, cutting an undulating silhouette against the flat orange earth as they perform mind-boggling feats of endurance with nobility, grace, and a mysteriously knowing smile.

What's perhaps more beautiful, and even more important, are the truths expressed through the humble lives of the azalai, the miners, and the nomads: that wealth is not a prerequisite for joy or self-respect; that commerce does not have to be founded upon greed; that each moment is ours in which to create delight, regardless of our circumstances; that living in balance with the natural world is the key to long-term survival; that it's possible to embrace tradition and modernity for what they each have to offer, without forsaking either.

If humanity *is* playing a role in a larger drama, and if it is our fate to save ourselves from destruction and rise to a new level of conscious interaction with the planet and each other, these seem like precisely the truths we'll have to discover to get there.

I didn't know how to reconcile my desire for my friends and others like them to live the lives of their choosing with my equally fervent hope to see the caravans march forever into the future. If one happens, it seems likely that the other can't. If left to me, I couldn't justify denying Saharans education, health care, and economic opportunity for the sake of preserving the salt trade. But neither would I be eager to contribute to the demise of the Caravan of White Gold. I wrestled with this dilemma, trying to think up a way to have both until my brain gave up, defeated. I hoped that in the future, when the world someday invites the azalai to leave the trail they've ridden for a thousand years, the Saharans will prove to be smarter than me.

In the afternoon, we passed the village of Agouni, from where the call to prayer that had so surprised me on my first morning in the desert had been broadcast. From here on, we encountered shepherds keeping watch over their herds from beneath the shade of thorn trees and crossed paths with men on camelback heading into the desert. Timbuktu felt close.

At sunset, Lamana proposed stopping for the night, but said that if I wanted to, we could continue on into the city. I asked how long it would take, and he said three to four hours. It was easily doable and hardly would have pressed me to my limits. But it felt right to spend one final evening in the Sahara, knowing it would be the last one. Moreover, from a purely pragmatic perspective, I preferred the thought of pulling into Timbuktu and finding a hotel in the daylight.

We camped on a sandy, flat-topped hill, about fifty yards from the rutted tire tracks that ran between Timbuktu and Agouni. When the camels were unloaded, Walid and Lamana spotted people they knew passing on the road and went to talk to them, while I scoured the area for fuel. The pickings were slim—most of the branches on the thorn trees were still alive, and there wasn't much camel dung. At last I spotted some piles of dried donkey dung, similar to but much bigger than camel turds; I was sure they'd burn well. When my friends came back up the hill and saw what I was collecting, they told me to throw it away.

"What are you talking about? It'll burn fine," I said.

"Yes, it'll burn, but we never cook over donkey shit," Lamana said.

"But you cook over camel shit?" I asked.

"Yes. Camels eat only plants. Donkeys eat everything, including garbage and human feces. The camel dung is clean. The donkey dung is poison."

I threw it away and continued my search for fuel. Even after five weeks on the trail, I was still learning.

The night was cool but not cold. The clear sky, pierced with countless stars, glowed faintly in the light of the waxing half-moon. Our proximity to town had a palpable effect on our mood as we sat around the flickering fire. Rather than intrepid travelers in the midst of an endless wilderness, we seemed like a few friends out on a recreational camping trip. We were each aware that this was our last night together, that the adventure was coming to a close, that by this time the following day we'd have gone our separate ways. We ate, talked lightly, and laughed. At one point, Lamana asked what I was looking forward to most about getting back to civilization. Without hesitation, I replied, "Chicken."

As Walid prepared to pour the tea, an old man with a single camel wandered into our camp and asked if he could join us. We invited him to sit, and he did. It was no intrusion; rather, it was satisfying to offer some hospitality to a stranger before leaving the desert.

I awoke in the morning to the lilting prayers of our nighttime visitor, who sang his devotions in haunting tones over the sound of the crackling tea fire. Dawn had just arrived. I lay in my blanket watching a fluid palette of grays, blues, pinks, and yellows swirl in the sky, in sync with the hypnotic voice of our guest.

Oddly, I wasn't in a hurry to pack, load, and leave. Normally I'm impatient on the last day of an expedition; I like to get up, get going, and get the hell out, regardless of how much I enjoyed the trip. But not this morning. I waited until I heard the splashing of tea and sugar being mixed in the pot before rolling out of my blanket and walking a few feet to the fire.

When we finished our three glasses, we loaded our camels and hit the trail for the last time. It was the thirty-sixth day of the journey.

I walked in silence, devising a vague plan for my arrival in Timbuktu: find an affordable hotel, take a shower, eat a chicken. I felt energetic and strong. My mind was sharp, my spirits high.

After about two hours, I mounted Mabrouk. Since Walid was already riding and Mabrouk was tied to L'beyya's tail, the camel was moving at its full marching pace. Without causing it to slow or miss a step, I sprang onto its neck and smoothly slid atop its hump, my form worthy of any seasoned azalai.

Perched high on Mabrouk's hump, I could see Timbuktu's tallest buildings in the distance—the dark cone of a minaret, the steel lattice of a radio tower, both pointing toward the heavens. I was content to watch them get slowly closer, grow slowly higher, with no impulse to rush toward the comforts they promised. I felt none of the desperation that can set in when the end of something difficult appears on the horizon, when the mere sight of the finish line causes one's reserves of strength to drain away. We'd get there when we got there, and that'd be soon enough. I could soar with the Rukh as long as it cared to fly.

ACKNOWLEDGMENTS

From the time that my trip through the Sahara—and this book—was nothing more than an exciting idea, no one has been more supportive than my agent, Jennifer Joel, at ICM. During moments of doubt, when I questioned whether the risks and hardships of the journey would be worth undertaking, Jenn's unwavering belief in the value of the story provided the pivotal encouragement that tipped the balance in favor of my going. The publication of *Men of Salt* is due in no small part to the enthusiasm and integrity with which she represented it. I owe her more thanks than I can express here.

I'm grateful for the insightful feedback of my editor, Ann Treistman, who helped this book evolve from a rough manuscript to a finished work; the gentle conviction with which she made suggestions effectively persuaded me to reconsider at times when stubbornness or laziness got the better of me and I resisted making changes.

When Ann went on maternity leave, her assistant, Christine Duffy, helped fine-tune the manuscript, reading through it more times in fewer days than seems possible. She also shepherded the book through various stages of production with a care and efficiency for which I was most fortunate.

Two people whose contributions were indispensable to my understanding of Saharan trade in general and the salt trade in particular are

Dr. E. Ann McDougall (professor of history and classics and director of the Middle Eastern and African Studies Programme at the University of Alberta) and Dr. Ghislaine Lydon (assistant professor of history at UCLA), both Saharan experts. They provided me with copies of their work, both published and unpublished; took the time to consult with me by phone and e-mail; and turned me on to other sources as essential as they were esoteric, which I likely never would have found on my own. Thanks also to Dr. Susan J. Rasmussen, anthropology professor at the University of Houston, for sending me some of her published work on the Tuareg.

I'd also like to thank Arthur Gelb, mentor and friend, whose wise counsel helped recalibrate my perspective at difficult moments during the editing process, and who over the years has taught me much about being a better writer, and a better person. Thanks, too, to Howard Fishman, longtime friend, who first introduced me to Arthur and started a circuitous chain of events that ultimately led to the publication of this book.

To my parents, Gary and Ruth, I am deeply grateful for the understanding they have for the wanderlust in my soul, giving me encouragement and support, along with a few words of caution. And a big smile to Kelly Wolpert, who nourished me with laughter and cookies when my computer was off.

I send a heartfelt *shokran* to the azalai, the salt miners, and the people of Timbuktu, including historian Sidi Mohammed Ould Youbba, who took time from his busy schedule at the Centre de Recherches Historiques Ahmed Baba to answer my questions about the salt trade, and Jiddou Ag Almoustapha, a Tuareg leader, at whose home I drank many cups of tea while talking about the people and ways of the Sahara.

My deepest thanks go to Walid, Lamana, and Abdi, who opened the doors to a world beyond anything my imagination had conceived. I will never forget them or their kindness, and hope one day to see them again.

AUTHOR'S NOTES

Factual information within the chapters was gleaned from the following sources:

PREFACE

The first few paragraphs of the preface are based on what I saw with my own eyes, supplemented by information found in *Forbidden Sands: A Search in the Sahara* by Richard Trench, *Tribes of the Sahara* by Lloyd Cabot Briggs, and *The Quest for Timbuctoo* by Brian Gardner, as well as conversations with historian Sidi Mohammed Ould Youbba of the Centre de Recherches Historiques Ahmed Baba in Timbuktu. After much searching for answers to the mystery of the evolutionary advantages of one-humped versus two-humped camels in their respective environments, I finally found them not on the Internet, but in a book (of all places): Richard Bulliet's *The Camel and the Wheel*. The section on the value of salt and its uses as currency was based on sections of the doctoral dissertation of Ghislaine Lydon, Ph.D., called "On Trans-Saharan Trails: Trading Networks and Cross-Cultural Exchange in Western Africa, 1840s–1930s"; as well as a paper written by Dr. E. Ann McDougall, "Salts of the Western Sahara"—the paper from which I also learned about the other uses for and types of salt in the region.

CHAPTER 1

Essential to my understanding of Mali's overall economic situation was the piece titled "Overview: The Malian Path to Democracy and Development" by R. James Bingen, in the book *Democracy and Development in Mali*. Additional facts were acquired from *The New York Times Almanac*, the U.S. State Department's Web page on Mali, and the 2004 United Nations Human Development Report. The quote "the most distant place imaginable" and the date of its first recorded use as a synonym for Timbuktu comes from *The Oxford English Dictionary*. Information about the uses of contracts and "traveler's checks" in Saharan trade was found in Dr. Lydon's doctoral dissertation (mentioned above). My recounting of the history of Timbuktu and the journey of Gordon Laing was adapted mostly from Gardner's book (mentioned above), *The Quest for Timbuctoo*, and supplemented a bit by what I read in the book *Sahara* by Paolo Novaresio and Gianni Guadalupi (it should be noted that this last book contains some glaring factual inaccuracies—when I mention it as a source, it is always a secondary source that merely confirms what I've read in other sources, or is one from which I've taken a direct quote that has no historical importance). The interview with Wilfred Theisger to which I refer was in the January–February 2002 issue of *National Geographic Adventure*. The translation of the Sindbad story I read and quoted comes from *The Arabian Nights II*, by Husain Haddawy.

CHAPTER 2

Much of the information about the Saharan climate through the ages, and its animal life, was adapted from the books *Tribes of the Sahara*, by Lloyd Cabot Briggs; and *The Sahara*, by Jeremy Swift. Dinosaur-specific facts came from BBC News Online (May 31, 2001); CNN.com (May 31, 2001); a University of Chicago press release (November 11, 1998); and a Web site called Dino Land—which is where I found the story about the Tuareg chief who told the paleontologist where he could find "a lot of big camel bones lying around." I learned about the history of green tea in West Africa through e-mail correspondence with Dr. Lydon, as well as from her dissertation. The paragraphs about the dung beetles were based on what I learned from Swift's book (mentioned above) and two Web sites: "In Praise of Dung Beetles" at earthlife.net, and "Our Friend the Dung Beetle," a paper on the University of Waterloo site.

My primary source for facts about male and female headdress practices in Tuareg culture was Dr. Susan Rasmussen's paper "Veiled Self, Transparent Meanings: Tuareg Headdress as Social Expression"; the quote about the veil and pants being brothers is from Dr. Jeremy Keenan's book *Sahara Man*. My account of Saharan ethnicities and the similarities and differences between tribes is based on Dr. Lydon's dissertation (especially the hasani/zawaya distinction), a telephone conversation with Dr. McDougall, and the book *The Arab Conquest of the Western Sahara* by H. T. Norris. I compiled the account of camel breeding among the Azawad's tribes from those same sources, as well as conversations with Jiddou Ag Almoustapha, a Tuareg leader in Timbuktu. Aside from the oral accounts of Saharans, including Ag Almoustapha and Abdi Abdurahman, I learned about the Tuareg Rebellion and the plight of Saharan nomads from Kare Lode's "Mali Feature Study" in the online magazine *Accord*, and a paper called "Conflict and Conflict Resolution in the Sahel: The Tuareg Insurgency in Mali" by Lieutenant Colonel Kalifa Keita (Army of the Republic of Mali). I read about the Great Drought in *An Overview of Drought Strategies and Land Use in African Pastoral System* by Gufu Oba and Walter J. Lusigi, and heard much about it in personal conversations with Saharans.

CHAPTER 3

Sidi Mohammed Ould Youbba told me about the French improvements to Saharan wells. Facts about camels and their water needs came from Jeremy Swift's *The Sahara*, as well as the Web site for the Chaffee

Zoo. The historical information about camel domestication and the disappearance of the wheel in North Africa and the Middle East was found in Richard Bulliet's *The Camel and the Wheel*. I found the story of the first automobile crossing of the Sahara on the Citroën Web site, as well as a site devoted to Citroëns called Tractions in Switzerland. The information about the djinn was derived from a paper called "Friends of the Kel Essuf: Perspectives on Shamanism in Tuareg Mediumistic Healing," by Dr. Susan J. Rassmussen, as well as personal conversations with Jiddou Ag Almoustapha and other Saharans.

CHAPTER 4

I read about the fennec in Swift's *The Sahara*. Historical information about the founding of Araouane and the Sufi principles of the Kel Es-Suq was found in H. T. Norris's *The Tuaregs: Their Islamic Legacy and Its Diffusion in the Sahel*. Information about Sidi al-Mukhtar and the Kunta came from the same source, as well as a paper by Dr. E. Ann Mc-Dougall called "The Economics of Islam in the Southern Sahara: The Rise of the Kunta Clan." This was supplemented by material from Dr. McDougall's unpublished manuscript titled "Salt and Saharans in the Pre-Colonial Development of Mali-Mauritania, 1600–1900."

CHAPTER 5

Facts about the Tanezrouft were derived from Swift's *The Sahara* (as was the information about the "reg"), *Trench's Forbidden Sands*, and About.com. The quote about the desert being a place not for living but for traveling through was found in Novaresio and Guadalupi's *Sahara*.

CHAPTER 6

The history of the Tegaza salt mines and their abandonment in favor of Taoudenni was found in Dr. McDougall's paper "Salts of the Western Sahara: Myths, Mysteries, and Historical Significance."

CHAPTER 8

Facts about the forced marches in Romania and Transnistria during World War II were culled from *The Holocaust in Romania* by Radu Ioanid.

CHAPTER 10

The number of languages in the world and the percentage that are endangered was found in *Light at the Edge of the World* by Wade Davis. (Though the thoughts and feelings I express may mirror Davis's in places, I came to them on my own, before I ever read his book.)

BIBLIOGRAPHY

BOOKS

The Compact Edition of the Oxford English Dictionary. Glasgow/New York: Oxford University Press, 1971.

Briggs, Lloyd Cabot, *Tribes of the Sahara.* Cambridge, MA: Harvard University Press, 1960.

Bulliet, Richard, *The Camel and the Wheel.* New York/Oxford: Columbia University Press, Morningside Edition, 1990.

Davis, Wade, *Light at the Edge of the World.* Washington, DC: National Geographic, 2002.

Gardner, Brian, *The Quest for Timbuctoo.* New York: Harcourt, Brace, and World, Inc., 1968.

Haddawy, Husain, *The Arabian Nights II.* New York/London: W. W. Norton and Company, 1995.

Ioanid, Radu, *The Holocaust in Romania: The Destruction of Jews and Gypsies Under the Antonescu Regime, 1940–1944.* Chicago: Ivan R. Dee, 2000.

Keenan, Jeremy, *Sahara Man.* London: John Murray, 2001.

Mahfouz, Naguib, *Arabian Nights and Days.* New York: Doubleday, 1995.

Norris, H. T., *The Arab Conquest of the Western Sahara: Studies of the Historical Events, Religious Beliefs and Social Customs Which*

Made the Remotest Sahara a Part of the Arab World. Beirut:
Librairie du Liban, 1986.

————, *The Tuareg: Their Islamic Legacy and Its Diffusion in the Sahel.*
Oxford: Aris & Phillips, 1975.

Novaresio, Paolo, and Gianni Guadalupi, *Sahara.* San Diego: Thunder
Bay Press, 2003.

Swift, Jeremy, *The Sahara.* Amsterdam: Time, Life, Inc., 1975.

Trench, Richard, *Forbidden Sands: A Search in the Sahara.* Chicago:
Academy Chicago, 1978.

Wright, John W., editor, *The New York Times Almanac 2001.* New
York: Penguin Reference, 2000.

PAPERS, ARTICLES, AND DISSERTATIONS

Bingen, R. J., "Overview—The Malian Path to Democracy and
Development," in *Democracy and Development in Mali.* East
Lansing: Michigan State University Press, 2000.

Lydon, Ghislaine, "On Trans-Saharan Trails: Trading Networks and
Cross-Cultural Exchange in Western Africa, 1840s–1930s."
Dissertation: Michigan State University, 2000.

McDougall, E. A., "Camel Caravans of the Saharan Salt Trade: Traders
and Transporters in the Nineteenth Century," in *The Workers
of African Trade*, C. Coquery-Vidrovitch and P. Lovejoy.
Beverly Hills, CA: Sage Publications, 1985.

————, "The Economics of Islam in the Southern Sahara: The Rise
of the Kunta Clan," in *Rural and Urban Islam in West Africa*,
N. Levtzion and H. Fisher, editors. Boulder, CO: Lynne
Reinner Publishers, 1986.

————, "Salts of the Western Sahara: Myths, Mysteries and Historical
Significance." *International Journal of African Historical Studies*
xxiii, 1990.

Rasmussen, Susan J., "Friends of the Kel Essuf: Perspectives on
Shamanism in the Tuareg Mediumistic Healing." *Cultural*

Survival Quarterly, summer 2003.

————, "Veiled Self, Transparent Meanings: Tuareg Headdress as Social Expression." *Ethnology* 30, no. 2, 1991.

Shnayerson, Michael, "The Man Who Walked Through Time: Wilfred Thesiger." *National Geographic Adventure*, January–February 2002.

ELECTRONIC ARTICLES AND WEBSITES

"Crossing the Sahara: 1922–1923." Citroen.com, *http://www.citroen.com/CWW/en-US/HISTORY/ADVEN-TURE/CrossingTheSahara/*

"Dromedary Camel." The Chaffee Zoo, *http://www.chaffeezoo.org/animals/camel.html*

Eberli, Daniel, "1994 an Anniversary of a Famous Company: 75 Years of Citroën Automobiles; 60 Years of Citroën Traction Avant." Tractions in Switzerland, 1994, *http://www.traction.ch/history/hist_ctr_e.html*

Gwynn-Jones, Terry, "Bill Lancaster: Lost in the Sahara." About.com, 2002 (originally published in *Aviation History* in January 2000), *http://africanhistory.about.com/library/prm/bllostinsahara1.htm?terms=Tanezrouft*

"Huge Fish-Eating Dinosaur Emerges from the Sahara." University of Chicago News Office, November 11, 1998, *http://www-news.uchicago.edu/releases/98/981111.suchomimus.shtml*

Keita, Kalifa, "Conflict and Conflict Resolution in the Sahel: The Tuareg Insurgency in Mali." Monograph: Strategic Studies Institute of the U.S. Army War College, May 1998, *www.carlisle.army.mil/ssi/pdffiles/PUB200.pdf*

Kellan, Ann, "Second-Largest Dinosaur Found in Egypt." CNN.com, May 31, 2001, *http://archives.cnn.com/2001/TECH/science/05/31/egypt.dinosaur/*

Lode, Kare, "Mali Feature Study." Conciliation Resources: Accord #13,

2002, *http://www.c-r.org/accord/peace/accord13/mapea.shtml*

"New Species of Primitive Dinosaur Found in Niger." Dino Land, November 13, 1999, *http://www.geocities.com/CapeCanaveral/Galaxy/8152/seren-odino.html*

Oba, G., and W. J. Lusigi, "An Overview of Drought Strategies and Land Use in African Pastoral Systems." Overseas Development Institute, March 1987, *http://www.odi.org.uk/pdn/papers/23a.pdf*

"Our Friend the Dung Beetle." University of Waterloo Department of Science, *http://www.science.uwaterloo.ca/~ja2macne/412paper.html*

Ramel, Gordon, "In Praise of Dung Beetles." *http://www.earthlife.net/insects/dung.html*

"'Striking' Dinosaurs Found in the Sahara." BBC News Online, November 11, 1999, *http://news.bbc.co.uk/1/hi/sci/tech/516012.stm*

United Nations Human Development Report, 2004, *http://hdr.undp.org/reports/global/2004/pdf/presskit/HDR_PKE_HPI.pdf*

Whitehouse, David, "Dinosaur Heaven Reveals Wonders." BBC News Online, May 31, 2001, *http://news.bbc.co.uk/1/hi/sci/tech/1362194.stm*